RELIGION, EDUCATION AND GOVERNANCE IN THE MIDDLE EAST

Global Interdisciplinary Studies Series

Series Editor: Sai Felicia Krishna-Hensel
Interdisciplinary Global Studies Research Initiative,
Center for Business and Economic Development,
Auburn Montgomery, USA

The Global Interdisciplinary Studies Series reflects a recognition that globalization is leading to fundamental changes in the world order, creating new imperatives and requiring new ways of understanding the international system. It is increasingly clear that the next century will be characterized by issues that transcend national and cultural boundaries, shaped by competitive forces and features of economic globalization yet to be fully evaluated and understood. Comparative and comprehensive in concept, this series explores the relationship between transnational and regional issues through the lens of widely applicable interdisciplinary methodologies and analytic models. The series consists of innovative monographs and collections of essays representing the best of contemporary research, designed to transcend disciplinary boundaries in seeking to better understand a globalizing world.

Also in the series

New Security Frontiers
Critical Energy and the Resource Challenge
Edited by Sai Felicia Krishna-Hensel
ISBN 978-1-4094-1979-2

Cities and Global Governance
New Sites for International Relations
Edited by Mark Amen, Noah J. Toly, Patricia L. McCarney
and Klaus Segbers
ISBN 978-1-4094-0893-2

Order and Disorder in the International System
Edited by Sai Felicia Krishna-Hensel
ISBN 978-1-4094-0505-4

Legacies and Change in Polar Sciences
Edited by Jessica M. Shadian and Monica Tennberg
ISBN 978-0-7546-7399-6

International Order in a Globalizing World
Edited by Yannis A. Stivachtis
ISBN 978-0-7546-4930-4

Religion, Education and Governance in the Middle East

Between Tradition and Modernity

Edited by

SAI FELICIA KRISHNA-HENSEL
Auburn University at Montgomery, USA

Routledge
Taylor & Francis Group

LONDON AND NEW YORK

First published 2012 by Ashgate Publishing

Published 2016 by Routledge
2 Park Square, Milton Park, Abingdon, Oxfordshire OX14 4RN
711 Third Avenue, New York, NY 10017, USA

First issued in paperback 2016

Routledge is an imprint of the Taylor & Francis Group, an informa business

British Library Cataloguing in Publication Data
Krishna-Hensel, Sai Felicia.
Religion, education and governance in the Middle East : between tradition and modernity.
– (Global interdisciplinary studies series) 1. Middle East–Civilization–21st century. 2. Middle East–Politics and government–21st century. 3. Religion and politics–Middle East. 4. Political culture–Middle East. 5. Democracy and education–Middle East.
I. Title II. Series
956'.054–dc23

Library of Congress Cataloging-in-Publication Data
Religion, education, and governance in the Middle East : between tradition and modernity / [edited] by Sai Felicia Krishna-Hensel.
    p. cm. — (Global interdisciplinary studies series) Includes bibliographical references and index.
ISBN 978-1-4094-3986-8 (hardback : alk. paper)
1. Islamic education—Political aspects—Middle East. 2. Islam and politics—Middle East. I. Krishna-Hensel, Sai Felicia.
 LC910.3.R45 2012
 320.956—dc23

2012016623

ISBN 13: 978-1-138-27168-5 (pbk)
ISBN 13: 978-1-4094-3986-8 (hbk)

Contents

List of Figures and Tables

Figures

Tables

List of Contributors

Sai Felicia Krishna-Hensel, Director, Interdisciplinary Global Studies Initiative, Auburn University at Montgomery, USA

Alise Coen, Assistant Professor, Department of Political Science, Emory & Henry College, Emory, VA, USA

Deina Abdelkader, Assistant Professor, Department of Political Science, University of Massachusetts, Lowell, MA, USA

Vânia Carvalho Pinto, Assistant Professor, Institute of International Relations, University of Brasilia, Brazil

Benedetta Berti, Associate Fellow, Institute for National Security Studies (INSS), Lecturer, Tel Aviv University, Israel

Kürşad Turan, Assistant Professor, Gazi University, Ankara, Turkey

Sultan Tepe,Associate Professor, Department of Political Science, University of Illinois at Chicago, IL, USA

Yusuf Sarfati, Assistant Professor, Department of Politics and Government, Illinois State University, Normal, IL, USA

Ebru Tekin, Boğaziçi University, İstanbul, Turkey

Introduction
The Middle East—Modernity, Religion, and Governance

Sai Felicia Krishna-Hensel

The Middle East has always been a geopolitically strategic region. The region's distinctive cultural and political divisions present a mosaic of states that do not lend themselves to simplistic interpretations. Developments in the region continue to remind us of the importance of understanding the complex forces that are driving change across a wide variety of societies. The world's attention is drawn to the area not only due to its geographical location, and its possession of critical energy resources, but also because evolving socio-political patterns are a rich source for comprehending social change.

The continuity and dominance of traditional cultures in the region have sometimes been interpreted as signs of regression, and rejection of modernity. Nevertheless, it is important to approach the discourse on modernity from the foundation of historical tradition, in order to comprehend the development of innovative social, religious, and political institutions in the region. As is the case in other examples of regional development, the Middle East has constructed its contemporary institutions on a foundation of traditional social arrangements, values, philosophical assumptions, and everyday practices that are deeply rooted in its cultural heritage.

The patterns of political thought, the evolution of institutions, and the interaction between the customary patterns and Western influence have often been the basis of analysis of the Middle East as a whole. This line of reasoning reveals a vastly underrated diversity of experience and culture that makes for an unexpected complexity in interpreting developments in the region. The demolition of stereotypical interpretations is a by-product of the acceptance that there is not only diversity of cultures, but also diversity of interpretation, and execution of religious directives within the states of the region. The emergent pattern is one of sincere efforts to grapple with the desire for progress, while retaining some of the basis of existing cultural and political practices.

Interpreting modernization in the Middle East from the perspective of time and space introduces the importance of not only indigenous cultural differences but also local circumstances as factors underlying the process of change. This approach places developments in the region within the discourse of the concept of multiple modernities, that increasingly focuses on how universal assumptions of modernity accommodate local forms (Eisenstadt 2000). A related premise is that Westernization and modernity can be differentiated as distinct progressions with different results in societies. This opens the way to a meaningful assessment of the role of tradition and culture in the process of change. Thus, rather than taking a judgmental approach towards achievement of levels of modernity, it is possible to think in terms of whether local forms of modernity that are appropriate to the indigenous traditions are being developed. Evaluating modernization solely in terms of the Western paradigm of progress ceases to be central to the understanding of the process. The dynamic between the external archetype and local cultures results in a resilience in shaping institutions that are more effective in serving the needs of the region's citizens.

A significant premise of the study of modernization has been that there is generally a confrontational attitude between the local and the universal, with the outcome often being interpreted in terms of success or failure. In doing so, the local has been relegated to being an obstructionist feature. The projection for modernization, construed in linear terms, sees the connections between societies as direct avenues of influence in an international system configured in terms of differing levels of power. While historically, the cultures and institutions of dominant powers have been either transplanted or diffused, the process has not been viewed in judgmental terms, until the discourse turns to modernization. The Western powers were now seen as the exemplar to be followed by the colonies and other societies with commercial or military ties. Resistance or rejection of this exemplar was viewed as backward looking. The insertion of globalization into this perspective has uncovered the complexity underlying the criteria for assessing change. Linear patterns have been replaced by a criss-cross of lines in which the direction of influence can often run both ways. There is then a discernible variance between earlier imperatives of modernization and the imperatives of globalization.

The transformation of societies has its basis in ideological outreach, economic imperatives, and political power. The dominant factor in the process has thus far been the secularization of power and the compartmentalization of religion from other forces. Scientific knowledge imbued the individual and the state with a new understanding of their power in society. A modern state, and its modern citizens, could make their own destiny based on rational thought and independent of religious sanction. The primacy of the state as an instrument of modernization was assumed until the introduction of new actors and external influences that challenged this premise. The emphasis shifted to examining a wide range of components that went into the process of political transformation as well as a movement away from a linear interpretation of change.

The resurgence of Islam at the end of the twentieth century could not be explained in terms of classic modernization theory. The Islamic revival was too complex to be rationalized simply in terms of tradition and needed to be placed in the context of specific Middle Eastern societies. The emphasis on specific local conditions would have enabled the understanding of tactics that were used to address them. Islamic civilization's struggle to maintain political and social viability over the centuries reflected the important role played by religious renewal. Muslim civilization has had to contend, and is still contending, with perennial problems of internal cohesion and also with the threat of being overwhelmed by external economic, cultural, and political forces. The reaction to modernity has ranged from the wholesale adoption of Western practices and values to the selective use of Western ideas. The result has been the embrace of technical and social reforms associated with modernity while simultaneously asserting national identities. A predictable reaction has been the reassertion of Middle Eastern social and religious ideals, and, in some cases, the rejection of modernity as inimical to Islam. During the post-World War II period, diverse strategies and conflicting interpretations of cultural values and historical symbols emerged.

The Islamic revival does not have a common manifest. Conservatives concentrate their efforts on a traditional version of Islam, discouraging any radically new interpretations of the faith. Fundamentalists, on the other hand, advocate a return to a lost purity in religious practice, envisaging a reimposition of Shari'a law and Koranic education, as well as discouraging rejection of traditions of belief and ritual that do not fit the concept of uncorrupted Islam.

The desire to restore purity to Islam is shared by the modernists as well as fundamentalists. Modernists have been more receptive to the idea of a society grounded in Koranic principles while simultaneously adjusting to change. Fundamentalists are less sanguine about progress which is seen as diluting the purity of Islam. The divergence is based upon the literal interpretation of doctrine and the spirit underlying the principles. While this dichotomy reveals the ongoing discussion in the region, it is unclear as to which position is most likely to be widely adopted. Local historical and cultural traditions are likely to influence the direction of the discourse.

The current Islamic resurgence is the consequence of the interaction of many historical and doctrinal forces. It has sought to overcome the diminution of Islamic influence over the centuries perceived by many as the invasion of Islam by foreign influences, and Western technology. The response of the Umma was to advocate a return to original principles as the most effective path to restore Islam. This was underscored by the reality that most of the successful Middle Eastern political movements of the twentieth century were not reflective of the aspirations of the general populace. The motivating force of political change was instead centered on the acquisition and distribution of power amongst new elites. Islam remained subordinated to the secular goals of modernist policy and ideology and religious aspirations were excluded from civil practice and by extension, political authority.

Modernization came to be equated with technical progress and Westernization, devoid of an indigenous ethical foundation. As secular institutions increasingly replaced religious administered schools, Westernization was viewed as a socially corrupting influence. The Westernization of the urban population effectively created an enclave of society that was alienated from the rural populace. Predictably, the revival of Islamic values and tradition, resulted in conflict with the ruling elites. The religious revival was conjoined with the quest for political and social identity as the societies in the region approached the challenges of a changing world in uniquely different and often contradictory ways.

A thoughtful analysis of the Middle East requires an understanding of the synergism between tradition and modernity in the region as it adapts to a globalizing world. Religious education and activism continue to remain significant factors in the modernization process and the development of modern governance in the states of the Middle East. The chapters in this volume explore the historical and contemporary role of religious tradition and education of political elites and governing agencies in several major states as well as generally in the region. The relationship between democracy and authority is examined to provide a better understanding of the complexity underlying the emergence of new power configurations. As the region continues to respond to the forces of change internationally, it remains an important and intriguing area for analysts.

The increasing emphasis on understanding how transnational forces, originating and operating outside the traditional domain of the state, wield influence on states' policy decisions and outcomes underlies Alise Cohen's chapter on global governance. She suggests that although international relations scholars have begun explore the challenges posed by transnational religious movements, diasporas, and phenomena associated with the "new Arab media," to state authority in the Middle East, there is as yet much less scholarship relating such transnational challenges to the study of Global Governance. Building on Craig Murphy's observation that Global Governance has been "poorly done and poorly understood," Chapter 1 examines three manifestations of Islamist transnationalism in the Middle East to consider the empirical and theoretical implications for Global Governance: the Muslim Brotherhood, Hamas, and Hizbullah. Empirically, these case studies present several trends regarding societal expectations of, and organizational competition over, governance in the Middle East. Theoretically, the chapter addresses the debate regarding what constitutes "Global Governance" and explores the tension between national and transnational elements of Islamist authority in the Middle East. Her analysis of global governance, Islamism, and authority endeavors to explore the interrelationships between these factors.

Deina Abdelkadir's chapter on modernity, Islam, and religious activity examines the common assumption that Islam and its followers are antithetical to modernity. Chapter 2 explains the continuing emphasis in contemporary literature on the need for the separation between faith and reason as a pre-requisite to modernization. She suggests that another end result of this predisposition to separate faith from reason was the negation of all theoretical Islamic works as sources of understanding the underlying dilemmas of modernization. This chapter addresses this gap in the literature, in search of a bridge between faith and reason from within Islamic literature. She concludes that rather than adopting historically and culturally foreign concepts, Muslim societies would need to redefine and reshape their own needs and goals according to their cultural and religious beliefs. Modernity thus becomes human empowerment because it concerns the needs and ambitions of a people seeking their advancement and progress.

Vânia Carvalho Pinto's study of the United Arab Emirates suggests that the combination of international challenges with the desire to forge a certain image of nationhood has been at the core of the UAE's nation-building project ever since the establishment of the country in 1971. The association of a strong religious and cultural symbolism with traditional rule has always marked this project, but this synergy was amplified in three key moments. The first was in response to the wave of popular interest in the religious roots of culture, which led rulers to amplify their traditional and religious credentials. The second was after the Iraqi invasion of Kuwait in 1991, an event that shook prevailing ideas about Arab solidarity and led rulers to strive for the consolidation of their national projects. The third occurred after 2001, as a result of the close international scrutiny brought about by the "war on terror," which led to intense self-examination in the UAE's society as a whole. Building on the analysis of these three moments, Chapter 3 argues that a close continuity can be observed in the basic underpinnings of the UAE national project, and in turn also in the international image that the UAE seeks to project, one based on the ideas of tolerance and cultural-religious observance. This analysis of the interrelated dynamics of culture, religion and nation in the United Arab Emirates provides valuable insight into the complexity underlying the modernization process in the region.

In Chapter 4, Benedetta Berti argues that foreign powers have always had an important role in supporting and shaping Lebanese internal as well as foreign policy, and the country has historically served as a playground for regional powers to test their reciprocal political and military strength. In this sense, the political and geo-strategic significance of Lebanon far exceeds its relatively small size, and all the main regional players have over the years battled each other to gain power and influence over this small Middle Eastern state. Being at the center of much broader regional dynamics has taken its toll on Lebanon. Specifically, this chapter analyzes the current ethnic and religious strife taking place in Lebanon through the lens of the destabilizing effect played by foreign powers. The study focuses on the role and influence of external players, including Saudi Arabia, Iran, Syria, and Israel, on the internal balance of power within Lebanon, assessing how these actors contribute to enhancing the existing ethnic and sectarian fragmentation, which, in turn, impacts the stability and governability of the country. The analysis further discusses the implications of this dynamic on the regional balance of power.

The role of the Muslim Brotherhood and the Islamic Action Front in Jordan is the focus of Kürşad Turan's analysis of the sources of instability in the Middle East; in Chapter 5, he traces the causes to both international and domestic factors. Internationally, he focuses on interventions by non-regional actors in search of influence and natural resources, pointing out that these interventions traditionally changed the balance in the region, leading to more authoritarian regimes which are both more predictable and more easily controlled. Domestically, he suggests that very few countries experienced democratic regimes and even those limited experiments failed to last long enough to make a significant impact. As a result, regardless of the label they adopt, the majority of political systems in the region remained patrimonial. The author emphasizes the importance of political structure to understanding political instability in the region, suggesting that patrimonial systems allow for a relatively small group to have access to power. In these situations, recruitment and advancement are not based on merit, but on close proximity to the ruler. The emphasis on personalism comprises an attempt to guarantee the loyalty of political elites to the source of that power, the ruler of the country. The structure leads to a system of political elites that permanently excludes large segments of the population. He suggests that comprehensive change, often involving violence, is the only solution to a system grounded in the inability to obtain power or become a relevant political actor based on objective qualifications. The chapter examines the process that led to the formation of Jordanian political elites. It also explores the most recent challenge posed to the Jordanian regime by the Muslim Brotherhood and its political wing, the Islamic Action Front. Finally, it reviews the developments of the Arab Spring and how it relates to the Jordanian situation.

Sultan Tepe's study of the micro-foundations of religious parties' (im)moderation explores the transformative effects of different levels of commitment in political parties. The author suggests that the inclusion-and-moderation thesis evaluates the transformative power of political context and negotiations among main political actors. He further argues that the process of moderation and its hybrid nature is often overlooked. In Chapter 6, he seeks to illustrate how the phases of moderation and immoderation coexist in many parties' trajectories of transformation. Using examples from Israel and Turkey's main religious parties, this study seeks to understand the micro-mechanisms of party change that lead to both moderation and immoderation. To disentangle the role of political context, leadership and supporters, the analysis focuses on a case study that attempts to map out the role that leadership and supporters' positions play in the critical decisions of Israel's and Turkey's main religious parties. He concludes that this explains the eventual change in the parties' overall ideological positions in substantial ways. Using a set of policy statements and public opinion studies (for example, the Israeli National Election Survey and Turkey's KONDA surveys), the analysis attempts to answer questions such as where do the supporters of religious parties stand on so called "critical issues"? When do religious parties follow their supporters? When do they take independent decisions? How and when do their decisions radicalize their positions?

In approaching the study of religious education from a case study perspective, Yusuf Sarfati's analysis of the politics of religious education in Turkey in Chapter 7 provides insight on the theoretical debate in comparative politics regarding the role of institutions and ideas in shaping political outcomes. Historical institutionalists maintain that political institutions constrain the behavior of political actors by providing incentives. Hence, political actors follow the rules, or regularized practices with rule-like qualities of their institutional context, and respond to the incentives produced by these rules while making their political decisions. While these insights of the institutionalists are important for understanding the effect of the institutional context on the political actors' decisions, this school of thought is not attentive to the role culture and ideas play in politics.

Ebru Tekin's examination of the evolution of biosafety policies in Turkey is a case study of governance processes. Chapter 8 explores a specific aspect of modernization: the introduction of market and law-making mechanisms into the dynamic between state and society. This study serves to bring out the complexity of modernization as the state's control of institutional change encounters the growing influence of diverse actors and groups on the modernization process. The author emphasizes the role of uncertainty in modern governance as the state interacts with external actors that are often difficult to place within the local context. This analysis of the governance process in a articulating biosafety policy reveals the limited participation of non-state actors in the decision-making process. Successful governance is heavily dependent on accountability and this is hard to establish in the context of multiple actors and institutions, both external and internal.

The studies in this volume take an interdisciplinary perspective in seeking to understand the intricacies of modernization in traditional societies as they meet the challenges of a globalizing world. The contributors provide an insightful analysis of a complex environment that would be of interest to students, scholars, and practitioners. The work is particularly timely as we seek to comprehend the rapidly evolving political developments in the region.

References

Appadurai, A. (1996) *Modernity at Large: Cultural Dimensions of Globalization.* Minneapolis: University of Minnesota Press.

Curtis, M. (1981) *Religion and Politics in the Middle East*: Boulder, Colorado: Westview Press

Eisenstadt, S.N. (2000) Multiple Modernities. *Daedalus* 129 (1), 1–29

Eisenstadt, S.N. (ed.) (2003) *Comparative Civilizations and Multiple Modernities.* Leiden: Brill

Larrain, J. (1994) *Ideology and Cultural Identity: Modernity and the Third World Presence.* Cambridge: Polity Press

Chapter 1

Global Governance, Islamism, and Authority in the Middle East

Alise Coen

Introduction

International Relations (IR) is increasingly concerned with how transnational forces, originating and operating outside the traditional domain of the state, wield influence on states' policy decisions and outcomes. While IR scholars have begun to uncover the myriad challenges to state authority in the Middle East, derived from transnational religious movements, diasporas, and phenomena associated with the "new Arab media," little work has related such transnational challenges to the study of Global Governance. Bearing in mind Craig Murphy's observation that Global Governance has been "poorly done and poorly understood," this chapter examines three manifestations of Islamist transnationalism in the Middle East to consider the empirical and theoretical implications for Global Governance: (1) the Muslim Brotherhood; (2) Hamas; and (3) Hizbullah. Empirically, these case studies present several trends regarding societal expectations of, and organizational competition over, governance in the Middle East. Theoretically, the chapter addresses the debate regarding what constitutes "Global Governance" and explores the tension between national and transnational elements of Islamist authority in the Middle East.

In his assessment of what constitutes Global Governance, Craig Murphy (2000: 796) describes a "global polity" comprised of neoliberal ideology, growing networks of transnational public and private regimes, global intergovernmental organizations, and transnational organizations that "[carry] out some of the traditional service functions of global public agencies." Relevant to the latter category of global governance activities, IR scholars focusing on the Middle East have observed a spectrum of political actors and phenomena that increasingly challenge the traditional functions of the State. Marc Lynch (2006: 21), for example, analyzes the emergence of a new, transnational Arab public sphere "defined by the rapidly expanding universe of Arabs able and willing to engage in public argument ... within an ever-increasing range of possible media outlets." This new public sphere, facilitated by new technologies, is increasingly able to disrupt the traditional state monopoly over the flow of information, pressuring Arab political elites to provide greater justification for their positions.

On a similar note, Fred Halliday (2005: 232) uses the term "transnational" to identify activities and spaces in Middle Eastern societies "that are not controlled by the state and which derive much of their strength and character from interaction with the external." Halliday discusses nationalist movements, diasporas, political violence, and media influences in this context, and additionally identifies Islamist movements as manifestations *par excellence* of transnational ideology and organization. As an important caveat, he notes that the origins and operations of these Islamist movements "lie very much *within* the specific societies in which they originate" (ibid.: 241). This chapter examines the theoretical and empirical implications of Islamist transnationalism for Global Governance, paying particular attention to the paradoxical nature of Islamism: on one hand, the rhetoric, ideology, and "social movement" aspects of political Islam appear supranational in many ways. On the other hand, important organizational and operational dimensions of Islamism remain very much territorially and nationally bound. In both cases, it is apparent that Islamist movements play an important role in the "disaggregation" of authority observed by Rosenau (2005) to be a worldwide process. Attention is also paid to the ways in which Islamist organizations challenge the traditional functions of the State. Here, the chapter seeks to illuminate the undermining of the State particularly in the realm of the provision of basic social services. By challenging traditional authority in this and other arenas, Islamist movements are poised to compete with the State over claims of good governance.

This chapter will proceed in four stages. First, the conceptualization of Islam as an inherently "transnational space" will be discussed. Secondly, the notion of Islamic governance *vis-à-vis* Islamism will be explicated to address those aspects which are aptly described as "transnational" or "global," particularly on the issue of reestablishing a supranational Islamic caliphate, and those aspects which are perhaps better described as nationally and territorially bound. Third, the chapter will examine three case studies of Islamist transnationalism in the contexts of the Muslim Brotherhood, Hamas, and Hizbullah. Finally, the chapter will conclude with an assessment of the trends observed across these three cases and their implications for future trajectories of global governance in the Middle East.

Islam as a Transnational Space

In considering the implications of transnational Islamism for Global Governance, it is important to address those elements of Islam itself which might be aptly described as "transnational." In his study of Islam as a transnational public space, John Bowen (2011: 202) identifies five elements of Islam which he characterizes as "universal": the concept of a worldwide *umma* (Muslim community), the use of Arabic as a primary language of scholarship and prayer, the system of Islamic global jurisprudence, the annual *Hajj* to Mecca, and an encouraged Islamic consciousness which "transcend[s] specific boundaries and borders." The first point is heavily related to the latter, as both connote attributes of Islam which organically facilitate a transplanetary mindset. Indeed, the pan-Islamist movement has capitalized on the concept of the *umma* to emphasize spiritual unity over nationally or territorially bound identities. This global consciousness has in many ways been intensified, negotiated, and reconstructed by new media technologies, which have opened up areas of contestation and debate theologically, politically, and with regard to identity construction. Peter Mandaville (2001) refers to this phenomenon as the creation of a "new umma consciousness," in which the monopoly on religious knowledge is increasingly broken down and Islamic virtual communities increasingly constitute new spaces of interaction.

Historically, the *Hajj*, as a pillar of Islam, has facilitated regular interaction of Muslims from diverse territorial spaces. Intrinsic to this religious obligation of pilgrimage is the uniting together of followers despite geographical separation or isolation. As such, it can be considered an organically transnational attribute of Islam. With regard to the third element identified by Bowen, the "universality" of Islamic jurisprudence, an important caveat should be noted. The *madhab* (schools) of Islamic legal thought are undeniably transnational in their geographic scope, with the influence of the Sunni Hanafi school, for example, transcending polities in the Middle East, Southern Europe, the Indian subcontinent, and Central Asia. At the same time, the division among these schools of jurisprudence in many ways limits their universality. While the influence of the Hanafi school spans multiple territorial polities, so too does the influence of the Shafi'i school, Maliki school, and, to a lesser extent, the Hanbali and Shi'a Ja'fari schools. No one *madhab* garners universal legitimacy, yet most of them are transnational in their reach.

Additionally significant is the historical presence of Islam across multiple geographic regions. In this way, Islam was substantially transnational by as early as 710 AD, with the Umayyad conquest of the Iberian Peninsula in Europe. Measuring transnationalism purely in terms of migration and the demographic movement of Muslims across the globe fails, however, to capture transnational Islam as "the existence and legitimacy of a global public space of normative reference and debate" (Bowen 2011: 199–200). For scholars like Bowen and Mandaville, transnational Islam connotes the creation of a supraterritorial space comprised of systematic debates, discussions, and reflections by Muslims via transnational socioreligious networks, institutions, and new media technologies.[1] Contemporary cyber communities like *IslamOnline.net* and *Ummah Forum* exemplify this aspect of transnational Islam. These websites provide users with interactive educational tools pertaining to Islam and the Qur'an and host discussion forums on issues ranging from marriage proposals to politics. The UK-based *Ummah Forum*, for example, hosts an "Ummah Lounge" that enables users to create discussion threads on any topic, such that one may engage in debates over collective identity issues by pondering "Who counts as a *kafir* [unbeliever]," or negotiate the significance of religious holidays in a discussion entitled "What does *Eid* mean to you?" *IslamOnline.net*, founded by prominent Egyptian Islamist Shaykh Yusuf al-Qaradawi and administered from offices in Doha and Cairo, offers educational tools, youth portals, and discussion forums in both English and

---

1   For further discussion on the role of transnational media and communication in Muslim identity construction, see Allievi and Nielsen (2003).

Arabic, and additionally provides commentary and analysis of news events that affect the daily lives and governance of Muslims living in Africa, Asia, Europe, and the Middle East ("IslamOnline.net: Independent, Interactive, Popular" 2008). The English website of *IslamOnline.net* offers a forum oriented specifically towards "Euro-Muslims," enabling users to actively construct and deconstruct this hybridized identity.

From Transnational Islam to Transnational Governance

In shifting to a discussion of transnational governance, it is important to distinguish the concept of a worldwide *umma* (Muslim community) in Islam from that of a supranational Muslim state. The latter, in particular, has generated a great deal of debate among Muslims thinkers. Some Muslim scholars, such as 'Ali 'Abd al-Raziq (1998: 32), have argued that Islam does not specify any particular form of government: "The Glorious Qur'an supports the view that the Prophet, peace be upon him, had nothing to do with political kingship. Qur'anic verses are in agreement that his heavenly work did not go beyond delivering the Message, which is free of all meanings of authority." 'Abd al-Raziq goes so far as to argue that the Qur'an *prohibits* Muslims from believing that the Prophet was calling upon his followers to establish a political state, as Muhammad's message should be "untainted by anything that has to do with government" (36). Similarly, Egyptian jurist Muhammad Sa'id Al-'Ashmawi (1998: 56) avers that "political conceptions of religion are extremely dangerous for Islam and for its *shari'a*," insisting that calls for an Islamic state have no theological basis in Islam.

On the other end of the spectrum are those who insist that Islam, and its foundational texts, *requires* Muslims to establish a political system, though the nature of this system has been heavily debated. Many scholars agree that calls for the reestablishment of a global Islamic caliphate by some contemporary Islamists and, in particular, transnational jihadists, exaggerate the extent to which such a polity ever existed. As many critics of the Ottoman Caliphate pointed out after its abolition in 1924, the "real Caliphate" was in existence for only three decades after the death of the Prophet, and the imposed political structure which lasted for centuries after was maintained largely by brute force for utilitarian rather than theological purposes (Enayat 2005: 83). This "fictitious Caliphate" was limited not only in its legitimacy but also in its territorial scope. During the ninth and tenth centuries, for example, the 'Abbasid dynasty struggled not only with the growing influence of Shi'a regimes, such as the Fatimids, but additionally with the fact that Sunni Muslims living in Spain and Morocco continued to recognize the Umayyads of Cordoba as their caliph (Bennison 2009: 43). Moreover, after the fall of 'Abbasid rule, most members of the *umma* in Central Asia, Persia, and Africa did not recognize the Ottoman Caliphate or perceive themselves as part of a unified, transnational structure of Islamic political authority.

As an alternative to the establishment of a modern caliphate, contemporary Islamists have put forth calls for establishing "Islamic states." Islamism (that is, political Islam) provides the primary means by which we may transition from a discussion of transnational Islam into a discussion of transnational Islamic governance. Islamism has been aptly defined by Mohammad Ayoob (2008: 2) as "a form of instrumentalization of Islam by individuals and organizations that pursue political objectives." The emergence of contemporary Islamism traces back to the colonial period of the nineteenth century, when religious reformers such as Jamal al-Din al-Afghani and Muhammad Abdu advocated pan-Islamic unity and a "return" to the Islam of the Prophet and the *Rashidun* to address contemporary challenges in Muslim societies, particularly with regard to the struggle against foreign occupation and the dilemma of reconciling Islam with Western modernity. Building on the ideas of al-Afghani and Abdu, though ultimately reformulating their orientation, Rashid Rida, Hasan al-Banna, and Abul Ala Mawdudi transformed Islam into a modern political ideology.

While substantial majorities in predominantly Muslim countries believe *Shari'a* should provide "a" source of legislation (Esposito and Mogahed 2007), Islamism does not unambiguously dominate the political ideology of the majority of the global Muslim population. In majority-Muslim countries in the Middle East, for example, one observes a spectrum of self-identified "Islamists" competing for political power with a spectrum of self-identified "liberals," "leftists," "nationalists," and "secularists" who happen to be Muslim. Hybridized versions of these political ideologies are also active in Muslim-majority polities, as seen in the cases of the "Islamic Left" and "liberal Islam," the latter of which has most notably gained ground in Egyptian politics under the term *wasatiyya* (centrism) (Browers 2009: 48). Furthermore, the majority of European and North American Muslims are not Islamists; rather, they have been described as "culturalists," meaning they interpret their Islamic faith as primarily ethno-historical and cultural, as "a family tradition and a source of identity, but not as the center of their lives" (Vidino 2010: 10).

Pertinent to the trajectory of Global Governance, it is noteworthy that the majority of Islamists do not seek the destruction of the territorially defined nation-state. As Lee (2010: 14) observes, "their victory ... would perhaps be the ultimate legitimation of political modernity," as it would signify "the nationalization of Islam." The category of Islamists who have taken the most rejectionist stance towards the existence of the modern, territorially defined system of states is that of the "transnational jihadists." Unlike the vast majority of Islamist groups who can be conceptualized as "mainstream" given their rejection of violence and willingness to participate in electoral systems of governance, "transnational jihadists" are distinguished by their global scale of operations as well as their willingness to use force, particularly against the "far enemy" (Gerges 2009).

Al-Qaeda is the most prominent example of a transnational jihadist network, and has famously called for both the reestablishment of the Islamic Caliphate and the disassembling of the territorial nation-state system in the Muslim world. Bin Laden has described the latter as a Western/American imperialist "scheme" imposed on Muslim societies to weaken and divide them. This rejection of the contemporary state system with regard to the Muslim world has led scholars like Barak Mendelsohn (2005) to conclude that al-Qaeda's brand of Islamism poses a challenge to the very nature of the international system by calling into question its most fundamental organizing principle: territorially bound state sovereignty.

Another transnational Islamist group, Hizb ut-Tahrir, similarly calls for the revival of the caliphate but must be distinguished from al-Qaeda in that it does not advocate the use of force. Established by Palestinian Shaykh Taqiuddin al-Nabhani in Jordanian-controlled East Jerusalem in the early 1950s, Hizb ut-Tahrir envisions the peaceful restoration of an Islamic Caliphate as a central component in reshaping Muslim society and governance. While its objectives have been presented in universal, pan-Islamic terms, its members have demonstrated an inclination to initiate the caliphate restoration project in the Arab world, and it has a "small but committed" following in Indonesia (Fealy 2004; Ward 2009). The vision of Hizb ut-Tahrir has very limited support, and the organization is described by Ayoob (2008: 140) as operating "on the fringes of Islamist political activity, with very little impact on the day-to-day political and social struggles in the vast majority of Muslim countries." Thus, while the political objectives of this transnational Islamist group are certainly global in scope, the implications of its "fringe" influence on Islamist Global Governance should not be exaggerated.

The more popular governance objective among Islamists calls for the establishment of an "Islamic state," which ultimately borrows from and reinforces territorial nationalism more than rejecting it. Rashid Rida is considered the father of the modern conception of the Islamic state. Rida emphasized the logistical barriers to reestablishing the Caliphate, including the determination of who was qualified to legitimately rule over all Muslims, where the Caliphate's capital would be located, and how different sects of Muslims would be allowed to follow their own rules. In proposing to reorganize the Caliphate, Rida essentially suggested a new entity with new institutions (Enayat 2005: 115). Rida's outline for an Islamic state consisted of the following: (1) government implementation of *shura* (consultation) between the ruler and the ruled to ensure democracy; (2) a constitution inspired in its general principles by the Qur'an, the Sunna, and the experiences of the *Rashidun* (the first four "rightly guided" caliphs); (3) legislation which implements both *Shari'a* as well as "positive law," so long as it does not contradict *Shari'a*; and (4) a Caliph (that is, head of state) "elected by the representatives of all Muslims from a group of highly trained jurisconsults" (ibid.: 121).[2]

The Islamist pioneers who followed Rida had their own visions of Islamic polities. Mawdudi used the phrase "theo-democracy" to describe his preferred political system. Rather than seeking to recreate the Caliphate of the *Rashidun*,

---

2   Enayat also notes that, according to Rida's vision of the Islamic State, faith would be an individual matter, non-Muslim minorities would have secure access to work and worship, and women would be equal to men in all arenas of social engagement outside the leadership of the home.

Mawdudi borrowed heavily from Western representative institutions. This can be seen in his "tripartite division of governmental functions among the principal organs of the Islamic state" (Ayoob 2008: 68). In his vision of an institutional separation of powers, Mawdudi described a legislature, judiciary, and popularly elected executive responsible for interpreting and implementing *Shari'a*. According to Mawdudi, this interpretation need not confirm to earlier theological and jurisprudential rulings, so long as new interpretations could be legitimized by *qiyas* (analogy). Al-Banna's formula for an Islamic state similarly sought to adapt Western representative institutions to Islamic governance. Specifically, al-Banna envisioned a strong executive, a consultative council with limited legislative functions, and an independent judiciary. Like Rida, he emphasized a constitution inspired by the Qur'an, a government operating in accordance with *shura* (consultation), and a "social contract" between the ruler and ruled. Al-Banna's blueprint for an Islamic state has been described as "a quasi-democratic, representative system" guided by a minimalist and flexible definition of "Islamic" (Ayoob 2008: 71).

With the basic tenets of these conceptualizations of Islamic governance established, it is worth revisiting the question of globality. Here, there is some ambiguity as to how transnational or global in scope these conceptualizations were. On one hand, scholars have observed that al-Banna perceived the Muslim Brotherhood "not as a political party but rather 'as an idea and a creed, a system and a syllabus ... not bounded by a place or group of people'" (Vidino 2010: 40). On the other hand, the Muslim Brotherhood under al-Banna functioned very much as a localized political party, shaped by the distinct political atmosphere of a territorially defined Egypt. Al-Banna's attempts to create a multinational organization were ultimately disabled by the repressive policies of the Egyptian regimes under which it operated. More recently, in 1982, a formal international organization of the Muslim Brotherhood was attempted, but ultimately failed due to travel bans and security restrictions on Arab branch members, as well as a general perception of Egyptian domination (ibid.: 38–9). While the degree to which mainstream Islamists today are actively seeking transnational or global Islamic states is questionable, how these organizations challenge the authority and legitimacy of the states in which they operate and contribute to a transnational Islamic space has important implications for Global Governance. This chapter will now turn to an assessment of three case studies of Islamist organizations: the Muslim Brotherhood, Hamas, and Hizbullah.

Islamist Organizations and Global Governance

The Muslim Brotherhood

Founded by Egyptian activist Hassan al-Banna in 1928, the establishment of the Muslim Brotherhood (*al-Ikhwan al-Muslimin)* in Egypt was a watershed moment for political Islam as the ideology and philosophy of Islamism was translated into a grassroots organization. The formation of the *Ikhwan* was in many ways a reaction of al-Banna to the British political and military presence in Egypt and to the ruling elite's perceived collaboration with their "colonial masters" (Ayoob 2008: 66). In this way, the *Ikhwan's* origins were shaped by al-Banna's view that Islam and nationalism were fully compatible, and that the regeneration of Islam internationally began with its regeneration in Egypt. Al-Banna's Islamist vision was a "bottom-up" process in which Egyptians would first come to internalize Islamic values at the grassroots level and then gradually transform the nature of the social and political order. While al-Banna's view of an Islamic state was discussed in the previous section of this chapter, it is worth reiterating that he felt the existing constitutional parliamentary framework of the Egyptian political system could be adapted to conform to Islamic principles.

While the organization underwent a period of militancy under the leadership of Sayyid Qutb in the 1950s and 1960s, the Muslim Brotherhood today can be categorized as a "mainstream" Islamist organization, given that it has renounced the use of violence and actively seeks to participate in the electoral politics of the Egyptian political system. This participatory brand of political Islam advocated by the *Ikhwan* in Egypt has been termed "Islamic Constitutionalism." Islamic Constitutionalism resembles classical liberalism in that the state is to be constrained by law, citizens are to actively participate in lawmaking, and the law is to apply equally to the ruler and the ruled. While Islamic Constitutionalism envisions "liberal" governance in these ways, there are also crucial components emphasizing "Islamic" governance: First, its "Islamic" elements are evident with regard to the *purpose* of state. While Western liberalism emphasizes limiting state power to the extent that its primary responsibility is to maintain order, Islamic Constitutionalism additionally vests the state with the moral obligation of implementing *Shari'a* and enhancing the piety of the community. In this way, Islamic Constitutionalism requires a much more invasive state than that required by classical liberalism or democratic theory (Rutherford 2006: 727). Secondly, Islamic Constitutionalists draw heavily on Islamic concepts for lawmaking, such as *maslaha* (public good), *ijtihad* (interpretation), *ijma* (consensus), *qiyas* (analogy), and *talfiq* (synthesis). Secular or "man-made" laws are permissible so long as they do not contradict Islamic law, and are in fact viewed as necessary components to the legislative process in light of the recognition that the Qur'an and Sunna are silent on many details of governing a state (ibid.: 711).

In advocating a transformation of the Egyptian state to reflect these elements of Islamic governance, the Muslim Brotherhood is challenging the status quo political order. However, its rise in popularity under the former Mubarak regime was rooted as much if not more in its social welfare and educational activities than in its philosophical formula for an Islamic state. As noted by Abed-Kotob (1995), the provision of social services has long been a key strategy of the Muslim Brotherhood in order to gain legitimacy among the Egyptian public. These social services include the establishment and operation of charitable schools, hospitals, medical clinics, care centers for orphans and widows, and vocational training for the unemployed; these are made available to Egyptians regardless of ideology or religious observance. Despite its lack of an official party license under the former Mubarak regime, the Muslim Brotherhood ran an estimated 20 percent of the 5,000 or so legally registered NGOs and associations in Egypt ("Egypt: Social Programmes," 2006).[3] Denis Sullivan (1994: 58) summarizes the growth of such Islamic private voluntary organizations in Egypt as follows:

> Islamic private voluntary organizations (PVOs) and other groups are attempting to fill the void left by a government that is increasingly unable to devote its limited resources to a plethora of problem areas: education and training, housing, health care, agricultural and industrial productivity, employment, and transportation ... Whether the grass-roots, *social* organizations [of the Egyptian Islamic movement] ... pose a challenge to governmental legitimacy is an important concern of the Egyptian government and its supporters.

Here, Sullivan justifiably links the activities of Islamist groups like the Muslim Brotherhood to a failure on the part of the state to meet the basic social needs and expectations of its citizens. This notion of "filling a void" in state governance is similarly observable in the cases of Hamas and Hizbullah.

Hamas

Established by Sheikh Ahmad Yassin as the political arm of the Palestinian Muslim Brotherhood in 1987, Hamas has been conceptualized as an "Islamist National Resistance" group given its discrete territorial objectives and its maintenance of an armed wing to carry out acts of political violence and self-described "resistance" activities against Israeli occupation. The political ideology of Hamas thus affords an interesting compatibility between Palestinian nationalism and commitment to the idea of a universal *umma* (Ayoob 2008: 114). This hybridization of political Islam and nationalism has become increasingly prevalent in the Arab world since the decline of secular pan-Arab nationalism, epitomized in the defeat of Egyptian and Syrian-led forces by Israel in 1967. As an "Islamist National Resistance" organization, Hamas engages in several realms which necessarily factor into an assessment of its implications for Global Governance. First, it engages actively in Palestinian civil society, taking on many social and charitable endeavors which resemble those of private volunteer organizations in other contexts. Secondly, it operates as a political party in the occupied territories, and won a major electoral victory against Fatah in the 2004–06 municipal and legislative elections.[4] Finally,

---

3   Many of the associations were registered under different names and associated with less well-known members of the *Ikhwan*.

4   Hamas operations in the West Bank have been severely impacted by the outbreak of violence between Hamas and Fatah after the 2006 elections. Many Hamas members elected to office in the West Bank were forced, amidst this violence, out of office and fled to

Hamas engages in violent "resistance" activities—described as "terrorism" by Israel and the United States—via its armed wing, the Qassam Brigades. This militant wing of the organization has vied for prestige *vis-à-vis* other nationalist groups in the territories by employing suicide bombings, kidnappings, and other violent tactics since 1994 (Bloom 2004).

The examination of the extent to which Hamas represents a broader trend of Islamist organizations challenging "state" authority is complicated by the lack of a formal Palestinian state apparatus. However, if one considers the Fatah-dominated Palestinian Authority (PA) as the internationally recognized administrative body of the Palestinians, or takes the Fatah-dominated Palestinian Liberation Organization (PLO) as the organization vested with legitimate authority by the international community to represent the Palestinian people, one may indeed conceptualize Hamas as challenging the de facto "state" authority. The PLO, established in 1964, was officially declared the sole legitimate representative of the Palestinian people by both the Arab League and the United Nations in 1974. The PLO additionally gained recognition by Israel and the United States as legitimately representing the Palestinians during the Oslo peace process in 1993, which led to the establishment of the Palestinian Authority as a formal administrative body in 1994. Hamas, on the other hand, has been delegitimized as a negotiating partner by both Israel and the United States, and has not been afforded the official recognition granted to the secular, Fatah-dominated PLO by either the United Nations or the Arab League. Indeed, a great deal of its popularity stems from the extent to which Hamas has been perceived as an alternative to the official, internationally recognized Palestinian Authority.

With regard to its platform for an "Islamic State," Hamas advocates an executive, judicial, and legislative branch; the latter is envisioned as consisting of a popularly elected *shura* (consultative) council, with legislation inspired by the general principles of *Shari'a* law as well as secular sources of legal and scientific knowledge in matters where *Shari'a* is silent. Hamas emphasizes *shura* (consultation) and *ijma* (consensus) via regular popular elections as conditions of legitimate authority; as such, the organization often describes its project for an Islamic state as "shura democracy" (Gunning 2009: 59).[5] The creation of this Islamic Palestinian state is viewed as a gradual, organic process which would ultimately be affirmed by national referendum. In this way, Hamas takes a "bottom-up" approach to Islamization, emphasizing, as natural precursors to the creation of an Islamic state, the socialization of Palestinians into recognizing and internalizing the importance of Islamic principles and the creation of institutional and economic foundations for a Muslim polity (ibid.: 91).

Gaza. At the time of writing, Hamas retains Gaza as a stronghold while Fatah has a greater presence in the West Bank.

5   As Gunning notes, citizenship would be granted to all citizens of the Islamic state, including women, regardless of religious affiliation, though women could not run for head of state (ibid.: 62).

This "bottom-up" approach to Islamization has manifested itself in an array of social action initiatives. Hamas's prioritization of social development can be seen, for example, in its creation of an extensive infrastructure of charitable social services for the poor, including vocational training, health care, and education. Education began to suffer during the first *intifada*, when schools were closed down for months at a time as PLO-affiliated leadership declared that the general strikes applied also to schools. Hamas, however, exempted educational establishments from participation in the strikes and issued a statement in 1989 (periodic statement no. 45) titled, "Read, in the name of thy God, the Creator. Learning and studying are a sacred right that we safeguard" (Hroub 2000: 238). Hamas additionally established orphanages, nurseries, relief societies, medical clinics, *zakat* (alms) committees, and sports clubs (ibid.: 233–5).The charitable services provided by Hamas have distinguished it from its secular PLO counterpart. As Israeli policies towards the occupied territories hardened and the Palestinian economy languished, the PA appeared increasingly unable to deliver basic social services to the Palestinian people, particularly to those living in the congested refugee camps and shantytowns of Gaza. In light of these PA shortcomings, Hamas's network of charitable services moved in to "fill the void" (Ayoob 2008: 125).

These social services provided by Hamas have contributed to its competitiveness as a political party. Within four months of coming to power in 2004 in the West Bank town of Bidya, Hamas councilors brought in new transformers to repair the village's electricity, and additionally replaced the village's outdated and ineffective water pipe infrastructure. Other newly elected Hamas councilmen constructed new town entrances, installed streetlamps, reinforced roads, and cleaned beaches and streets (Gunning 2009: 152–3). Hamas has undoubtedly capitalized on the public demand for such projects, which the Fatah-led government too often failed to provide. In contrast to the PA's reputation of corruption and ineffectiveness, these social services have enabled Hamas to establish a reputation of efficiency and accountability, even among segments of the Palestinian public which do not agree with its religious vision or its traditionally militant stance *vis-à-vis* the peace process.

This brings us to a third dimension of the organization: its armed wing. Were Hamas to engage only in charity, social services, and electoral participation, it could perhaps be categorized as a "mainstream" Islamist organization, like the Muslim Brotherhood in Egypt. However, it is worth reiterating that Hamas evolved into an organization distinct from the Palestinian Brotherhood in the context of the first *intifada*, which shaped its self-perception as an entity engaged first and foremost in "resistance" to Israeli occupation. That "resistance" was perceived by Hamas members as necessitating something beyond politics and social action can be seen in the decision to create the Izz al-Din al-Qassam Brigades in 1992, which began carrying out "martyrdom" operations in 1994. The Qassam Brigades have been designated a terrorist organization by the United States, Israel, the United Kingdom, Australia, and the European Union, and have made Hamas the central target of Israel since the 2000 al-Aqsa *intifada*. Public support for this violent resistance among the Palestinian population has varied, depending on the political and temporal context, and in recent years, Hamas has curtailed its suicide bombing operations. While the extent to which Hamas is directly responsible for recent rocket fire into Israel from Gaza is debatable,[6] the organization's refusal to disassemble its armed wing continues to hamper its recognition by the international community as a legitimate representative of the Palestinian nationalist movement. Its use of violence, or at least its insistence on the option to use violence, thus continues to challenge the PA's monopoly on the legitimate use of force.

Hizbullah

Like Hamas, Hizbullah is multifunctional and can be categorized as an "Islamist National Resistance" organization. Hizbullah emerged shortly after the Israeli invasion of Lebanon in 1982, and for 18 years engaged in "resistance" activities against the Israeli occupation. Its nationalist and irredentist origins distinguish it from transnational jihadist organizations, though its maintenance of an armed wing and engagement in political violence precludes its classification as a "mainstream" Islamist group. Its activities in the realm of charitable and social services highlight similarities with private volunteer organizations, while its entrance into and subsequent successes in the Lebanese confessional parliamentary system reveal its importance as a Shi'a political party. It is to some extent part of the state, but also challenges Lebanese state authority in important ways. Hizbullah's relationship with the state is further compounded by the fact that it receives significant material and ideological support from external political actors, particularly Iran and Syria.[7]

For nearly the first decade of its existence, Hizbullah was defined by its role as a clandestine militia, influenced in part by the Lebanese civil war but shaped primarily by its fight against the Israeli military occupation of southern Lebanon. The Israeli occupation bolstered support for Hizbullah even among those that did not share its ideological orientation and Islamist vision, and the Israeli troop withdrawal in 2000 solidified the perception among many Lebanese that Hizbullah was "the only Arab force capable of compelling Israel to cede conquered Arab territory" (Ayoob 2008: 122). This underscores the extent to which Hizbullah has challenged a fundamental expectation of the State—that its official military wields the sole legitimate use of force and is better prepared to do so than any non-state

---

6   At the time of writing, Hamas claims to be actively engaged in preventing rocket fire at Israel from rogue individuals by deploying its security forces along the Gaza–Israel border. For example, see "Hamas Vows" (2011).

7   It is important to emphasize that despite this external support, it is inaccurate to characterize Hizbullah as merely a "puppet" of the Iranian or Syrian regimes. For example, Hizbullah has had to share its Shi'a parliamentary seats with Amal to ameliorate Syrian fears that Hizbullah might acquire too much power and ultimately harm Syrian interests. For Ayoob (2008: 121), this indicates "an acknowledgement on the part of Damascus that it could not control Hizbullah."

apparatus. On the contrary, many Lebanese have looked to Hizbullah's soldiers as an alternative to a seemingly impotent Lebanese army.

In 1992, Hizbullah began to transform itself into a mainstream political party, participating in parliamentary elections and adapting its ideological stances in the process. Perhaps most significantly, Hizbullah has grown to accept the confessional parliamentary nature of the Lebanese political system, actively forming coalitions with non-Islamist and non-Muslim parties and distancing itself from its original goal of establishing a Shi'a Islamic polity (ibid.: 122). This pragmatism has enabled Hizbullah to control a large parliamentary bloc of 14 deputies, out of a total of 128 national legislators, and garner 60 percent of municipalities in southern Lebanon (Flanigan and Abdel-Samad 2009: 123). In this regard, Hizbullah has a significant amount of national political power and is thus part of the Lebanese state. Hizbullah's political success has emanated not only from its armed resistance of Israeli occupation, but additionally from its vast network of social services.

Lara Deeb (2008: 67) describes Hizbullah as "the political party in Lebanon that best responds to its constituents' needs and desires in the country, both politically and economically." It does so primarily via its highly organized system of health and social service organizations, which cater mostly to the country's Shi'a communities, but sometimes benefit non-Shi'a citizens as well. This system is comprised of a Social Unit, Education Unit, and Islamic Health Unit; many of the service organizations operating under these umbrella branches are registered with the Lebanese government as NGOs (Flanigan and Abdel-Samad 2009: 124).[8] Hizbullah's social institutions provide monthly support to the poor in the form of nutritional, educational, housing, and healthcare assistance. Hizbullah also supports orphanages, war damage reconstruction projects, medical clinics, garbage collection operations, water treatment facilities, and low-cost hospitals, including a school for children with Down's syndrome (Deeb 2008: 67).[9] The war damage reconstruction efforts, which are carried out by Hizbullah's "Jihad Construction Foundation," proved essential after Israel's aerial bombardment of Lebanon in the summer of 2006. Similarly, Hizbullah's "Foundation for the Wounded" provides aid to civilians injured during Israeli assaults, while its "Martyrs' Foundation" grants financial and social assistance to the families of "martyrs" killed during combat with Israeli military forces.

As of 2009, Hizbullah's Islamic Health Unit operated three hospitals, 12 health centers, 20 infirmaries, and 20 dental clinics. Hizbullah's health unit has also embarked on projects to offer free health insurance and prescription drug coverage by partnering with local pharmacies. It is worth noting that Hizbullah's

---

8   The authors point out that this NGO status enables easier collaboration with partner organizations that are circumspect of the "Hizbullah" name.

9   As Deeb observes, other social welfare-oriented organizations operate alongside Hizbullah, including those affiliated with Fadlallah, family associations, and Shi'a women's organizations.

Health Unit has been so successful in meeting the public health needs of Lebanese citizens that several government-run hospitals in southern Lebanon and the Bekaa Valley requested it take over their operations (Flanigan and Abdel-Samad 2009: 125). This underscores the extent to which Hizbullah operates as a "state within a state," or a "state within a *non-state*" as Deeb (2008) proposes, filling a void left by the State in poor Shi'a areas of the country. The varied sources of public support Hizbullah receives across Shi'a, Christian, and Druze segments of the population are ultimately rooted in the organization's presentation of an alternative to the status quo governance and/or identity supplied by the Lebanese state, either in terms of religious orientation, social welfare infrastructure, or military defense.

Trends Across Cases

Several important patterns can be observed from this examination of the Muslim Brotherhood in Egypt, Hamas in the Palestinian Territories, and Hizbullah in Lebanon. First, in all three cases, the Islamist organization in focus either rivals or outperforms the state/official administrative apparatus in the provision of basic social services, particularly with regard to the poor. In the Lebanese case, Flanigan and Abdel-Samad (2009: 128) summarize this phenomenon as follows: "Decades after the end of the civil war, the Lebanese government remains inert, unable to provide for many of the basic needs of its population. In this vacuum, Hezbollah has emerged to become one of the country's most important and competent service providers." Similarly, the social services and institutions provided by the Muslim Brotherhood have in many regards addressed a fundamental "void" left by the Egyptian state. This void is perhaps intensified in the Palestinian case, as there is no formal state apparatus; in this context, the educational, medical, and infrastructure services provided by Hamas have enabled many Palestinians to view the organization as better adept at meeting basic governance expectations than the Fatah-dominated Palestinian Authority.

Secondly, in the cases of Hamas and Hizbullah, these Islamist organizations additionally challenge the official source of authority with regard to its monopoly on the legitimate use of force. In the Palestinian territories, Hamas fighters have engaged in direct battles with Fatah/PA security forces. The engagement of the Qassam Brigades in suicide bombing operations and other such tactics of political violence challenges existing international norms regarding the use of force against civilian targets; in designating civilians as legitimate casualties of its struggle for national liberation, Hamas is challenging the status quo juxtaposition of state versus non-state use of force, in which the former is traditionally constructed as morally sanctioned in its application of violence and, to some extent, in its infliction of civilian casualties, whereas the latter is traditionally constructed as unauthorized to use any matter of force and is designated with the "terrorist" descriptor. In light of the failure of diplomatic negotiations with Israel to produce a fully sovereign, contiguous Palestinian state, Hamas has presented Palestinians with an alternative framework of national liberation which employs (or at least reserves as a possibility) violence as a tactic of resistance.[10] In Lebanon, this challenge to state authority is more direct, as Hizbullah maintains its armed wing despite the existence of an official Lebanese army. While Hizbullah's use of kidnappings, hijackings, suicide bombings, and other unconventional warfare tactics against Israel has challenged international norms regarding appropriate and/or legitimate use of force, its perceived victories as a paramilitary actor in driving Israel out of south Lebanon in 2000 and inflicting substantial casualties in its war with Israel in 2006 are especially relevant in underscoring the extent to which it challenges state authority in this realm.

Third, all three cases highlight a "national-transnational paradox" in that the examined Islamist organizations exemplify a fundamental tension among their aspects which strive, on one hand, to be detached from territorially defined space and nationality but are, on the other hand, locally and translocally bound reifications of the nation-state. On the issue of creating an "Islamic state," for example, all three organizations examined in this chapter illustrate Ayoob's (2008: 72) observation that the Muslim Brotherhood's model for an Islamic polity "takes the existence of sovereign states as given and does not attempt to replace them by a universal polity." Territorially defined nationalism factors prominently into Hamas's vision of political Islam, as it seeks to liberate occupied land for the creation of an independent Palestinian state. Moreover, in its pragmatic competition for political power in the Lebanese confessional system, Hizbullah appears to have moved a significant distance from its original objective of an Islamic state. As such, the nationally and territorially defined operations and objectives of these organizations must be weighed against the external support they receive and the ideological influence they wield across several Arab and majority-Muslim polities. While occasional rhetoric indicates these groups seek to establish supranational Islamic polities in which territorial boundaries among Muslims dissolve, the utopian vision of installing a global Caliphate appears diluted, if not completely subsumed, by local territorial considerations.

The national-transnational paradox is intensified by the observation among scholars of political Islam that these organizations are in many ways part of a broader, supraterritorial social movement. Janine Clark (2004: 942), for example, approaches the study of Islamic social institutions in Egypt, Jordan and Yemen from the theoretical framework of social movement theory, conceptualizing these institutions as webs or networks of linkages loosely bound by the same ideology and symbols. This perspective envisions Islamist groups across the globe, and particularly those which have established extensive networks of private voluntary organizations, as engaged in a symbolic political protest against the ruling secular state. Likewise, in his analysis of the "new Muslim Brotherhood in the West,"

---

10   At the time of writing, some analysts believe that the PA's bid for statehood at the United Nations is primarily an attempt to bolster domestic credibility in light of its dwindling authority ("Palestine Statehood," 2011), while the hesitation of Hamas to support this bid underscores the entrenchment of its competition with the PA ("Palestinian Statehood Bid," 2011).

Vidino (2010: 39) defines the Brotherhood as "a global ideological movement in which like-minded individuals interact through an informal yet very sophisticated international network of personal, financial, and especially ideological ties."

In justifying this definition of the Brotherhood in Europe and North America as adherence to a set of ideas and methods rather than formal membership or affiliation, Vidino (2010) observes a host of shared characteristics among Islamist networks transnationally with regard to: methods of education and political activism; tactics of "Islamizing knowledge" via the translation, publication and dissemination of Islamist texts; frequent interactions with other Islamists via international conferences and collaborations; and membership in Islamist "superstructures" like the Federation of Islamic Organizations in Europe (FIOE). Also supporting this construction of the Muslim Brotherhood as a global movement are the statements of prominent members, like Egyptian *Ikhwan* member Abd El Monem Abou El Foutouh, who has described the Brotherhood as "an international school of thought" given its establishment of informal networks of groups and individuals who share a similar vision for Islam and the future (ibid.: 42).

If one views the Muslim Brotherhood and other mainstream Islamist groups in this fashion, focusing on the scope of their connections, collaborations, and shared ideological perspectives, there is much evidence for Islamist transnationalism. This is particularly so with regard to the role of new media technologies, discussed in the first section of this chapter. Related to the role of new technology in facilitating a globalized Islamism, there additionally appears to be a globalized discourse of Islamic activism. While Ayoob (2008: 16) is careful to emphasize the extent to which various Islamist groups are locally and territorially bound, he nonetheless acknowledges the globalization of a shared Islamist rhetoric: "The various Islamist movements take recourse to similar vocabulary because they draw their inspiration from the same sources and also because this vocabulary is familiar to their audiences." All three cases of Islamist groups examined in this chapter employ the common slogan "Islam is the solution" in their endeavors to demonstrate the superiority of an Islamist polity to a more secular administrative body that appears to have neglected the needs of its most disenfranchised citizens. In their charitable and social action initiatives, these groups also utilize the shared rhetoric of *da'wa,* which literally means "the call" to Islam, but is perhaps better defined as "activating Islam through deed in all spheres of life" (Clark 2004: 948). Finally, all three of these groups utilize participationist rhetoric emphasizing the importance of citizen involvement in governance, though the specific formulation of this rhetoric is very much tied to the discrete local circumstances of each organization.

Future Trajectories of Authority and Global Governance

The shared emphasis by Islamist movements on civic and electoral participation may be a manifestation of their resistance to productive power; as Barnett and Duvall (2005: 23) observe, "knowledgeable actors become aware of discursive tensions … and use that knowledge in strategic ways (e.g., deconstructing or inverting the discourse) to increase their sovereignty, control their own fate, and remake their very identities." Islamists have undoubtedly recognized the extent to which their detractors have sought to delegitimize them by characterizing them as anti-modern and anti-democratic. In this way, their emphasis on democratic procedures and progressive social action may have emerged in part as a response to their critics and to the broader power imbalance between the "Muslim world" and "the West," in which the latter has socially produced the capacities and identities of the former. At the same time, it is clear today that the focus by many Islamist groups on civic and electoral participation is driven by two mutually constituting realities. First, these Islamist groups have become political pragmatists in their competition to maximize power. Secondly, populations in majority Arab and Muslim polities in the Middle East have growing societal expectations of access to democratic mechanisms of governance.

If states in the region continue to fail in providing their citizens with such mechanisms, as seen in the case of Egypt, and to a lesser extent, in the case of the Shi'a in Lebanon, Islamist sources of opposition will continue to garner legitimacy. However, as the recent revolutions in Egypt and Tunisia illustrate, Islamist groups do not monopolize the voices of opposition or the calls for democratic governance, and typically form coalitions with non-Islamist groups that share their vision for a less oppressive state.[11] On a related note, if states in the region continue to fail in providing their citizens with adequate access to basic social goods, Islamist movements will continue to achieve popularity by filling this void. All three cases examined in this chapter underscore this trend, and suggest that state authority in the Middle East will be undermined by Islamist movements so long as this reality creates a vacuum in the arena of social services. This is related directly to Craig Murphy's (2002: xv) observation that "governance" implies "a concept of power that emphasizes capability, power as the ability to do things." In situations where states or official administrative bodies are unable to "get things done," Islamist groups are poised to compete with these actors over claims of good governance.

With regard to the legitimate use of force, the future trajectory of both state and international authority in the Middle East is ambiguous. On one hand, the evolution of groups like Hamas and Hizbullah indicate a trend of moderation with regard to political questions of governance. While not officially changing its charter, Hamas additionally appears to have moderated on the issue of a two-state solution.[12] On

---

11   As Rutherford (2006: 720) discusses, this coalition-building strategy for the Muslim Brotherhood dates back to the 1980s, when its members were able to win seats in the Egyptian Parliament through alliances with the Wafd, Liberal, and Labor parties. Similarly, in the buildup to the recent ousting of President Mubarak, the *Ikhwan* acted in conjunction with leftists, secularists, nationalists, and others. This coalition across ideologies manifested itself most clearly in opposition activities organized by *Kifeya* (Enough).

12   For example, Khaled Meshaal told former President Jimmy Carter in 2008 that Hamas would accept a Palestinian state on the 1967 borders and would accept the right

the other hand, both groups refuse to abolish their armed wings or abandon their unconventional warfare tactics, as they feel this element of militant "resistance" is integral to their continued legitimacy in the arenas of nationalist and/or irredentist struggles. Given the lack of a formal state apparatus in the case of Hamas, its armed wing is perceived by members of the organization as a necessary instrument for engaging in asymmetric warfare with Israel. In light of the Israeli withdrawal of troops from southern Lebanon in 2000, Hizbullah justifies the continued existence of its armed wing by pointing to continued Israeli presence on a sliver of disputed border territory, Sheba'a Farms. However, it seems likely that Hizbullah will cling to its paramilitary activities regardless of this disputed piece of land, as it perceives its armed resistance as an important ingredient in its promise to defend Lebanese sovereignty. As such, the Westphalian norm holding the state to be the only actor legitimately authorized to use violence will likely remain challenged in both of these contexts. It is also noteworthy that the authority of international institutions of governance such as the United Nations and the Geneva Conventions will likely remain challenged in these contexts; for example, both Hamas and the Israeli government have been accused of committing "war crimes" in Gaza during their December 2008 battle ("Human rights in Palestine," 2009).

Finally, the implications of this analysis suggest that most Islamist movements in the Middle East are actively seeking to be *part of the state* and to transform it on these terms, rather than seeking to *overturn the state* or to replace it with a supranational structure of governance. In this way, Islamist movements in the region are aptly termed "transnational" as they have material and ideological elements spanning multiple states, but are still very much envisioning their own rise to power within the context of the territorially defined nation-state system. The most significant exception to this trend is found on the transnational jihadist end of the Islamist spectrum, in which networks like al-Qaeda view themselves as waging a violent global struggle that rejects the division of the Muslim world into sovereign nation-state polities. While groups like al-Qaeda are often highlighted as examples *par excellence* of transnational networks of people tied together despite the limitations of national borders,[13] it bears reiterating that they represent the fringe minority of Islamists worldwide.

That many Islamists are striving to share power with state authorities affirms Wilkinson's (2002: 2) conceptualization of Global Governance:

---

of Israel to live as a neighbor if such a peace deal were approved by a national Palestinian referendum ("Hamas Ready," 2008). Similarly, in November 2008, Gaza Hamas leader Ismail Haniyeh reiterated to a group of European parliamentarians that Hamas was willing to accept a Palestinian state within the 1967 borders ("Haniyeh: Hamas Willing," 2008).

13   For example, Juergensmeyer (2002: 153) discusses Islamic movements in general as "especially" holding the illusion of being engaged in global struggle, but focuses primarily on al-Qaeda and religious terrorists as examples of "e-mail ethnicities."

… global governance can be thought of as the various patterns in which global, regional, national and local actors combine to govern particular areas. Global governance, then, is not defined simply by the emergence of new actors or nodes of authority; instead it comprises a growing complexity in the way in which its actors interact and interrelate.

This increasingly complex amalgam of interrelations is evident in the interactions of Islamist groups, which often operate political parties, social institutions, and in some cases paramilitary wings, with state actors (or in the case of Hamas, with actors officially recognized by the international community as representing the Palestinian people in lieu of a formal state).

References

'Abd al-Raziq, A. (1998). "Message Not Government, Religion Not State," in Kurzman, C. (ed.), *Liberal Islam: A Sourcebook* (Oxford: Oxford University Press).

Abed-Kotob, S. (1995). "The Accommodationists Speak: Goals and Strategies of the Muslim Brotherhood of Egypt," *International Journal of Middle East Studies* 27(3): 321–39.

Al-'Ashmawi, M.S. (1998). "Sharia: The Codification of Islamic Law," in Kurzman, C. (ed.), *Liberal Islam: A Sourcebook* (Oxford: Oxford University Press).

Allievi S. and Nielsen, J. (eds) (2003). *Muslim Networks and Transnational Communities in and across Europe* (Boston, MA: Brill).

Ayoob, M. (2008). *The Many Faces of Political Islam: Religion and Politics in the Muslim World* (Ann Arbor: University of Michigan Press).

Barnett, M. and Duvall, R. (2005). "Power in Global Governance," in Barnett, M., and Duvall, R. (eds), *Power in Global Governance* (Cambridge: Cambridge University Press).

Bennison, A. (2009). *The Great Caliphs: The Golden Age of the 'Abbasid Empire* (New Haven, CT: Yale University Press).

Bloom, M. (2004). "Palestinian Suicide Bombing: Public Support, Market Share, and Outbidding," *Political Science Quarterly* 119(1): 61–88.

Bowen, J. (2011). "Beyond Migration: Islam as a Transnational Public Space," in Volpi, F. (ed.), *Political Islam: A Critical Reader* (London and New York: Routledge).

Browers, M.L. (2009). *Political Ideology in the Arab World: Accommodation and Transformation* (Cambridge: Cambridge University Press).

Clark, J. (2004). "Social Movement Theory and Patron-Clientelism: Islamic Social Institutions and the Middle Class in Egypt, Jordan and Yemen," *Comparative Political Studies* 37(8): 941–68.

Deeb, L. (2008). "Hizballah and its Civilian Constituencies in Lebanon," in Hovespian, N. (ed.), *The War on Lebanon: A Reader* (Northampton, MA: Olive Branch Press).

"Egypt: Social programmes bolster appeal of Muslim Brotherhood" (2006, 22 February). Retrieved on September 12, 2011 from <http://www.irinnews.org/report.aspx?reportid=26150>.

Esposito, J. and Mogahed, D. (2007). *Who Speaks for Islam: What a Billion Muslims Really Think* (New York: Gallup Press).

Enayat, H. (2005). *Modern Islamic Political Thought: The Response of the Shi'i and Sunni Muslims to the Twentieth Century* (London: Macmillan Press).

Fealy, G. (2004). "Islamic Radicalism in Indonesia: The Faltering Revival?" *Southeast Asian Affairs*, 104–21.

Flanigan, S.T. and Abdel-Samad, M. (2009). "Hezbollah's Social Jihad: Nonprofits as Resistance Organizations," *Middle East Policy* 16(2): 122–37.

Gerges, F. (2009). *The Far Enemy: Why Jihad Went Global* (Cambridge: Cambridge University Press).

Gunning, J. (2009). *Hamas in Politics: Democracy, Religion, Violence* (New York: Columbia University Press).

Halliday, F. (2005). *The Middle East in International Relations: Power, Politics, and Ideology* (Cambridge: Cambridge University Press).

"Hamas ready to accept 1967 borders" (2008, April 22). Retrieved September 16, 2011 from <http://english.aljazeera.net/news/middleeast/2008/04/2008615098393788.html>.

"Hamas vows to halt rocket fire at Israel" (2011, January 19). Retrieved September 12, 2011 from <http://www.theworld.org/2011/01/hamas-vows-to-halt-rocket-fire-at-israel/>.

"Haniyeh: Hamas willing to accept Palestinian state with 1967 borders" (2008, November 9). Retrieved September 12, 2011 from <http://www.haaretz.com/news/haniyeh-hamas-willing-to-accept-palestinian-state-with-1967-borders-1.256915>.

Hroub, K. (2000). *Hamas: Political Thought and Practice* (Washington, DC: Institute for Palestine Studies).

"Human rights in Palestine and other occupied Arab territories: Report of the United Nations fact finding mission on the Gaza conflict" (2009, September 15). Retrieved on September 16, 2011 from <http://www2.ohchr.org/english/bodies/hrcouncil/specialsession/9/docs/UNFFMGC_Report.pdf>.

IslamOnline.net (English), retrieved on September 20, 2011 from <http://discover.islamonline.net/English/index.shtml>.

"IslamOnline.net: Independent, Interactive, Popular" (2008), *Arab Media and Society* 4. Retrieved on September 16, 2011 from <http://www.arabmediasociety.com/index.php?article=576andprintarticle>.

Juergensmeyer, M. (2002). "The Global Dimensions of Religious Terrorism," in Hall, R.B. and Biersteker, T. (eds), *The Emergence of Private Authority in Global Governance* (Cambridge: Cambridge University Press).

Lee, R. (2010). *Religion and Politics in the Middle East: Identity, Ideology, Institutions, and Attitudes* (Boulder, CO: Westview Press).

Lynch, M. (2006). *Voices of the New Arab Public: Iraq, Al-Jazeera, and Middle East Politics Today* (New York: Columbia University Press).

Mandaville, P. (2001). "Reimagining Islam in Diaspora: The Politics of Mediated Community," *International Communication Gazette* 63(2–3): 169–86.

Mendelsohn, B. (2005). "Sovereignty Under Attack: The International Society Meets the al Qaeda Network," *Review of International Studies* 31: 45–68.

Murphy, C. (2000). "Global Governance: Poorly Done and Poorly Understood," *International Affairs* 76(4): 789–803.

——(2002). "Foreword: Why Pay Attention to Global Governance?" in Wilkinson, R., and Hughes, S. (eds), *Global Governance: Critical Perspectives*(London: Routledge).

"Palestine statehood team 'a cause of concern'" (2011, September 22). Retrieved on September 22, 2011 from <http://english.aljazeera.net/indepth/features/2011/09/201192212910587149.html>.

"Palestinian statehood bid: Why Hamas has stayed on sidelines" (2011, September 20). Retrieved on September 22, 2011 from <http://www.csmonitor.com/World/Middle-East/2011/0920/Palestinian-statehood-bid-Why-Hamas-has-stayed-on-sidelines>.

Rosenau, J. (2005). "Global Governance as Disaggregated Complexity," in Ba, A. and Hoffman, M. (eds), *Contending Perspectives on Global Governance: Coherence, Contestation and World Order* (New York: Routledge).

Rutherford, B. (2006). "What do Egypt's Islamists Want? Moderate Islam and the Rise of Islamic Constitutionalism," *Middle East Journal* 60(4): 707–31.

Sullivan, D. (1994). *Private Voluntary Organizations in Egypt: Islamic Development, Private Initiative, and State Control* (Gainesville: University Press of Florida).

Ummah Forum. Retrieved on September 20, 2011 from <http://www.ummah.com/forum/forumdisplay.php?10-Ummah-Lounge>.

Vidino, L. (2010). *The New Muslim Brotherhood in the West* (New York: Columbia University Press).

Ward, K. (2009). "Non-Violent Extremists? Hizbut Tahrir Indonesia," *Australian Journal of International Affairs* 63(2): 149–64.

Wilkinson, R. (2002). "Global Governance: A Preliminary Interrogation," in Wilkinson, R. and Hughes, S. (eds), *Global Governance: Critical Perspectives* (London: Routledge).

Chapter 2

Modernity, Islam, and Religious Activism

Deina Abdelkader

Introduction

If one compares post-colonial literature to contemporary literature on modernization, one will find quite a few similarities: first, the belief in the Weberian definition of modernity that necessitates an "ideal" type of authority, that is, the legal rational type. The second similarity is the Cartesian conjecture on the separation of faith from reason. The definition of modernity thus becomes an unattainable goal for any society that professes faith, whether Catholic, Jewish, or Muslim. Thus modernity is not necessarily tied to consumption, as in Lerner's writing in the late 1950s about the Middle East, nor is it tied to being stuck in the feudal stage as in leftist writings about the Asiatic Mode of Production theory. Modernity is not also necessarily also a byproduct of separating church from state as Weberian modernists would assert. Is it possible then, in this context, to assert that all Catholics are against "modernization"? Can we also assert that Israel, a state that defines itself as the homeland of the Jewish people, as "anti-modern"? Obviously one cannot make those assertions. Modernity should not be used as a unilateral schema and yardstick in any given society because it is loaded with subjectivity; rather modernity should be defined as the empowerment of peoples to live a better life according to their own definition of what a better life is, without infringing on anyone's rights.

However, it is assumed that Islam and its followers are antithetical to modernity. The reasons for those assumptions are numerous. First, the foundations on which colonialism started were built on the dehumanization of the indigenous populations. Secondly, post independence, the Cold War defined the relationship between the developed and less developed worlds which had its repercussions on the Muslim world. Third, with the rise of Islamic activism in the late 1970s (after the 1979 Iranian Revolution), the literature on modernity again emphasized the contradiction between modernity and Islam, based on the Iranian experience. Fourth, Samuel Huntington's "Clash of Civilizations" (1993) again emphasized the differences between Islam and its followers, and the Judeo-Christian tradition in terms of modernization and democratization. Fifth, the role Muslims played in their writings, whether they were mainstream like Qutb, or marginal, stated that an Islamic community has to be run by the "Sovereignty of God" (Hakimiyat Allah).

Hakimiyat Allah, literally, means God's rule or the sovereignty of God, but what the term really means is man's interpretation of how to respect and uphold God's laws. In different parts of the Muslim world, Qutb's ideas about the "sovereignty of God" have been taken literally. Unfortunately, not only have Qutb's words affected Muslim understanding of the role of religious laws, they have also influenced the West's perception of Islam as inimical to the idea of the "sovereignty of the people," a cornerstone in practicing democracy. The distinction thus emphasizes the antithetical nature of the faith to democracy and modernization.

Contemporary literature still emphasizes the necessity of the separation between faith and reason as a prerequisite to modernization. A negation of all theoretical Islamic works therefore was also the end result of this predisposition to separate faith from reason.

In Foucault's "What is Enlightenment?" he discusses the tendency to confuse two concepts: the "Enlightenment" and "Humanism." He explains that the Enlightenment is a well-defined "set of events" that took place in Europe and he stresses its historical specificity (Rabinow 1984: 43). He defines "humanism" as a set of "conceptions of man borrowed from religion, science, or politics" (ibid.: 44). Foucault concludes that "I think that, just as we must free ourselves from the intellectual blackmail of being for or against Enlightenment we must escape from the historical and moral confusionism that mixes the theme of humanism with the question of the Enlightenment" (ibid.: 45).

Foucault's argument clearly identifies the rigidity of the Enlightenment ideology and its followers. The Enlightenment focuses on secularization as a prerequisite for modernity and democratization, that is, the ideal type of authority, as Max Weber would phrase it. Contemporary moderate Islamists are wary of the Enlightenment philosophy's dichotomy and intolerance of differences.

Not all western theorists have thought that the "Great Separation," as Mark Lilla refers to the faith/reason dichotomy in his 2007 book *The Stillborn God*, is necessary to modernize. Even Jean Jacques Rousseau—the father of the French and American revolutions—was radical in his belief that religion plays an important public role in democratic political life.

Lilla recognizes that Rousseau distances himself from the dogmatic understanding and practice of faith, and instead stresses the universal role of human conscience. This is precisely why Orthodox Christians would feel threatened by his ideas, because they are universal in nature (Lilla 2007: 128). Rousseau writes: "Take up again the religion of your fathers. Follow it sincerely, since it is simple, holy and can be made consistent with both morality and reason" (ibid.: 130).

In fact, the rigid constructs and dichotomy between faith and reason, and also between liberal democratic practices and religious mores are critiqued by Rousseau, De Tocqueville, and many contemporary political theorists, for example, Mark Lilla and Cheryl Hall. Lilla shows that when the Enlightenment philosophy broke away from the Church and its authority, the result was an absolute distancing of divine revelation from public policy. Lilla argues that this decisive blow to "political theology" was and continues to be a challenge in western societies.[1]

Lilla criticizes the western political-ideological fixations that result from the separation of politics and theology:

> These [stories] are legends about the course of history, full of grand terms to describe the process supposedly at work- modernization, secularization, democratization, the 'disenchantment of the world', 'history of the story of liberty' and countless others. These are the fairy tales of our time ... *The Stillborn God* is not a fairy tale. It is a book about the fragility of our world, the world created by the intellectual rebellion against political theology in the West. (Ibid.: 6).

Furthermore, Lilla stresses the failure to recognize the political-theological connection in western thought. He says that the separation of religion from politics depends on "self-restraint," and "That we must rely on self-restraint should concern us. Our fragility is not institutional, *it is intellectual*" (ibid.: 7–8).

Lilla points out not only that this rigid separation is relatively new in the West but also, and more importantly, that the founders of liberal democracy never intended for that great separation or dichotomy to happen. Lilla cites Rousseau's allegory of the Vicar to substantiate his claim that the father of liberal democracy and one of the main "social contract" theorists was not for the rigidity of the current liberal intellectual milieu.

In agreement with Lilla, I also wish to emphasize that Alexis de Tocqueville, Rousseau's student and the father of the world's "ideal" liberal democracy (the United States), agreed with his mentor. In de Tocqueville's second essay on America, Part 1, chapter 4, he writes: "In my opinion, I doubt whether man can ever support at the same time complete religious independence and entire political freedom and am drawn to the thought that if a man is without faith, he must serve someone and if he is free, he must believe" (de Tocqueville 2003: 512).

De Tocqueville warns against the danger of abandoning faith because total equality between men also has the adverse effect of awakening "dangerous

---

1   "By attacking Christian political theology and denying its legitimacy, the new philosophy simultaneously challenged the basic principles on which authority had been justified in most societies in history. That was the decisive break. The ambition of the new philosophy was to develop habits of thinking and talking about politics exclusively in human terms, without appeal to divine revelation or cosmological speculation. The hope was to wean Western societies from all political theology and cross to the other shore ... Our experiment continues, though with less awareness of why it was begun and the nature of the challenge it was intended to meet. Yet the challenge has never disappeared" (Lilla 2007: 5).

instincts ... It exposes their souls to an excessive love of material enjoyment" (ibid.: 512). He believed that excessive equality must be controlled or checked by religion in a democratic society. In describing American religiosity, he wrote that they "practice their religion without shame or weakness but one generally observes at the heart of their zeal something so calm, so methodical, and so calculated that the head rather than the heart leads them to the foot of the altar" (ibid.: 615).

Discussions and arguments about the public role of religion have continued into contemporary political thought, whether one refers to post-modernists, or feminists, or even earlier on historically, with the Romantic era in European thought, that gave us intellectuals such as Nietzsche, Bergson, Sorel, Durkheim, and Pareto. Contemporary examples of intellectuals who challenge the theoretical status quo include Roxanne Euben, in her work *Enemy in the Mirror: Islamic Fundamentalism and the Limits of Modern Rationalism* (1999), and Jurgen Habermas, a student of the Frankfurt School. In his debate with Joseph Ratzinger (Pope Benedict XVI), Habermas argues that "secular knowledge cannot disregard and dismiss religion as 'irrational'" (Habermas and Ratzinger 2006: 50–51). It is interesting that in this debate, the Pope recognizes that "The Islamic cultural sphere, too, is marked by similar tensions. There is a broad spectrum between the fanatical absolutism of a Bin Laden and attitudes that are open to a tolerant rationality" (ibid.: 74). That is, the Pope recognizes the tolerant discourse of what I define as the liberal/moderate trend in modern Islamic thought.

Cheryl Hall's *The Trouble with Passion: Political Theory Beyond the Reign of Reason* (2005) exemplifies a feminist critique of the great divide between reason and passion. She establishes a connection between liberal theory and "Western political structures, processes, and cultures" and criticizes their influence on public life. The underlying argument of her book is that "passions" have a positive role to play in society. If this positive role is not recognized, she warns, the result is "the perpetuation of gender inequality in politics and the stifling of political innovation" (Hall 2005: 36).

Hence, after examining Rousseau, de Tocqueville, Foucault, Euben, Lilla, Habermas, and Hall, there is agreement from different fields of study on the importance of religion in public life. The link between secularization and modernization is frail, which brings the discussion of modernization to more profound assumptions about how we currently explicate the word.

The deeply biased question addressed to Islamists is whether they would abandon faith for reason in pursuit of modernization. The bias in this context is that by "reason" critics mean "Enlightenment" rationalism, which categorically rejects any role for religion in political life.[2]

---

2   Ernest Gellner identified himself as an "Enlightenment rationalist fundamentalist" as opposed to "Muslim Fundamentalists" (Gellner 1992).

This chapter addresses this gap in the literature, in search of a bridge between faith and reason from within Islamic theory.

Public Welfare, as a legal principle, was the essence of discussion on "modernity" in Islam, starting in the nineteenth and twentieth centuries with al-Afghani and, after him, his student Muhammad 'Abduh in their publication *Al-'urwa al-wuthqa*. The debate on the liberal interpretation of the sources of Islamic law, however, started in the very early days of Islam. The inclusion of principles such as Public Welfare (*maslaha*)[3] started with the leaders of the four Sunni law schools: Abu Hanifa, Ibn Malik, al-Shafi'i and Ibn Hanbal. The legal debates that extended thereafter were also reflective of how "liberal" the legal scholar *(faqih)* was at the time.

This legal/political principle is mostly discounted in the western discourse on modernity, as Euben indicates in *Enemy in the Mirror*. In order to gain a preliminary understanding of the grievances and the writings of Muslim theoretical work and Islamists today, more attention and focus is needed on this historical debate on Public Welfare and the end goals of Shari'a *(maqasid al-shar')*. Analyzing Public Welfare and the end goals of Islamic law is also imperative for a culturally sensitive discourse on modernity and Islam.

The debate on Public Welfare expresses the adaptability and flexibility of Islamic legal doctrine and links it consequently to the discourse on modernity.

Islam, Islamic Activism, and Modernity

A society governed by "legal-rational authority," according to Weber, was equated with the quintessential modern/developed society. Not only was the original theory partial, but also the offshoots of its application to the Muslim world reflected some weaknesses; for example, Ansari's writing (1986) stresses that Egypt's "stagnation" is primarily caused by the predominance of "traditional" authority in Egypt. Another example of using the Weberian paradigm is Dekmejian's analysis of Abdel Nasser's success as a leader, which he links to Nasser's "charismatic leadership":

---

3 These two legal concepts are used interchangeably in *fiqh* works, as Sardar indicates: "Traditionally, Muslim scholars have focused not on *istislah*, but its more general form, *maslaha*, which means a cause, a means, an occasion, or a goal which is good ... Its [*maslaha*'s] use as a principal tool of promoting the Shari'a is based on the argument that good is lawful and that lawful must be good. On the basis of such reasoning, traditional Muslim scholars developed a whole array of *maslaha* categories, some of which required direct evidence from the Qur'an and the Sunna while others could lead to binding legal sanctions on the basis that they clearly promote a noted ethical criterion such as preservation of life, property, promotion of Islamic mores and sound reasoning of the Shari'a [that is, the End Goals of Shari'a]" (Sardar 1985: 113). Therefore, the principle of Public Welfare will be used in the rest of this chapter to refer to both *maslaha* and *maqasid* (the End Goals of Shari'a).

> If a leader is committed to the destruction of the status quo, his subsequent quest for legitimacy must proceed along lines substantially different from those prevalent in the previous system. One possible way such a leader may legitimize his rule is by what Weber calls charismatic authority. (Dekmejian 1971: 3)

In an effort to distinguish between societies that are governed according to the "legal-rational" authority model as opposed to the "charismatic" model, Dekmejian stresses the "inability of democratic man to conceptualize such a foreign experience" (ibid.: 3). This statement reflects a bias in Dekmejian's writing, because he is oblivious to the fact that charisma plays a role in western political life as well. In a later publication, Dekmejian writes about the rise of Islamic movements:

> The ideologies of these movements are both comprehensive and rigid, reflecting the responses of typically charismatic leaders to situations of crisis. It is no mere accident that fundamentalist movements in various political contexts have acquired spiritual and sociopolitical potency when two interrelated conditions are met: the appearance of a leader of charismatic propensity and a society in deep turmoil. Significantly, the Islamist movements of the past have satisfied both of these conditions. The Islamist movements of the present are no exception. (Dekmejian 1985: 25)

Dekmejian later writes that al-Banna (the founder of the Muslim Brotherhood in Egypt) "typifies Weber's charismatic leader" (ibid.: 81). It is problematic in Dekmejian's work to explain the political success of both Nasser and the Muslim Brotherhood's al-Banna by reference only to the charismatic nature of their leadership. That is, the charismatic nature of the leader could only be taken as one among many variables that explain the political success of such movements.

Apart from the stress on the type of authority, stability, and institutionalization, the discourse on modernity was also tainted with cultural biases.[4] In defining what is modern, Lerner writes:

> This [modern living] requires in behavioral terms, a population equipped for production and consumption—a population quite different in its style of life from the rural folk who planted cotton seeds before the rich waters of the Nile arrived and picked cotton puffs when they receded. Needed are people who, among other things, read and write, tell time, change underwear, and go to the

---

4   In Lerner's *Passing of Traditional Society*, he uses the number of newspapers circulated as an indicator for education and literacy in Egypt. However, some familiarity with the culture would clarify that this is not a suitable indicator because one newspaper is read by many people in coffeeshops, barber shops, or posted on public notice boards, and so on.

movies. These are the people who make things, sell to others and buy things made by others. (Lerner 1958: 260)

The post-World War II views on modernity primarily dealt with a predominantly secular elite in the Middle East: the young nationalists of the newly created Middle Eastern states. Over time, however, the Islamists who were part of the national struggle for independence in many instances in the Middle East started to reappear on the political scene, which caused a new genre of literature on modernity to develop. The post-World War II discourse on modernity was prevalent mostly in the late 1950s and up to the late 1970s. It was towards the end of the 1970s, especially with the Iranian Revolution in 1979 and the assassination of Sadat in 1981, that attention became focused on the rise of Islamic activism, or Islamic "revival." As a result, studies on Islamic activism and its causes were on the increase. One repeated causal explanation of Islamic activism, presented at the end of the 1970s until current times, is that these societies are reacting to the advent of "modernity." Piscatori's work, for example, illustrates the causal relation mentioned above:

> The process of development has been a contributing factor. It has stimulated the revival in two main ways: (a) it has often strained the social and political fabric, thereby leading people to turn to traditional symbols and rites as a way of comforting and orienting themselves, and (b) it has provided the means of speedy communication and easy dissemination of both domestic and international information. (Piscatori 1986: 27)

The link between Islamic activism and modernity is a common theme in these writings. Vatikiotis explains that Islamic resurgence is caused by the "disaffection" with the change imposed on these societies by the advent of "modernity" (Vatikiotis 1981: 193). The "disaffection" that Vatikiotis and others refer to is summed up in a comment by Gilles Kepel about Islamic activist movements: "Education has taught them [Islamists] the mannerisms of modern life but not its techniques and spirit" (Kepel 1985: 235).

All these perspectives have a common supposition: that Islamic movements are byproducts of the "universal crisis of modernity," "rapid development," and so on. By defining Islamic activism as a product or reaction, the analyst implicitly judges these movements as an adverse and inimical reaction to modernization and development. That is, by assuming that Islamic activism is caused by discomfort with modernization, such explanations also assume that Islamic activism, as a social movement, is discordant with modernization and development.

In these writings, the link between Islamic activism and modernity is vague, because "modernity" as a concept is not universal. The definitions of modernization and development are not theoretically clear, and comparative studies differ on what development and change comprise in any Third World country. To assume that rapid change, development, and modernization are causal factors in Islamic activism is theoretically dubious, since there is no clear conception of a unilateral schema of modernization/economic development. In relation to the first common supposition previously mentioned, Islamic activism is perceived as a regressive force, even though there are no clear definitions or empirical studies that specify what constitutes "rapid modernization." Even though there are numerous studies on the stagnation of development in the Middle East and other Muslim regions, Islamic activism is explained as a phenomenon that is against development and change. The authors referred to explain Islamic activism as a regressive, traditionalist, and stagnant movement against the forces of development and change. Islamic activism is not the only phenomenon that is explained away by the so-called "crisis of modernity." Religious differences are also linked to the perceived threat to western "modernity" from Islamic civilization. Lewis writes:

> We are facing a mood and a movement far transcending the level of issues and politics and the governments that pursue them. This is no less than a clash of civilization—the perhaps irrational but surely historic reaction of an ancient rival against our Judeo-Christian heritage, our secular present, and the world-wide expansion of both. (Lewis 1990: 60)

Huntington writes:

> In Eurasia the great historic fault lines between civilizations are once more aflame. This is particularly true along the boundaries of the crescent-shaped Islamic bloc of nations from the bulge of Africa to central Asia. Violence also occurs between Muslims, on the one hand, and Orthodox Serbs in the Balkans, Jews in Israel, Hindus in India, Buddhists in Burma and Catholics in the Philippines. Islam has bloody borders. (Huntington 1993: 34–5)

Another assumption is that western-style democracy is a component of modernity. However, Miller claims that Arabs and Muslims could never value or commit to democracy and justice, because historically Arabs and Muslims were never ruled democratically (Miller 1993: 46). Another example of tying faith to democracy is found in Huntington:

> A strong correlation exists between Western Christianity and democracy. Modern democracy developed first and most vigorously in Christian countries ... Democracy was especially scarce among countries that were predominantly Muslim, Buddhist, or Confucian. This correlation does not prove causation. Western Christianity emphasizes, however, the dignity of the individual and the separate spheres of church and state. In many countries, Protestant and Catholic leaders have been central in the struggles against repressive countries.

It seems plausible to hypothesize that the expansion of Christianity encourages democratic development. (Huntington 1991: 72–3)

Muslim Women and Modernity

In addition to the aforementioned criteria for measuring "development/ modernity" in Muslim societies, the question of women in Islam has also been used as a yardstick to measure the society's degree of development. The way Arab women dressed was the most often used sign of progress, that is, westernization or the lack of it. Anonymous women were those who were not westernized in dress; on the other hand, a miniskirt apparently gave a woman an identity and a university education. A 1979 article on Bahrain charted what the author called "feminine progress" in three generations of women sighted in the gold bazaar:

> Grandma moved like a shadow under layers of black ... Mother wore the same black aba, or cloak, but with exposed face and hands ... The youngest, in her teens, sported a fashionable red pantsuit. A red pantsuit signified feminine progress when compared to the veil. Readers need not know anything more about an Arab woman than that she wore a pantsuit or a veil; dress said it all. (Steet 2000: 133)

Nonetheless, in Elizabeth Fernea's film documentary "A Veiled Revolution" (1982), the women interviewed seemed actively and non-submissively to choose to veil.[5]

As Nilufer Gole notes, "The question of women lies at the center of the modernization mentality, which favored the Western notion of universality in opposition to tradition, and particularly, Islam" (Gole 1996: 29).[6] In agreement with Gole, I would like to add that because Muslim countries know how central the "women question" is to modernity, many Muslim statesmen have altered the way women dress overnight to send a message to the western world about what type of government they are. For example, in Syria in the 1970s, women's scarves were torn from their heads in public because Assad wanted to emphasize the secular and socialist nature of his Ba'athist regime. In Ataturk's and the

---

5   The author is aware that there are differences from one Muslim country to another in the amount of freedom enjoyed by women to wear what they please, but writings about Islam and the veiling of women do not take these differences into account.

6   It is quite common in children's literature to generalize; for example, in a book about international costumes and culture, a Middle Eastern woman is dressed in "traditional" garb where she is in a long dress and has a feather on her head (Smith 2000: 4).In another fairy tale for grades 2 and 3 the author, out of the context of the story (titled "Arabian Days"), writes: "In Arabian society, women were not eq equal to men but could own property and were often educated" (Kerven 2000: 47).

Shah's era, the wives of public officials were forbidden from wearing the veil. Both leaders were trying to impress the western world with their perceived "modernity." After the 1979 Iranian Revolution, Iranian women were forced to wear the veil, regardless of their creed, and again this was imposed to emphasize the Islamic nature of the state. Therefore, women in the Muslim world were utilized to emphasize the nature/ideology of the state and to carry on the discourse on modernity with the western world.

The fixation in the western world about veiling is not a new phenomenon, it actually pre-dates colonialism in the Muslim world, and Orientalists' observations' exemplify this:

> The East is full of secrets—no one understands their value better than the Oriental; and because she is full of secrets she is full of entrancing surprises. Many fine things there are upon the surface: brilliance of colour, splendour of light, solemn loneliness, clamorous activity; these are only the patterns upon the curtain which floats for ever before the recesses of Eastern life: its essential charm is of more subtle quality. As it listeth, it comes and goes; it flashes upon you through the open doorway of some blank; windowless house you pass in the street, from under the lifted veil of the beggar woman who lays her hand on your bridle, from the dark, contemptuous eyes of a child; then the East sweeps aside her curtains, flashes a facet of her jewels into your dazzled eyes, and disappears again with a mocking little laugh at your bewilderment; then for a moment it seems to you that you are looking her in the face, but while you are wondering whether she be angel or devil, she is gone.
>
> She will not stay—she prefers the unexpected; she will keep her secrets and her tantalizing charm with them, and when you think you have caught at last some of her illusive grace, she will send you back to shrouded figures and blank house-fronts. (Mabro 1996: 49)

In a more revealing manuscript by Lucie Paul, quoted in Judy Mabro's anthology of Orientalist writing: "Under the arcades of the Avenue de France the veiled women of the common people go into the shops. Beside these women wrapped up from head to toe, whose eyes cannot always be seen but are always seeing, I have the feeling of being naked" (ibid.: 50).

Apart from the utilization of women in the discourse on modernization, the lives and rights of women in the Muslim world did not change by taking off the veil: for example, in Turkey, Iran, and Egypt, the women did not get their suffrage until they fought for it, although all three countries were secular at that point. The women's position in those secular, "modernized" countries did not benefit them or change their status. Thus, the patriarchal culture remained and dominated the public discourse, even though those countries were secular.

On a different note, the fixation of the West on the Muslim women's veil as a sign of oppression is in total disconnect with the real issues that affect Muslim women's daily lives like family laws: divorce law, child custody law, and so on.

Therefore, on many levels, women have suffered from getting caught in the discourse on modernity; from the western side, they are seen as submissive and in need of protection/defense, so that the discourse is patronizing. On the other hand, domestic patriarchy is utilized as explained above to testify to a state's "modernity," apart from neglecting women's rights in other respects.

At this juncture, I would like to ask a question: why did the literature on modernity take such stances *vis-à-vis* Muslim societies? There could be a number of reasons. (1) The separation of church and state (which was a consequence of European historical events and experiences) is taken as an ideal form of government and organization. That is to say, any other form was deemed "irrational" and "traditional," as opposed to the Enlightenment's "rationality" and thus "modernity." (2) The West has an overwhelming perception (unfortunately reinforced after the 9/11 attacks) that Muslims—the Other with a capital O—are united in their cause, and more importantly, that Muslims represent a common threat to the western world. This perceived threat is reflected clearly in the literature on Islamic activism and it is more of a political stance than a concern for modernity and development in Muslim societies. (3) Realpolitik interests in the area have compounded the difficulty of representing Muslim societies and their faith.[7]

Separating church and state, and the "rational" from the "irrational," has been constantly used as a measure of Muslim societies' ability to modernize (Esposito 1992: 233). The definition of rationality in this context is linked to post-Enlightenment Cartesian thought. Euben writes:

> ... the reflex to dismiss fundamentalism as irrational or pathological is not merely a product of the almost habitualized prejudices and fears operative in the relationship between "the West" and "Islam" but, as I have argued, also a function of the way a post-Enlightenment, predominantly rationalist tradition of scholarship countenances foundationalist political practices in the modern world. (Euben 1999: 14)

Haddad and colleagues emphasize this in an earlier writing:

> In order to understand the dynamic of revival, we need more analysis of the issues being raised in the current debate over the reinstitution of the Shari'ah in countries such as Egypt, Jordan, Tunisia, Algeria, and Indonesia. Given the fact that the public discussion of these issues uses familiar Islamic language and themes, scholars have been tempted to dismiss the revivalists as seeking

---

7 Fawaz Gerges highlights this in his work America and Political Islam: Clash of Cultures or Clash of Interests? (1999).

to return the Muslim community to the seventh century. It is clear that for most revivalist writers, however, this is not the case, and the exegetical and contextual analysis of the language they are using makes it clear that they are seeking a better understanding of the problems besetting their societies and of the ways in which traditional Islamic sources can be interpreted so as to help solve them. (Haddad et al. 1991: 15)

These attempts at solving contemporary problems in Muslim societies, as referred to above, are starting to gain proper expression in literature about Muslim societies, Islamic law, and modernity. Although the majority of literature on Muslim societies, Islamic activism, and modernity tends to focus on the issues referred to earlier in this chapter, there is a normative transformation in the discourse concerning modernity in Muslim societies. Contemporary examples of this transformation are Euben's work and also Richard Khouri's.[8] Khouri takes a major step in his recognition that there is a "meeting ground" for "modernity" and Islam, stressing that both lack universality unless the best elements of both are combined (Khouri 1998: xxxvi). Khouri acknowledges Zia Goklap's work about "*urf*" [custom] as an important legal principle in Islamic law, but does not delve deeper in Islamic legal matters.

The Principle of Public Welfare and End Goals of Shari'a: Its Origins and Exegesis

For clarification purposes, and to establish the connectivity of Islamic law with "modernity," I will focus on principles in Islamic legal thought called *maslaha* (Public Welfare) and *maqa'sid al-shar'* (the End Goals of Islamic law). These principles are advocated by modern and current Islamic writers such as Qutb (1991), al-Bayyumi (1992), al-Darwish (1992), al-Turabi (1980), and al-Qaradawi (1973, 1981). Even extremist groups, such as al-Jama'at al-Islamiyya (responsible for violence against foreigners and public figures in 1993 and 1994), and individuals like Shaykh 'Abd al-Rahman (1989: 154), write of the End Goals of Shari'a as an important legal principle.

The principle of Public Welfare is very pertinent to the synthesis between modernity and Islam with which Khouri and others are grappling. These principles of Islamic legal thought gain weight and importance in the discourse about modernity for two reasons: (1) they have been researched and discussed from the rise of Islamic legal thought until current times, and (2) they are still advocated by contemporary Islamists (whether they are violent or nonviolent

---

8   Khouri raises this issue in *Freedom, Modernity and Islam:* "The marginality of critical voices at Western universities who are also unequivocally religious, and the preponderance of orientations inimical to Muslims among most critics of the excesses of positivism, materialism, and rationalism, only augment their fears" (Khouri 1998: 312–13).

groups), as indicated earlier. Islamic legal thought (*fiqh*) indicates that many legal scholars advocated the principle of Public Welfare and the End Goals of Islamic law: for example, al-Juwayni (d. 1085), al-Ghazali (d. 1111), al-Razi (d. 1209), al-Amidi (d. 1233), al-Salmi (d. 1261), al-Qarafi (d. 1285), Ibn Taymiyya (d. 1327), al-Shatibi (d. 1388), Ibn al-Qayyim al-Jawziyya, and al-Tufi.

It is interesting to note that the differences between the *fuqaha* "were not related to whether they accepted Public Welfare as a source of law or not, but rather to the degree to which they used reason alone to acknowledge Public Welfare without considering the textual sources *(nusus)*: the Qur'an and the Sunna" (Abu Zahra 1952: 404).[9] There are three different kinds of *maslaha*:

> (1) recognized *maslaha (maslaha mu'tabara)*: the *maslaha* that has been clearly stated in the Qur'an and the Sunna, or has gained the consensus *(ijma')* of the fuqaha'; (2) nullified *maslaha (maslaha mulgha)*: the *maslaha* that is in clear contradiction to the Qur'an and the Sunna, and does not have the support of the *fuqaha'*; (3) conveyed mas*laha (maslaha mursala)*: the *maslaha* that is not in explicit agreement or disagreement with the Qur'an or the Sunna or the *ijma* of the fuqaha'. (Shalabi 1943: 281)

These legal scholars used Public Welfare and the End Goals of Islamic law interchangeably, that is, Public Welfare is defined as a primary and imperative component of Islamic jurisprudence in the absence of textual reference.

A brief history of *fiqh* (Islamic jurisprudence) and the four legal Sunni schools and their different views on Public Welfare is needed at this point. The differences that existed in early Islamic jurisprudential writings are almost impossible to discern in this day and age. However, for the purpose of this chapter, it is necessary to explain the importance and consensus of the four schools. The four Sunni schools of law are the Malikis, the Hanafis, the Shafi'is, and the Hanbalis. The Malikis and the Hanafis were the first founders of other *fiqh* schools. Malik was a contemporary of Abu Hanifa and lived in the Hijaz (part of contemporary Saudi Arabia) from 93 to 179 AH. Abu Hanifa lived in what is now Iraq from 70 to 150 AH (al-'Alwani 1988: 31). Malik and Abu Hanifa did not write about their practices, but their students wrote later about their teachings and practices. Al-Shafi'i (one of the leaders of the four *madhahib)* was the first to write of *usul-al-fiqh* in his books *Al-risala* (The Message), and later, *Al-'umm* (literally "mother," but in this context, "The Origin"). Al-Shafi'i refused to take Public Welfare as an independent source of law because it did not restrict itself to the

---

9 In Islamic legal doctrine, there is a distinction drawn between two concepts: (1) *qati'yyat* (absolutes), that is to say, the issues that are clearly discussed and stated in the Texts *(nusus)* and are therefore binding on the Muslim community; and (2) *zaniyyat* (conjectures), that is, things that are alluded to in the text in terms of spirit and are not clearly identified, for example, rulership. The spirit of rulership is clearly talked about; however, the exact form of government and governmental organization is not.

basic religious sources such as the Qur'an and the Sunna. Rather, the principle of Public Welfare (*maslaha*) seemed to al-Shafi'i to be a concept totally dependent on human reasoning, which separated it from religion altogether (al-Buti 1966: 377). In a primary source, al-Shafi'i (n.d.: 273) writes:

> Whoever gives his legal opinion *fatwa* with no restraint or qiyas [analogy], is in fact saying: I do what I please, even if it is against my belief-thus going against the Qur'an and the Sunna ... I have not seen an incident where the people of knowledge [the *fuqaha'*] allowed the people of reason to give their legal opinions, since the people of reason have no knowledge of *qiyas* from the Qur'an and Sunna or *ijma'* and the usage of analogical reasoning. (al-Buti 1966: 375)

Thus al-Shafi'i was more conservative in his conception of Public Welfare, for he feared its encroachment upon the importance of the textual sources of the law. Al-Shafi'i equated conveyed Public Welfare with recognized Public Welfare, because he believed that the sacred Texts covered all issues pertaining to people's welfare. Therefore, al-Shafi'i could not conceive of a legal issue that would fall outside the boundaries of the Texts (ibid.: 375).

Malik, on the other hand, took Public Welfare as an exception to the rule. Therefore, although he was misunderstood by many (especially his student al-Shafi'i), he did not call for using the principle of nullified Public Welfare (that is, Public Welfare that goes against the letter of the textual sources of Islamic law), but applied the Public Welfare principle when there was no reference in the Texts to the issue in question. That is, Malik took Public Welfare as an alternative only when the Texts and legal consensus (*ijma'*) did not provide an answer. This, in principle, agrees with al-Shafi'i's contentions and worries.

Abu Hanifa was in agreement with his contemporary, Malik, because he took Public Welfare to be an independent source of law. He too was therefore liberal in his interpretation and usage of the Public Welfare principle.

Ibn Hanbal also takes the Public Welfare principle to be a subsidiary source of law and an extension of the End Goals of Shari'a (ibid.: 369). As an example of rulings that upheld Public Welfare as a guiding jurisprudential principle, during the period of the second Caliph 'Umar Ibn al-Khattab's leadership, a man stole bread several times. He was therefore faced with the Islamic penalty of severing the hand that stole the bread. However, Caliph 'Umar questioned the justice of this sentence because that year was a year of famine. Consequently, the man was freed because: (1) using human reasoning, Caliph 'Umar was following the spirit of the law rather than the letter of the law; (2) Caliph 'Umar was said to have adopted and practiced the principle of Public Welfare in this instance—that is, if he as a ruler could not provide for the man's basic needs, he could not penalize him for stealing the bread. Thus, strict Islamic law is not upheld if it contradicts Public Welfare.

So the connection between Public Welfare and the End Goals of Shari'a and modernity is that they allow religious scholars to exercise human reasoning more freely, thus permitting the analysis and adjustment of old customs to the needs of modern life. Although the essence of religious teachings is left untouched, the usage of Public Welfare allows for reinterpreting the faith without going against its primary sources—the textual sources (the Qur'an and the Sunna). For example, the use of drugs is prohibited in Islam, even though there is no direct mention of it in the *nusus* (the Texts). This prohibition is derived from the use of human reasoning: if alcohol is prohibited because it affects the alertness and awareness of the human mind, drugs should also be prohibited.

If Muslim polities enforce Shari'a laws, they will have to come to terms with the principle of Public Welfare because it is a legal principle and part of Islamic jurisprudence. However, rather than adopting historically and culturally foreign concepts, Muslim societies would need to redefine and reshape their own needs and goals according to their cultural and religious beliefs. Modernity thus becomes human empowerment because it concerns the needs and ambitions of a people seeking their advancement and progress.

Conclusion

In closing, I will give two examples that indicate the dangerous divide that has plagued the discourse on modernity and Islam. First, Gellner, who identifies himself as an "Enlightenment rationalist fundamentalist," claims that "When dealing with serious matters, when human lives and welfare are at stake, when major resources are being committed, the only kind of knowledge which may legitimately be used and invoked is that which satisfies the criteria of Enlightenment philosophy" (Gellner 1992: 90).

Secondly, Bernard Lewis, in his book *What Went Wrong?*, writes "Today, for the time being, as Ataturk recognized and as Indian computer scientists and Japanese high-tech companies appreciate, the dominant civilization is Western, and Western standards therefore define modernity" (Lewis 2002: 150).

I would like to end this chapter by raising some questions and issues. (1) How much has the mainstream discourse on modernity changed since the 1950s? (2) If we equate modernization with the cultural globalization of the world, if we reduce the human and historical advancement of the West to superficial elements such as styles of dress, and "going out to the movies," do we also, in creating this superficial modernity, contribute to the creation of a superficial Islam? Did the attempts at the cultural globalization of the world also lead to the Talibanization of parts of the Muslim world?

Are we contributing to this ideological polarization by focusing on Lewis's view that "the dominant civilization is Western and Western standards therefore define modernity"? Is "modernity" a unilateral path?

After the fall of the Soviet Union, political science as a field shifted its focus from "modernization" to "democratization" and some used the term interchangeably; however, what is of relevance is that the commonalities found in the discourse are numerous. The central commonality to both is that paradigmatically we are still adamant about the divide between faith and reason, and the necessity to abandon the latter in public life before we can bestow those efforts with the description "modern" or "democratic":

> We tell ourselves stories about how our big world came to be and why it is destined to persist. These are legends about the course of history, full of grand terms to describe the process supposedly at work- modernization, secularization, democratization, the "disenchantment of the world," "history as the story of liberty," and countless others. These are the fairy tales of our time ... *The Stillborn God* is not a fairy tale. It is a book about the fragility of our world, the world created by the intellectual rebellion against political theology in the West. (Lilla 2007: 6)

The binding ties of our contemporary paradigm lie at the heart of what Huntington calls a "clash of civilizations"; it is not because there are inherent specifications to faith (in this case, Islam), rather it is because we chose to annihilate faith in our public discourse and to relegate it to its classic Weberian private irrational realm.

References

English Sources

Almond, Gabriel A. (1982). *Progress and Its Discontents* (Berkeley, CA: University of California Press).
Ansari, Hamid (1986). *Egypt the Stalled Society* (Albany: State University of New York Press).
Apter, David E. (1965). *The Politics of Modernization* (Chicago, IL: University of Chicago Press).
Binder, Leonard (1971). *Crises and Sequences in Political Development* (Princeton, NJ: Princeton University Press).
De Tocqueville, Alexis (2003). *Democracy in America and Two Essays on America* (London: Penguin Books).
Dekmejian, Hrair (1971). *Egypt Under Nasser* (Albany: State University of New York Press).
—— (1985). *Islam in Revolution* (Syracuse, NY: Syracuse University Press).
Eisenstadt, S.N. (1966). *Modernization: Protest and Change* (Jerusalem: Hebrew University).
—— (1973). *Tradition, Change and Modernity* (New York: John Wiley & Sons).

Esposito, John L. (1992). *The Islamic Threat: Myth or Reality?* (Oxford: Oxford University Press).

Euben, Roxanne (1999). *Enemy in the Mirror* (Princeton, NJ: Princeton University Press).

Gellner, Ernest (1992). *Postmodernism, Reason and Religion* (London: Routledge).

Gerges, Fawaz (1999). *America and Political Islam: Clash of Cultures or Clash of Interests?* (Cambridge: Cambridge University Press).

Gole, Nilfur (1996). *The Forbidden Modern* (Ann Arbor: University of Michigan Press).

Habermas, Jurgen and Ratzinger, Joseph (2006). *Dialectics of Secularization: On Reason and Religion* (San Francisco, CA: Ignatius Press).

Haddad, Yvonne Y., Voll, John Obert and Esposito, John L. (1991). *The Contemporary Islamic Revival: A Critical Survey and Bibliography* (New York: Greenwood Press).

Hall, Cheryl (2005). *The Trouble with Passion: Political Theory Beyond the Reign of Reason* (New York: Routledge).

Huntington, Samuel (1991). *The Third Wave* (Norman: University of Oklahoma Press).

—— (1993). "A clash of civilizations?" *Foreign Affairs* 72(3) (Summer): 22–50.

Kepel, Gilles (1985). *The Prophet and Pharoah* (London: Saqi Books).

Kerven, Rosalind (2000). *Aladdin* (New York: Dorling Kindersley Publishing).

Khouri, Richard (1998). *Freedom, Modernity and Islam* (Syracuse, NY: Syracuse University Press).

Lerner, Daniel (1958). *The Passing* of *Traditional Society* (Glencoe, IL: The Free Press).

Lewis, Bernard (1990). "The roots of Muslim rage," *Atlantic Monthly* 266 (September): 47–60.

—— (2002). *What Went Wrong?* (Oxford: Oxford University Press).

Lilla, Mark (2007). *The Stillborn God: Religion, Politics, and the Modern West* (New York: Alfred Knopf).

Mabro, Judy (1996). *Veiled Half Truths: Western Travelers' Perceptions of Middle Eastern Women* (New York: I.B. Tauris).

Miller, Judith (1993). "The challenge of radical Islam," *Foreign Affairs* 77(2) (Spring): 43–56.

Parsons, Talcott (1977). *The Evolution of Societies* (Englewood Cliffs, NJ: Prentice Hall).

Piscatori, James (1986). *Islam in a World of Nation-States* (Cambridge: CambridgeUniversity Press).

Rabinow, Paul (1984). *Foucault Reader* (New York, Pantheon Books).

Sardar, Ziauddin (1985). *Islamic Futures: The Shape of Ideas to Come* (New York: Mansell).

Smith, Rebbeca (2000). *The Ultimate Barbie International Dolls* (New York: Dorling Kindersley Publishing).

Steet, Linda (2000). *Veils and Daggers* (Philadelphia, PA: Temple University Press).

Vatikiotis, P.J. (1981). "Islamic resurgence: a critical view," In Alexander Cudsi and Ali Hillal Dessouki (eds), *Islam and Power* (Baltimore, MD: Johns Hopkins University Press).

Arabic Sources

Abd al-Rahman, 'Umar (1989). *Mithaq al-'amal al-islami* (Cairo: Maktabat Ibn Kathir).

Abu Zahra, Muhammad (1952). *Malik* (Cairo: Maktabat al-Anglu al-Misriyya).

Al-Alwani, Taha Jabir (1988). *Uusul al-fiqh* (Herndon: International Institute of Islamic Thought).

Al-Bayyumi, Ibrahim (1992). *Al-fikr al-siyassi li-al-imam Hassan al-Banna* (Cairo: Dar al-Tawzi' wa'l Nashr al-Islamiyya).

Al-Buti, Muhammad (1966). *Dhawabit al-maslaha fial-shari'a islamiyya* (Damascus: al-Maktaba al-Amawiyya).

Al-Darwish, Salih (1992). *Hiwarat Rachid al-Ghannouchi* (London: Khalil Media Services).

Al-Qaradawi, Yusuf (1973). *Shari'at al-islam* (Beirut: al-Maktab al-Islami).

—— (1981). *Al-sahwa al-islamiyya bayna al-juhud wa-al-tataruf* (Qatar: Dar al-Umma).

Qutb, Muhammad (1991). *Hawla tatbiq al-shar'a* (Cairo: Maktabat al-Sunna).

Al-Shafi'i (n.d.). *Al-umm* (n.p.).

Shalabi, Muhammad (1943). *Tahlil al-ahkam* (Cairo: Matba'at al-Azhar).

Al-Turabi, Hasan (1980). *Tajdidal-fiqh al-islami* (Beirut: al-Matba'a al-Ahliyya).

Chapter 3

The Interrelated Dynamics of Culture, Religion, and Nation in the United Arab Emirates

Vânia Carvalho Pinto[1]

Introduction

> The UAE is like a tree that has been protected by its leadership so that it will
> grow strong and bear fruit in abundance.[2]
> Sheikh Mohammed bin Rashed al-Maktoum, Ruler of Dubai

The utilization of cultural and religious symbolisms in the strengthening of traditional systems of rule within the Arab Gulf in general, and in the United Arab Emirates in particular, have been the object of considerable academic attention over the past years.[3] In the case of the UAE, two dimensions have received particular attention in this regard: first, the state's proactive association of valued tribal personal characteristics with the persona of the ruling sheikhs (see for example, Onley and Khalaf 2006, Davidson 2005: 70–82, Khoury 1980: 136–41); and, secondly, the contemporary state-led recreation of traditions through public events and festivals as a means to create a link between current life in the UAE and its historical past (Khalaf 2000, Davidson 2008, 2009, Fox et al. 2006). This literature production has done much to enrich the field of Arab Gulf studies. It has aided in the understanding of issues as diverse as the sustainability of monarchical rule in contexts where fast-paced modernization was deemed to overturn them

---

1   The transliteration of words from Arabic into English follow the general rules of the International Journal of Middle Eastern Studies. Diacritical marks were removed and the common spelling of certain words such as 'sheikh' instead of 'shaykh' were favored so as to facilitate reading.

2   His Highness Sheikh Mohammed bin Rashid al Maktoum (Undated). *His Highness Quotes.* Retrieved July 31, 2011 from <http://www.sheikhmohammed.co.ae/vgn-ext-templating/v/index.jsp?vgnextoid=2b44142042525110VgnVCM1000007064a8c0RCRD&QueryPage-page=8>.

3   In this regard, see, for example, the edited volume by Eric Davis and Nicolas Gavrielides (1991) on statecraft in oil-producing states; it includes the Gulf but it is not restricted to it; as well as the more Arab Gulf-oriented volume organized by John Fox, Nada Mourtada-Sabbah, and Mohammed al-Mutawa (2006).

(for example, Gause III 2000: 167–86); the development of folklore and heritage revival (for example, Hurreiz 2002), and the study of the emergence of new globalized multicultural societies in the Arab Gulf, portrayed as a successful blend of the new and the old (Fox et al. 2006).

This extensive production has provided us with some very interesting analysis on the association between tribal qualities and political leadership in the case of the former, and with some vivid and very detailed descriptions on the recreation of culture in the case of the latter. However, what has received considerably less attention in analytical terms has been first, the ways through which these processes can be firmly located within a much larger, state-led, strategic nation-building project; and secondly, the extent to which the contents and contours of this national scheme were defined through an evolving, interactive process between state and society. The neglect of these dimensions has led to a certain lack of appreciation for the degree of consolidation already achieved by the Emirati national project (for example, Partrick 2009), an imbalance that this chapter seeks to address. Therefore, it will look at the issue of nation-building consolidation in the UAE by resorting to the analysis of three key interrelated moments during which the existing political system was particularly strengthened.

Based on the examination of these moments, this paper will suggest a chronological and phenomena-based typology through which the process of nation building in the UAE may be understood.[4] Such exercise is of relevance not only for the study of Emirati domestic politics, but of its international interactions as well. Indeed, several authors writing within the context of Arab states' foreign policy have already signaled the importance that a high degree of state formation and consolidation bears on a country's international standing and actions.[5] It follows that a more internally consolidated state, with a stronger self-image, will certainly hold different readings about available lines of action in the external domain than a self-perceived weaker state. Many of the justifications offered for the emergence of the so-called "Gulf moment" (Abdulla 2010, Ottaway 2010) in contemporary Arab politics rest precisely in the idea that the Arabian Peninsula states, having achieved a high degree of socioeconomic and human development that is unparalleled in the region, are now taking center stage in Arab politics and international finance. As a consequence, the core of Arab power is now depicted as shifting into the Gulf region (Abdulla 2010: 1–2). Ideas of self-image and nation-building consolidation have been, to my knowledge, absent from such evaluations, but it is certainly worthwhile to examine the extent to which the internal consolidation of the national project can serve as a backdrop to a more proactive, self-assured image and positioning of these states in the international sphere. This chapter does not

---

4   Previous explorations of this topic were undertaken in Carvalho Pinto (forthcoming 2012a and forthcoming 2012b).

5   It is the case of Gerd Nonneman's contribution on Saudi Arabia's foreign policy (2005/2006: 315–51), and of Raymond Hinnebusch's analytical framework for the study of the Arab states' foreign policies' (2002: 1–27).

claim to make such extensive examinations, but it will conclude by suggesting that using an analysis of the process of nation building as a departure point for the understanding of this new Gulf moment—in fact the Gulf countries' actions throughout the Arab Spring may be understood as part of it—may bring about significant insights to the understanding of these countries' contemporary foreign policies. Some ideas will be offered in this regard in connection to the case of the UAE, but these are merely of a preliminary nature. Not only is this not the main focus of the chapter, but also the very recent occurrence of the Arab Spring's events still precludes a more thorough examination.

The timeframe for the analysis presented here begins in 1971 with the country's foundation and ends in 2011 with the events of the Arab Spring. The analysis is based on an examination of primary and secondary literature, as well as insights collected during a research stay in the UAE in 2007–08.

The structure of the chapter is as follows: the first section offers some theoretical background for the analysis of nation building in the UAE, followed by a brief overview of the country's sociopolitical background and early development challenges. The following section looks at the ideational shaping of the nation through an examination of three key interrelated moments that led to a strengthening of traditional rule. The chapter concludes with a brief summary of the argument presented, as well as some comments on the usefulness of this perspective for an analysis of the Gulf moment, particularly concerning the Emirati case.

What is Nation Building?

Theoretical Background for the Analysis of the UAE Case

Nation building is a state-led, strategic action through which the leadership of a country seeks to create or maintain a national entity within a given territory. The main purpose is the survival of such an entity. In order to achieve that goal, the population must perceive the former as something that is worth striving for. This means that the state must be perceived as "useful," that is, actively responding to the needs of the population and being able to convey the vision that union rather than separation is a better "deal" for all those involved (Derichs 2005: 42).

Within the Emirati context, such a goal has been achieved by following a "needs-oriented" approach (Hippler 2005: 185) that consisted in the state's attempt, since independence, to fulfill the many socioeconomic needs of the region's inhabitants. Therefore, nation building in the UAE can be understood as having unfolded into three interrelated projects: the creation of a national society, the setting-up of a functional state apparatus, and the devising of a unifying national ideology (ibid.: 7–9). This definition allows for the capturing, in a very holistic manner, of the myriad of transformations that accompanied the formation of the UAE. On the one hand, it apprehends the extensive material and infrastructure changes that occurred in the country through the concept of state building while, on the other, it also encompasses the practical measures involved in the creation of a national society and in the devising of a persuasive and unifying national identity. The final two components are inextricably linked, as a national society comes about partly as a result of the success achieved with the formulation of a national ideology. A national community is also created as a result of state policy, involving, but not exclusive to, the establishment of a national educational system, a housing policy, and the establishment of a public employment service.[6]

The devising of a national ideology, which is the component that most interests us here, must be a strategic state-led endeavor, which must be inclusive, flexible, and displaying great openness in reacting to internal and external events. In the Emirati case, for such an undertaking to be successful, it had to incorporate not only the traditional elements of the region's cultural stock,[7] but also explain, in a way that made narrative sense and was adjusted to the people's worldviews, why life had changed beyond recognition in a short amount of time, what does it mean to be an Emirati, and how to manage "demographic imbalance"—an expression used to refer to the minority status of the indigenous population *vis-à-vis* the expatriate population (currently about 16 percent of the population).[8] I do not claim that the state narrative has managed to solve these problems in a fully coherent, convincing manner, but rather that many of these ambiguities have been, to a large extent, successfully incorporated into the national narrative. Feelings of tribal belonging are no longer seen as a challenge to the state, but rather they have been woven and incorporated into the concept of Emirati national identity.[9] In addition, the creation of the UAE was popularly seen as having a positive impact in daily life, a vital legitimizing factor of the new state.[10]

The strengthening of traditional rule has been part and parcel of this process. Especially in latter years, the ruling families have portrayed themselves as those who guided their society towards its current economic prosperity while protecting the cultural and religious traditions of the region. Formulated in this way, there is almost a coincidence between the ruling families (and more specifically, the

---

6   Michael Hill and Kwen Fee's volume (1995) address precisely these issues in the case of nation building in Singapore.

7   The concept of "cultural stock" refers to the ideational elements that are part of the cultural universe of the target group, such as values, beliefs, and ideologies. This definition was borrowed from the process of framing in the social movement research (Snow and Benford 2000).

8   UAEinteract (August 16, 2011). *Ajman population at over 262,000; Population up by 12,000 and Emiratis account for 16%.* Retrieved on August 16, 2011 from <http://www.uaeinteract.com/docs/Ajman_population_at_over_262,000;_Population_up_by_12,000_and_Emiratis_account_for_16/46426.htm>.

9   See Partrick (2009) for the opposite argument.

10   These elements of the national narrative (flexibility, openness to change, narrative familiarity, scope and centrality, incorporation of traditional forms of organization) were identified by Claudia Derichs (2005: 44) as indispensable elements for the success of ideational nation building.

figure of the ruling sheikhs), and the boundaries of the nation. While almost equating the nation with the ruling families has certainly served to strengthen the existing political system, it should also be borne in mind that the recrafting of symbols and traditions—of which the ruling tribal family is an indelible part—has also served to create and delimit a national core that was "offered" to the population as a sort of cultural guide, to orientate them amidst material and social change. As I will argue throughout this chapter, having such a "core" was a deeply felt necessity among the Emiratis given the vertiginous changes that their surroundings and ways of life had experienced in the past decades. In this sense, the national narrative sought to possess both narrative fidelity and centrality, two key ingredients in ideational nation building.

Within this wider project the periods during which traditional rule was strengthened corresponded to particular moments of cultural challenge. These moments are probably best conceptualized as overlapping waves, with one springing from the other. Since their fluidity renders them uneasy for chronological and phenomenological delimitation, temporal markers related to internal and regional events were incorporated so as to facilitate analysis. Hence, the first wave corresponds to the re-traditionalization trend of the late 1970s that started before the Iranian Islamic Revolution of 1979; the second wave corresponds to the cultural authenticity policies of the 1990s, that developed more strongly after the 1991 Iraqi invasion of Kuwait, and the third—the focus on cultural empowerment of the native population—has unfolded since the 2001 terrorist attacks.

The choice of these particular moments in time and their denominations reflect a certain research perspective. The use of terms such as "re-traditionalization," "cultural authenticity," and "cultural empowerment," signals that issues of cultural identity and belonging associated to the maintenance and reproduction of the indigenous minority's way of life are here considered to be the most elaborate and salient dimension of the Emirati national project. Such perspective is sustained by the fact that the native Emiratis have held a demographic minority status since the establishment of the country in 1971. Such standing in the overall composition of the country's inhabitants has thus generated a well-documented massive investment, both financial and emotional, into the maintenance of cultural practices whose observance have lent a high degree of consistency to the UAE national project and, by implication, to the crafting of a national identity.

Since the long journey of nation building begins with the establishment of the country and with the addressing of the many security, survival and national unification challenges, the next section will provide a brief overview of how all this has unfolded.

The Formation of the UAE

External Challenges, Domestic Fragmentation and Early Self-image

The United Arab Emirates is a country located in the south-east area of the Arabian Peninsula, bordering Saudi Arabia and Oman. Before the UAE reached independence, its regions were known as the Trucial States, a small collection of poverty-stricken sheikhdoms that had been under British domination since the nineteenth century. They became independent in 1971, in the aftermath of the British retreat from the Gulf region, and united to form the country of the United Arab Emirates. The emirates are Abu Dhabi, the largest and most affluent of the seven regions, which became the capital of the new country, and Sharjah, Ras al-Khaimah (RAK), Ajman, Umm al-Qaywayn (UAQ), Dubai, and Fujairah. Each of these emirates has its own ruling family: the al-Nahyan from Abu Dhabi, the al-Maktoum from Dubai, the al-Sharqi from Fujairah, the al-Nuaimi from Ajman, the al-Mua'lla from UAQ, and the two branches of the al-Qasimi from Sharjah and RAK.

Achieving recognition from its larger and more powerful neighbors was not an easy task. The formation of a very wealthy micro-estate in the Gulf region was not regarded with particular enthusiasm by the region's great powers, Saudi Arabia and Iran. Saudi Arabia declared its support in 1968 of the federative solution as long as such an alternative enjoyed US and the neighboring states' support, but it deferred recognition until 1974 on account of outstanding border disputes with Abu Dhabi (Taryam 1987: 71, 227).[11] As regards Iran, the country saw the British retreat from the Gulf as an opportunity to emerge as the dominant power in the Gulf region. Consequently, it immediately rejected the proposed plan for a federation of Emirates, describing it as "emanating from colonial origins" and representing British control in disguise (ibid.: 73–5).

The new country's ownership of large oil resources were also the subject of discussion, as larger Arab neighbors commonly expressed the opinion that these reserves constituted "Arab wealth," and therefore should "not belong to any particular little country but to the Arab people as a whole." They argued that "the few, with their wealth, should be incorporated into the many" (Lienhardt 2001: 11). The uncertainty of the regional situation was further accentuated by Iran's occupation, on the eve of independence in 1971, of Abu Musa and Greater and Lesser Tunb, three islands claimed by the emirates of Sharjah and RAK. This action showed the weakness of the new state, clearly displaying the UAE's inability to protect its own borders. The lack of a confrontational stand as regards Iran's actions in the Emirati government's early responses to this crisis have revealed that the UAE leadership appreciated the extent of its weakness and inability to confront its larger neighbor (al-Alkim 1989: 48).

---

11   For an account of the border disputes between Saudi Arabia and Abu Dhabi, see Hawley's account over the Buraimi Oasis dispute (Hawley 1970: 186–94).

While dealing with this external uncertainty, the Emirati leadership was also facing substantial challenges at home. The primary problem was one of a political nature and was related to the rulers' disagreements over the contours of the new state. Opinions differed regarding emirate-level contributions to the federal budget, and the division of power between the federation and each emirate—these differences were further heightened by internal border disagreements. Placing particular strain on the overall negotiations was the fact that some of the emirates had established direct relations with other countries—particularly Iran and Saudi Arabia—a political attribute that should have been exercised at the federal, not emirate level. The continuing interference from, and conversely, the reliance on other Arab countries to make judgments on UAE internal matters (many of them confidential, such as the unification of the armed forces) were serious factors undermining the UAE's sovereignty, and a particular source of tension in the relationship between Abu Dhabi, as the main architect of the union, and the other emirates (Taryam 1987: 77, 226–7). Due to the existing range of disagreements, it was felt that the only feasible solution was to follow a gradualist approach to political integration (ibid.: 218, Khoury 1980: 47–8, Khalifa 1979: 122–5). Therefore, a federal union was the solution that had garnered more consensus among other possible options that were being discussed at the time,[12] but nevertheless disagreements over the final form of the political arrangements still existed.

On the social level, the population was quite ill prepared, both in terms of educational qualifications and lifestyle, for the irrevocable alterations that were sweeping their country. Government support in this transition period was particularly important, for much of the population had lost their traditional means of livelihood and did not possess the necessary educational and technical skills to find jobs in the new economy. In addition, overwhelming poverty frequently gave rise to shifting loyalties to wherever rewards might lie; there was a danger that if living conditions did not improve and people felt that their lot had become worse with the federation, this would translate into lack of individual and tribal support for the new country. Indeed, having witnessed how living conditions in Kuwait and Bahrain had quickly improved as a result of oil revenues further reinforced the UAE's people's own aspirations for a better life (personal interviews, Sharjah, 2007–08). Within this overall context of poverty and deprivation, the state's utilization of the newly acquired resources to build infrastructure and to improve the inhabitants' lives was as much a political as a humanitarian imperative (Townsend 1984: 37).

Bearing these twin goals in mind, Sheikh Zayed al-Nahyan, the former Sheikh of Abu Dhabi, and first president of the federation (1971–2004), had in the pre-federation years, already begun delivering development assistance to the population of the other emirates. Such support continued in the following years, and the population, especially from more remote and poorer areas, began

---

12   For a succinct description of other envisaged solutions, see El Rayyes 1988: 69–70.

considering Abu Dhabi as their best hope for a better life. A popular stake in the new order was beginning to arise, emanating from the promise for a better future (Khalifa 1979: 75–7).

Feeling that the new country was something useful and worth striving for was already a good beginning for the crafting and fostering of an Emirati national identity. The political and economic benefits of being attached to Abu Dhabi were clear, but it was still necessary to give sustenance to this feeling by creating a national society.

This was an outstanding challenge considering the tribal diversity and fragmentation that characterized the region's population. Even though the common bond rooted in traditional Arab and Islamic values was a positive factor, trucial society was also divided into tribes, many of them still nomadic and often displaying a deep-seated dislike and suspicion of one another. The tribe had traditionally provided the cultural and ethnic frame of reference for the people (Khalifa 1979: 95), but for the purposes of creating a modern state, the primary focus of loyalty had to be shifted from the tribe into the modern state.

Therefore, from a nation-building perspective, these existing tensions had to be dealt with adequately. As already mentioned, the solution was to follow a "needs-oriented approach," of which the pre-federation development aid provided by Abu Dhabi was an early example. Since the former had been so successful in fostering attachment to the emirate, such policy was continued and expanded. From the provision of educational and health services to income-generating activities and infrastructural development (ibid.: 75, El Mallakh 1981: 64–73),[13] the presence of the newly created Emirati state was felt throughout the region, and the Emiratis could see their lives improving as a result.

These changes generated great excitement in the small Emirati community. Having seen how life had become better in Kuwait and Bahrain, the UAE population was "in a hurry to catch up with its neighbors." Their widespread aspirations "to be part of a modern twentieth century state" (Soffan 1980: 60–1), as well as of pursuing education and other available roads for "self-improvement" (personal interviews, UAE, 2007), were leading to the rapid disintegration of several social conventions. There was a widespread will to negate everything that was considered backward, and to be part of a more sophisticated world. In this sense, it was similar to the experiences in other countries of the Middle East and South Asia, where social modernization and the ending of certain life practices were associated with ideas of modernity, development, and civilization (Jayawardena 1994: 12). These aspirations for change that had largely sprung from certain feelings of personal and educational inadequacy to deal with the "modern world," were not exclusive to the Emirati population. A close reading of the Preamble of the Emirati Constitution that was signed upon independence in 1971 gives evidence that the UAE rulers shared similar feelings:

---

13   See also Cordes and Scholz 1980: 12–48; and Hill and Kwen Fee 1995, addressing similar issues in the nation-building process in Singapore.

... it is our desire and the desire of the people of our Emirates to establish a Union ... to promote a better life, more enduring stability and *a higher international status for the Emirates and their people*;

And whereas the realisation of the foregoing was our dearest desire, towards which we have bent our strongest resolution, *being desirous of advancing our country and our people to the status of qualifying them to take appropriate place among civilised states and nations.*[14]

The expressions "a higher international status for the Emirates and their people," and "qualifying the country and the people to take a place among civilized states and nations," indicate a very humble evaluation not only of the external image of the country, but also of the level of social development hitherto existing.

The Constitution Preamble makes a close link between development at home and self-image abroad. Since the projection of a new image abroad was dependent upon the "qualification" of the people and the country, this meant not only that the country had to be modernized, but its inhabitants as well. This was thus an important component in the creation of the "new" Emirati society.

While much of the "logistical" part of this process was achieved through the provision of services, the fostering of new ways of thinking was much aided by, for example, the rulers' encouraging of families to send and keep their children at school, boys and girls alike, and also by lifestyle examples of Arab expatriates originating from Egypt, Syria, Iraq, Lebanon, and Palestine. They played a very important part as role models for the Emirati population, who considered them to be "more skilled, better educated, more sophisticated and more experienced in dealing with the complexities of modern life" (Melikian 1988: 112–13). Their influence was felt in the introduction of colloquial expressions, in the changes to the conducting of religious observance, and also in interpersonal relationships. Many of these influences were channeled through the educational system (ibid.: 124–7), since expats held many of the teaching positions.

In the early years, the ongoing modernization of society did seem to be reinforcing, within the domestic space, a sense of the national capacity for "self-improvement." At a time of great optimism and, at the same time, great pain in adapting to new ways of living and thinking, this was a decade strongly oriented towards internal development. This did not mean, however, that the UAE was shying away from international involvement.

On the contrary, they were keen to show, at all possible occasions, that the UAE people had risen to the challenge of modernization and development. This plan had a very distinct gender dimension to it that I develop at length elsewhere but here it suffices to say that the participation of female Emirati delegations in international

---

14   Helpline Law: Legal Solution Worldwide (Undated). *The UAE Constitution* (emphasis added). Retrieved on July 31, 2011 from <http://www.helplinelaw.com/law/uae/constitution/constitution01.php>.

gatherings and organizations was meant to signal to other countries not only the level of progress that the Emirati state had achieved, but also its readiness to be part of the modern world (Carvalho Pinto 2012a (forthcoming)). There was thus a holistic approach to development, underpinned by Sheikh Zayed al-Nahyan's particular aspiration to create a state with prestige in both the Gulf and Arab areas (Taryam 1987: 208).

The Ideational Shaping of the Nation

The Re-traditionalization Wave of the Late 1970s

At the end of this early period of internal consolidation, some generalized uneasiness emerged in connection to the massive cultural shifts that the Emirati society was undergoing. These feelings were triggered both by material and social alterations to the population's ways of life as well as growing discomfort with the increased influx of foreign workers into the country. This was a phenomenon that began during the late 1960s, with the beginnings of the oil commercialization. Because native Emiratis were very small in number and not skilled enough to take up jobs in the modern economy, there were many opportunities for those that were looking for employment. Many non-Emiratis arrived looking for work, and their numbers have been increasing ever since.

Their growing numbers, the burgeoning of new sociocultural influences, together with a widespread adoption of a consumerist lifestyle, began to generate an insidious collective feeling among Emiratis that their indigenous culture was somehow being put aside for the sake of development. In this period and well into the 1980s, these sentiments were more of a loose recognition that the Emiratis, as a people, were "losing themselves," collectively and as individuals, in an upward spiral of abundance and materialistic yearnings (personal interviews, UAE, 2007–08).

Discontent with the rising number of foreigners became widespread as Emiratis increasingly felt that they could not continue as minorities in their own country; at the time, they only numbered about 22 percent of the total population. In the meanwhile, there was discontent with the uneven distribution of wealth (Abdullah 1980: 21). It is in this overall context of dissatisfaction that a wave of popular interest in the indigenous roots of culture and religion started to reemerge. This is not to say that traditional norms had completely disappeared in the UAE as a result of the modernization process. On the contrary, they had always been part of the community's social discourse and practice. For this reason, the trend is better understood as a pullback movement, a retreat from a situation that was emotionally and practically felt as having progressed too far. Therefore, not only in the UAE but also throughout the Gulf, the mid-1970s were characterized by the unfolding of an intellectual and cultural movement aimed at Islamic renaissance. The adoption and application of Islamic law became one of the most important issues of the 1980s and of the utmost significance to Gulf citizens (Al-Moqatei 1989: 139). In the United

Arab Emirates, this wave of re-traditionalization in the late 1970s can be understood as having more of an emotional rather than an intellectual content, since it was an indigenous culture's defensive reaction to socioeconomic change that was expressed in religious terms. This is unsurprising, since the traditional culture is popularly perceived as being completely enmeshed in Islamic values.

Since this phenomenon happened around the same time in several Muslim-majority countries (Bill 1984: 108–27), some connection to the spillover effects of the 1979 Iranian Islamic Revolution can be drawn. Indeed, the Islamic Revolution in Iran was being perceived in the UAE both as an example of the overthrow of an economically corrupt regime that should serve as a warning sign for the government (Abdullah 1980: 21), and also as an example of modernization taken too far, with the consequent powerful backlash.[15] In addition, there was widespread challenge from Islamist movements to governments across the Arab world; monarchs and presidents alike felt compelled to amplify their religious credentials, often through the sponsoring of Islamic projects. The Emirati case was no exception to this regional trend (al-Muhairi 1996: 352–5).[16]

The adoption and visibility of new behaviors, particularly among the expatriate community, caused significant anxiety among the Emiratis. Public drunkenness, rising crime rates, theft, brigandage, and apostasy were some of the areas to which the application of Islamic law sanctions were perceived as particularly fitting. In fact, rising criminality was popularly seen as a consequence of the abandonment of Islamic penalties (ibid.: 352–3).

It should be mentioned that modifications in gender relations brought about both by the expatriates' lifestyle as well as by the extensive changes to the situation of Emirati women, were seen by many as particularly troubling (Carvalho Pinto 2012a (forthcoming)). Fears associated with the emergence of "distasteful" cultural habits attributed to western-oriented development (Soffan 1980: 38), as well as with the liberalization of social norms that had the potential to break up the family, and the emphasis on material gains over personal and spiritual values (Bill 1984: 113), were perceived as especially worrisome.

Given the popular concerns that issues of morality and culture aroused in Emirati society, the government began its own process of "Islamization" of its laws. Butti Sultan al-Muhairi (1996: 352–5) pinpoints the beginning of this process in the UAE to a Council of Ministers resolution from January 17, 1978; the resolution stated that the Islamization of laws was not to be applied to areas that affected orderly economic development and its institutions. This shows the extent to which selective re-traditionalization was perceived as the way forward.

As already mentioned, given that rulers and population alike felt the appeal for the Islamization of laws (being also part of society, rulers should not be viewed as being immune to these societal trends), the re-traditionalization wave of the late 1970s

---

15 Nesta Ramazani (1985: 262) makes this insight for Saudi Arabia, but it can be generalized to the Emirati case.

16 See Bill (1984: 111) as regards Gulf states in general.

should be primarily seen as a domestic phenomenon. It may well be considered as the first truly challenging moment since the federation's establishment (at the time, only a decade old), when there was widespread popular uneasiness with cultural and material change. However, as the above shows, this overall process unfolded through a strong interface between society's wishes and the response given by public policymakers. In this sense, this wave may be considered as a crucial nation-building moment, whereby the leadership was able to respond to the wishes of the population, while at the same time renewing its legitimacy and strengthening its own credentials.

The Cultural Authenticity Policies of the 1990s

This process of self-questioning and attempts to hang on to traditional cultural roots continued throughout the 1980s. Having gone through the eight long years of the Iran–Iraq War (1980–88) and the insecurity and instability that followed, the Emirati people were yearning for a period of calm. But in 1990, the Iraqi invasion of Kuwait once again launched the region into turmoil (Abdulla 1994). This event profoundly challenged assumptions underlying Arab identity and solidarity.[17] The Gulf States had supported Iraq against Iran, often at their own risk, and Kuwait, the country that had helped Iraq the most, was now being invaded and its legitimacy brought into question.

At the same time, during the early 1990s, the consequences of the social dynamics identified in the previous section were already quite clear. The multiplicity of cultural influences, as well as the Emiratis' adoption of lifestyle habits from their fellow Arabs, had transformed UAE popular culture into an almost exclusive amalgam of foreign idioms, symbols, and practices (Lawson and al-Naboodah 2008: 15).

In 1991, Iraq invaded Kuwait and the ensuing political instability heightened the feelings of uncertainty associated with national identity and viability that had been boiling under the surface for nearly two decades (Abdulla 1994: 1–13). Once the Gulf War was over, the ongoing debates on cultural survival gained renewed emphasis. Within the UAE, the return to Islam became a means to regain one's true identity, as opposed to mimicry of the West. Within this vibrant atmosphere, the Islamists successfully captured the national discourse (al-Sayegh 2004: 113–17), and the offset of expatriate influence assumed particular importance.

Seeing that the external national legitimacy challenge that had afflicted Kuwait might one day also dawn upon the UAE, and that domestic calls for a stronger return to cultural and religious roots were being amplified, the UAE rulers had little choice but to step up the project of national consolidation. Great significance was

---

17   See Sayigh (1991: 487–507) for an assessment of the reasons that led to the 1990 Iraqi invasion of Kuwait.

attached to this project, since it was felt that after such rapid progress throughout the past decades, it was "now imperative to preserve the deep roots of society."[18]

The prevalence of this perspective among the leadership was translated into a widespread project of cultural and heritage revival aiming at the promotion of culturally "authentic" policies and practices. State encouragement was given to the setting-up of research centers, heritage areas, and societies, in order to stimulate the production and diffusion of knowledge about traditional culture (Lawson and al-Naboodah 2008: 15–30). Construction was increasingly influenced by Islamic architecture; old forts and homes were reconstructed; mosques were built; and traditional industries such as handicrafts revitalized (Bill 1994:108–27, Khalaf 2000: 243–61).[19] Old traditions such as camel races were revived and became massive public events where the rulers and the population could meet in a traditional tribal environment. Not only have these provided the link to the Emirates' historical past, but they also have served as a means to educate the younger generations about the lives and struggles of their ancestors (Khalaf, 2000: 243–4).

Modern means of communication have been central in propagating this idea of traditional culture, and serving as vehicles of nation building. The ruling sheikhs' generosity and crucial role in the maintenance of these cultural festivals was emphasized, as the following statement from the Emirati newspaper *al-Ittihad* from 1996 illustrates:

> Within the framework of the directives of His Highness Shaikh Zayed Bin Sultan al-Nahyan, The President of the State, and His Highness Shaikh Khalifa Bin Zayed al-Nahyan, The Crown Prince ... and because of their Highnesses' concern for the revival of our authentic popular heritage ... the preservation of our fathers' and ancestors' sport, and the protection of our authentic Arab customs and traditions, camel races were organized under the patronage of Sheikh Zayed ... .[20]

The imagery of the racetracks, with their rituals and poetry recitals, is meant to emphasize the role of the ruling sheikhs in promoting national development and safeguarding culture. The association between their generosity and the safeguarding

---

18   Statement by Sheikha Fatima Mubarak, the favored wife of the late Sheikh Zayed al-Nahyan upon her visit to the 1992 Annual Handicraft Exhibition. Shabaka alrahal alemaratia [Emirati Wanderer Network] (Undated). "Zayed the Millennial Legend/Women in Zayed Reign." Retrieved on June 15, 2009 from <http://www.uaezayed.com/zayed/zayed/zayed11e.htm>.

19   See Ouis 2002, Khalaf 2000: 243–61, Lawson and al-Naboodah 2008: 15–30, Fox et al. 2006, Hurreiz 2002, Rahman 2008: 31–9. There have been similar policies all around the Gulf area. For general accounts of this phenomenon, see, for example, Davis 1991: 1–35, Baabood 2008: 97–120. On Kuwait, see Longva 1997; on Bahrain, see Alkhozai 2008: 71–84.

20   No title (1996, April 26). *Al-Ittihad*, p. 3. Cited in Khalaf (1999: 102).

of cultural traditions has further strengthened their status and legitimacy (Khalaf 2000: 243–61), as well as the overall political system of which they are part.

For the Emirati population, what had previously been very diffuse reflections about loss of identity, and the search for "culturally authentic" ways of life, assumed a much more direct and specific focus as a result of this state-led cultural revival project.[21] The specifics of the reception of this multifaceted project are debatable, but in general terms, it can be said that this endeavor has enjoyed great resonance and popular backing among the Emiratis. Similarly to the first wave, it responded to the cultural anxieties of the population by offering a more or less strong and cohesive national core that strengthened the political system while at the same time lending greater substance to the definition of what it meant to be "an Emirati." In this sense, it was a continuation of the previous wave, but one in which both the scope of the problems at hand and the extent of the solutions offered were even more accentuated.

The Cultural Empowerment Wave (2001–)

Throughout the 1990s, cultural anxieties continued to reverberate throughout UAE society, reaching a high point with the terrorist attacks of September 11, 2001. This event became "a turning point for the Gulf states, for the way the world viewed them, for their own self-analysis, and for the religions within these states" (al-Sayegh 2004: 107–8, 118). This was so because the US's response to these attacks brought about massive international scrutiny of the Arab Gulf region as a whole, mainly focused on the perceived negative traits of the region's indigenous cultures. Hence, the combined outside pressures for democratization, the denigration of Arab culture for inciting violence, and the worldwide association of terrorism with the Islamic faith, dealt a severe blow to UAE society. The self-image that, over three decades, the Gulf's rulers and people had sought to construct, of a "model of peace and harmony in a war-torn region" characterized by its "multicultural, multiethnic societies and booming economies," was beginning to show signs of strain (al-Sayegh 2004: 118). As a country already so caught up in its own self-questioning, issues, which were already very much debated—such as the underpinnings of cultural and Islamic identity, the increasing westernization of daily life practices, and concerns about demographic changes—assumed even greater significance (ibid.: 107–8, 118).

Consequently, and responding to the intensity with which these matters were felt in society, the UAE government stepped up its cultural revival program. There was considerable spending on museums, open-air heritage villages, the staging of heritage events, and the sponsorship of traditional literary and cultural programs. In addition to the camel races mentioned above, a number of new festivals were also launched, generously sponsored by the rulers. For example, since 2003, an

---

21   A similar idea applied to the overall context of the Arab Gulf countries was similarly expressed by Davis 1991: 31.

annual hunting and equestrian exhibition takes place in Abu Dhabi, in addition to poetry readings and other activities (Davidson 2009: 133–5).[22]

The nostalgic evocation of the past has not been restricted to the elderly generations alone. Young Emiratis, as the generation most deeply affected by the sharp contrast between strong cultural concerns and rapid development, have also been turning to traditional culture, in search of clues to how to reconcile tradition with modernity. Within this context, "Islamization" has been but one way of seeking to harmonize their life conditions, characterized by international exposure and alien influences, with their own desires to leading 'culturally authentic' lives (Ouis 2002). The recurrence of veiling among females, in sharp contrast to the opposing tendency during the 1970s, as well as the expansion of the use of traditional attire among young males and females reflects the same tendency. The population's pursuance of more 'culturally authentic' ways of life has become one of the UAE's most significant features in recent decades. While this tendency towards the re-traditionalization of life practices has been unfolding since the late 1970s, it has been gradually assuming a more self-assertive tone in the past decade. Cultural observance is no longer a sign of backwardness, as in the early development years. In these cosmopolitan new Emirates, "Arabness is chic and not backward" (Fox et al. 2006: 49). There is a self-assurance that originates from a sense of history, structure, and knowing one's place in the world. The attempt to strike a balance between fast-paced economic modernization and the maintenance and recreation of traditions is being placed by the state at the core of national identity crafting. The blending of modernity and tradition are pretty much presented as part and parcel of the Emirati's distinctiveness, and not as a shying-away from the modern world. Such concern is not unwarranted, since UAE society feels itself to be under demographic and cultural siege. Stronger attachment to traditional and religious mores has been increasingly used as a shielding mechanism from what many perceive to be harmful influences. As a means to address these fears and simultaneously build a positive image of the UAE, the political leadership has been trying to construct a national ethos of tolerance, by stressing the example that the UAE can set for other nations, as an open-minded society, and as a "live example of tolerance and coexistence"[23] where many nationalities live together. This progressive image that is being built and deployed by the Emirati leadership seems to be directed at both domestic and international audiences. On the internal level, it seems to be meant to strongly convey to the population the ideals of tolerance and cultural respect, which are indeed essential for the stability of a country with more than 200 nationalities. On the external front, it is interesting that about forty years after independence, the self-image of the country that is being presented by the Emirati leadership is a positive

---

22   For more details on the cultural-religious components of domestic legitimacy in the Emirate of Dubai, see Davidson 2008: 173–6.

23   Ministry of Foreign Affairs. United Arab Emirates (2010). "UAE Foreign Policy: Tolerance and Coexistence." Retrieved on August 15, 2011 from <http://mofa.gov.ae/mofa_english/portal/b074766a-5507-43c7-9beb-3155a52e25b5.aspx>.

and modern one that is a far cry from the early 1970s assessment of the UAE as a country seeking to attain a status that would qualify it "to take appropriate place among civilized states and nations."[24] This shows that an intensive, state-led nation building was able, throughout time, to carve a very positive self-image, while at the same time departing from very humble beginnings in this regard. The variations from one phase of nation building to the other have surely also produced different self-images both in the domestic and international space. These, in turn, have certainly influenced the state's perceptions regarding available lines of action in the international domain,[25] although such scrutiny is beyond the scope of this paper.

From the above, it can be suggested that this radical difference in terms of the self-image that the UAE leadership is projecting both domestically and internationally can be largely ascribed to the success of the UAE nation-building project. Indeed, looking at international self-perception from the viewpoint of nation building does allow for the introduction of a measure of temporality and dynamism into the ways domestic and international capabilities are perceived in different moments in time. Maybe the so-called "Gulf moment" that was alluded to in the beginning of this chapter, and within it, the Gulf countries' actions during the Arab Spring, can be understood in this perspective. In the UAE's case, two key state actions were particularly striking considering that they came from a country that usually practices a very discreet diplomacy. The visibility of the UAE's commitment to sending of troops to Bahrain, as well as the open display of support for the former Egyptian president Hosni Mubarak in the form of the visit of the Emirati minister for foreign affairs, Sheikh Abdulla al-Nahyan, the Emirati President's half-brother, to Cairo in the height of the Tahrir Square protests, were quite surprising. In this regard, maybe the Arab Spring has offered the opportunity to visibly showcase the degree of internal self-confidence and state consolidation that has resulted from forty years of intensive and strategic nation building. Having consolidated the emotional boundaries of the nation-state and armed with a high sense of self-esteem, maybe the ascension of a new educated generation of leaders to whom feelings of inadequacy and discomfort with modernity are a distant tale, means that the UAE is ready to take on a more visible international role that is more in line with its current self-image. This newfound assertiveness may well be part of this "Gulf moment."

Returning to the domestic environment, the positive assessment that is being presented here should not overlook the fact that, as with many other nation-building projects in other settings, the Emirati endeavor was not without its shortcomings and insufficiencies. For example, the presentation of the blending of the old and the new as a successful feature of "Emirati-ness" does not appeal to many young Emirati women, who feel torn between their generation's lifestyle

---

24   Helpline Law: Legal Solution Worldwide. "The UAE Constitution." Retrieved on July 31, 2011 <http://www.helplinelaw.com/law/uae/constitution/constitution01.php>.

25   More or less similar ideas were expressed by Gerd Nonneman (2005/2006), Raymond Hinnebusch (2001), and Eric Davis (1991).

and its associated demands for professional success, and the restraints placed upon them as females. For many of them, this dimension of the national project appears as extremely contradictory and often unfair (see Carvalho Pinto 2012a (forthcoming)). Nevertheless, it can safely be said that the Emirati state-led nation-building endeavor was largely a success. It has been able to fulfill a gap in terms of providing a national identity core to the indigenous population, as well as of keeping its geographic integrity and standing as the only successful example of political union in the Arab world.

Conclusion

The successful unfolding of the material elements of the Emirati nation-building project was largely made possible thanks to the availability of oil resources. Their strategic utilization to fulfill the three state tasks inherent to national construction—building of infrastructure, creation of a national society, and the devising of a persuasive national narrative—were key to the survival of the country and its political system. The existing ruling families were able to renew their popular legitimacy through the pursuance of a needs-approach strategy to nation building that included the setting-up of a welfare state that catered to the health, housing, and income needs of the population. In parallel and on an ideational level, the role of the ruling families in the effective selection, shaping, and deployment of the constitutive elements of national identity were crucial in providing a national narrative that was largely forged in response to the cultural and, let's say, existential anxieties of the population. In a period of massive socioeconomic changes, this narrative continuity was quite important in the face of the spiraling modernization and socioeconomic changes, for it did offer the population a sense of steadiness and stability amidst their otherwise completely unrecognizable surroundings. The result of forty years of thorough, strategic nation building may well have given rise to a "Gulf moment" in Arab politics, a moment characterized by the Gulf States' emergence as economic and developmental powerhouses *vis-à-vis* their fellow Arab neighbors. The assertiveness of these countries during the Arab Spring, of which sending troops to Bahrain is the prime example, may be precisely an indication of such a moment. In the UAE's case, as the aforementioned Arab Spring examples, together with the 1971 and 2010 quotes from Emirati decision makers illustrate, a new international image born out of a successful nation-building process may well give rise to a future differing positioning in international politics.

References

Abdulla, Abdulkhaleq (2010). *Contemporary Socio-Political Issues of the Arab Gulf Moment.* Retrieved from London School of Economics, Kuwait Programme on Development, Governance and Globalisation in the Gulf States website: <http://www2.lse.ac.uk/government/research/resgroups/kuwait/research/papers/sociopoliticalissues.aspx>.

—— (2000). *The Arab Gulf States: Old Approaches and New Realities*. Abu Dhabi: ECSSR.

____(1994). "Gulf War: The Socio-Political Background." *Arab Gulf Quarterly*, 16(3): 1–13.

___(1980). "The Revolution in Iran Stimulated the Existing Contradictions in the United Arab Emirates". MERIP Reports, No. 85 (Feb.), pp. 19-22+25

Al-Alkim, Hassan H. (1989). *The Foreign Policy of the United Arab Emirates*. London: Saqi.

Alkhozai, Mohammed A. (2008). "An Aspect of Cultural Development in Bahrain: Archaeology and the Restoration of Historic Sites." In Alanoud Alsharek and Robert Springborg (eds), *Political Culture and Political Identity in the Arab Gulf States* (pp. 71–84). London: Saqi.

Baabood, Abdullah (2008). "Sport and Identity in the Gulf." In Alanoud Alsharek and Robert Springborg (eds), *Political Culture and Political Identity in the Arab Gulf States* (pp. 97–120). London: Saqi.

Bill, James A. (1984). "The Persian Gulf: Resurgent Islam." *Foreign Affairs* 63(1): 108–27.

Carvalho Pinto, Vânia (forthcoming 2012a). *Nation-Building, State, and the Gender Framing of Women's Rights in the United Arab Emirates (1971–2009)*. Reading, UK: Ithaca Press.

—— (forthcoming 2012b). "Der Bau der Nation vor dem Hintergrund von Diversität am Beispiel der Vereinigten Arabischen Emiraten." In F. Lenz and S. Schlickau. (eds), *Interkulturalität in Bildung, Ästhetik und Kommunikation*. Frankfurt am Main et al: Peter Lang.

Cordes, Rainer, and Scholz, Fred (1980). *Bedouins, Wealth, and Change: A Study of Rural Development in the United Arab Emirates and the Sultanate of Oman*. Tokyo: The United Nations University.

Davidson, Christopher M. (2009). *Abu Dhabi: Oil and Beyond*. New York: Columbia University Press.

—— (2008). *Dubai: The Vulnerability of Success*. New York: Columbia University Press.

—— (2005). *The United Arab Emirates: A Study in Survival*. Boulder, CO: Lynne Rienner.

Davis, Eric (1991). "Theorizing Statecraft and Social Change in Arab Oil-Producing Countries." In Eric Davis and Nicolas Gavrielides (eds), *Statecraft in the Middle East: Oil, Historical Memory, and Popular Culture* (pp. 1–35). Miami: Florida International University Press.

Derichs, Claudia (2005). "Shaping the Nation – Ideological Aspects of Nation-Building." In Jochen Hippler (ed.), *Nation-Building. A Key Concept for Peaceful Conflict Transformation?* (pp. 42–53). London and Ann Arbor, MI: Pluto Press.

Fox, John W. et al (eds) (2006). *Globalization and the Gulf*. London: Routledge.

Gause III, F. Gregory (2000). "The Persistency of Monarchy in the Arabian Peninsula: A Comparative Analysis." In Joseph Kostiner (ed.), *Middle East Monarchies: The Challenge of Modernity* (pp. 167–86). Boulder, CO and London: Lynne Rienner.

Hawley, Donald (1970). *The Trucial States*. London: George Allen & Unwin.

Hill, Michael, and Kwen Fee, Lian (1995). *Politics of Nation Building and Citizenship in Singapore*. London: Routledge.

Hinnebusch, Raymond (2002). "Introduction: An Analytical Framework." In Raymond Hinnebusch and Anoushiravan Ehteshamin (eds), *The Foreign Policies of Middle East States* (pp. 1–27). Boulder, CO: Lynne Rienner.

Hippler, Jochen (2005). "Violent Conflicts, Conflict Prevention and Nation-Building- Terminology and Political Concepts." In Jochen Hippler (ed.), *Nation-Building. A Key Concept for Peaceful Conflict Transformation?* (pp. 3–14). London and Ann Arbor, MI: Pluto Press.

Hurreiz, Sayyid Hamid (2002). *Folklore and Folklife in the United Arab Emirates*. London: Routledge Curzon.

Jayawardena, Kumari (1994 [1986]). *Feminism and Nationalism in the Third World*. London and Atlantic Highlands, NJ: Zed Books.

Khalaf, Suleyman (2000). "Poetics and Politics of Newly Invented Traditions in the Gulf: Camel Racing in the United Arab Emirates." *Ethnology* 39(3): 243–61.

—— (1999). "Camel Racing in the Gulf. Notes on the Evolution of a Traditional Cultural Sport." *Anthropos* 94: 85–116.

Khalifa, Ali Mohamed (1979). *The United Arab Emirates: Unity in Fragmentation*. Boulder, CO: Westview Press; London: Croom Helm.

Khoury, Enver M. (1980). *The United Arab Emirates: Its Political System and Politics*. Hyattsville, MD: Institute of Middle Eastern and North African Affairs.

Lawson, Fred and al-Naboodah, Hasan M. (2008). "Heritage and Cultural Nationalism in the United Arab Emirates." In Alanoud Alsharek and Robert Springborg (eds), *Political Culture and Political Identity in the Arab Gulf States* (pp. 15–30). London: Saqi.

Lienhardt, Peter (2001). *Shaikhdoms of Eastern Arabia* (Ahmed al-Shehi, ed.). Basingstoke and New York: Palgrave.

Longva, Anh Nga (1997). *Walls Built on Sand: Migration, Exclusion, and Society in Kuwait*. Boulder, CO and Oxford: Westview.

El Mallakh, Ragaei (1981). *The Economic Development of the United Arab Emirates*. London: Croom Helm.

Melikian, Levon (1988). "Arab Socio-Political Impact on Gulf Life-Style." In B.R. Pridham (ed.), *The Arab Gulf and the Arab World* (pp. 112–30). London, New York, and Sydney: Croom Helm.

Al-Moqatei, Mohammad (1989). "Introducing Islamic Law in the Arab Gulf States: A Case Study of Kuwait." *Arab Law Quarterly* 4(2): 138–48.

Al-Muhairi, Butti Sultan Butti (1996). "The Islamisation of Laws in the UAE: The Case of the Penal Code." *Arab Law Quarterly* 11(4): 350–71.

Nonneman, Gerd (2005/2006). "Determinants and patterns of Saudi Foreign Policy: 'Omnibalancing' and 'Relative Autonomy' in multiple environments." In Paul Aarts and Gerd Nonneman (eds), *Saudi Arabia in the Balance: Political Economy, Society, Foreign Affairs* (pp. 315–51). New York: New York University Press.

Onley, James, and Khalaf, Suleyman (2006). "Shaikhly Authority in the Pre-oil Gulf: An Historical–Anthropological Study." *History and Anthropology* 17(3): 189–208.

Ottaway, David B. (2010). "The Arab Tomorrow." *Wilson Quarterly* Winter: 48–64.

Partrick, Neil (2009). "Nationalism in the Gulf States." Retrieved from London School of Economics, Kuwait Programme on Development, Governance and Globalisation in the Gulf States website: <http://www2.lse.ac.uk/government/research/resgroups/kuwait/research/papers/nationalism.aspx>.

Ouis, Pernilla (2002). "Islamization as a Strategy for Reconciliation between Modernity and Tradition: Examples from Contemporary Arab Gulf States." *Islam and Christian-Muslim Relations* 13(3): 315–34.

Rahman, Nadia (2008). "Place and Space in the Memory of the United Arab Emirates Elders." In Alanoud Alsharek and Robert Springborg (eds), *Political Culture and Political Identity in the Arab Gulf States* (pp. 31–9). London: Saqi.

Ramazani, Nesta (1985). "Arab Women in the Gulf." *The Middle East Journal* 39(2): 258–76.

El-Rayyes, Riad N. (1988). "Arab Nationalism and the Gulf." In B.R. Pridham (ed.), *The Arab Gulf and the Arab World* (pp. 67–94). London, New York, and Sydney: Croom Helm.

Al-Sayegh, Fatma (2004). "Post-9/11 Changes in the Gulf: The Case of the UAE." *Middle East Policy* 11(2): 107–24.

Sayigh, Yezid (1991). "The Gulf Crisis: Why the Arab Regional Order failed." *International Affairs (Royal Institute of International Affairs)* 67(3) (July): 487–507.

Snow, David and Benford, Robert D. (2000). "Framing Processes and Social Movements: An Overview and Assessment." *Annual Review of Sociology* 26: 611–39.

Soffan, Linda Usra (1980). *The Women of the United Arab Emirates*, London: Croom Helm.

Taryam, Abdullah Omran (1987). *The Establishment of the United Arab Emirates 1950–85*. London, New York, and Sydney: Croom Helm.

Townsend, John (1984). "Philosophy of State Development Planning." In M.S. El Azhary (ed.), *The Impact of Oil Revenues on Arab Gulf Development* (pp. 35–53). London and Sydney: Croom Helm.

Chapter 4

Lebanon's Quest for Independence: Between Fragmentation, Political Instability, and Foreign Intervention

Benedetta Berti

Lebanon, a country with multiple and at times conflicting identities, often appears puzzling to outsiders. On the one hand, the small Mediterranean country is time and time again mentioned as a possible model for the Middle East: with a multicultural and pluralist society, a fundamentally liberal outlook—both culturally and economically—and a strong "outward orientation" (Gates 1998: 2), Lebanon stands out as a unique experiment in the region.

However, behind this rosy portrait, Lebanon's political and social structure still suffers from serious constitutional and institutional weakness. In particular, far from being a harmonious experiment in multiculturalism, Lebanese society is extremely fragile and fragmented along ethnic, religious, and sectarian lines.

In turn, this divided society has strongly impacted the country's political system and the government's capacity to exercise control and authority over all of its citizens and territory.

First, because identity politics are still very much the basis of Lebanon's political system, political parties tend to function according to a clientelist and community-based, rather than a nation-based, platform, thus failing to foster national unity. Secondly, the Lebanese political system—far from rejecting the divided and sectarian basis of its society—reproduces and enhances existing divisions by working on the basis of confessionalism. As a result, the government and the political system as a whole suffer from institutional weakness, and are often both ineffective and dysfunctional.

This unique combination of inter-sectarian tensions, societal divisions, clientelism, and institutional weakness make Lebanon particularly vulnerable to the influence of foreign powers. Direct and indirect foreign intervention has been a key pattern in Lebanese political life since the foundation of the modern Lebanese state, blurring the lines between domestic and foreign matters.

Lebanon's main sectarian groups have all developed ties with foreign actors and powers as a way to improve their domestic position with respect to the other sects. An important consequence of the ongoing relations between domestic sectarian groups and their foreign "patrons" is that, despite the small size and relative unimportance of Lebanon, a myriad of foreign powers have been invested in the country, often with profoundly conflicting agendas.

Of course, there are other reasons as to why each major regional power, from Syria, to Iran, to Saudi Arabia has been strongly involved in Lebanese domestic politics. In particular, Lebanon is geo-strategically important, and exercising influence over it is deemed key to shifting the regional balance of power.

The relationship between foreign patronage and state weakness is both entrenched in Lebanese modern history and self-reinforcing. Foreign interventions challenge and question the government's sovereignty and its ability to exercise control. What's more, by making Lebanon a surrogate for regional conflicts, the system becomes even more unstable and prone to periodical outbursts of violence, further eroding the state's ability to function.

Starting with this premise, this chapter looks at the role and influence of foreign intervention upon Lebanese domestic affairs, focusing in particular on understanding the shifts in the power dynamics following the Syrian withdrawal from Lebanon in 2005. More specifically, the research explores old trends and new dynamics behind the involvement of several major regional powers (Syria, Iran, and Saudi Arabia).

The Role of Syria in Lebanon since 2005: Old Interests, New Dynamics

The Roots of Syrian Involvement in Lebanon: Overview

Syrian interest in Lebanese affairs differs from that of any other foreign power active in Lebanon, because Syria alone de facto sees Lebanese politics as both a matter of foreign as well as domestic policy. This Syrian "exceptionalism," which leads the country to claim "distinctive relations" (*alaqat mumayyaza),* has both historical and ideological roots (Salloukh 2005: 14).

Ideologically, Syrian interest in Lebanon was backed by the notion of a "Greater Syria," an idea that was summarized by Hafez al-Assad who said, "Throughout history, Syria and Lebanon have been one country and one people" (Dawisha 1984: 229).

Historically, the relationship between the two countries has always been extremely strong, starting with the Lebanese-Syrian cooperation towards ending French occupation preceding the 1946 declaration of independence (Harris 1985).

In addition, geo-strategic considerations have also contributed to Damascus's stable interest in its neighbor's domestic politics. First, Lebanon is crucial for Syria's defense—with the country's view that "it is difficult to draw a line between Lebanon's security in its broadest sense and Syria's security" (Dawisha 1984: 229). This position partly accounts for Syrian interests in maintaining a strong foothold in Lebanon, especially given the Assad regime's fear that either Israeli or "Western" influence could become dominant in the absence of strong Syrian involvement—a development that is perceived as threatening to the internal stability of the regime.

In addition, it is difficult to disentangle Syria's involvement in Lebanon from its interests in the Arab–Israeli conflict. Over the past decades, Lebanon, as an intermediate arena between Syria and Israel, has been a critical area where political, and at times military, competition with the State of Israel has taken place. In turn, this has served a second very important interest of the Syrian government: to gain legitimacy, both internally and regionally, by strengthening its role as the main military and political foe of Israel. Finally, Syria has always had strong economic interests in Lebanon.

Therefore, due to historical, ideological, military, political, and economic reasons, Syria's interest in maintaining a strong role in Lebanon has remained stable in the past decades, although the means and strategies it has employed to attain this goal have shifted over time.

Syria's first direct intervention in Lebanon occurred during the bloody civil war that took place in Lebanon between 1975 and 1990. Following Damascus's military involvement in 1976, the Syrians remained highly engaged in the war. Through a combination of shifting alliances, political assassinations, reliance on proxies, diplomatic pressure, and direct military and political intervention, Damascus managed to gain a strong foothold on the war-torn country, while frustrating the ambitions of other foreign powers.

While the civil war years allowed Syria to impose its military presence on Lebanon, the termination of the conflict and the national reconciliation process that led to the Taif Agreement allowed Syria to truly consolidate its role in the Lebanese Republic. Taif recognized the "special relationship" between Lebanon and Syria, while authorizing Syrian troops to "thankfully assist" the Lebanese government to reassert its sovereignty" (Taif Agreement 1989). With these provisions, Syria de facto obtained a legal basis to maintain a military presence in Lebanon, together with the recognition of its special relationship with Lebanon and its role as "guarantor" of Taif.

In the 1990s, Syria worked to consolidate its military and political influence within Lebanon. This process of institutionalization of the Syrian role took place largely undisturbed, as foreign powers generally accepted Syria's limited hegemony on Lebanon as a *fait accompli*. What's more, in the early 1990s, the United States rewarded Syria for its cooperation during the Gulf War and for its willingness to enter negotiations with Israel by turning a blind eye on the country's strategy and tactics in Lebanon (Gambill 2010).

Taking advantage of this *laissez faire* attitude, Syria developed an intricate system to preserve its hegemony on Lebanon, a system grounded in military presence, intelligence infiltration of the Lebanese government, political control of key posts within the government, electoral manipulation, and silencing of political opposition.

This *Pax Syriana*, which held for over a decade, would, however, start to crumble in the new millennium, as new domestic, regional, and global dynamics gradually started shaking the foundations of Syrian power within Lebanon.

The year 2000 represented a watershed for the Syrians: Hafez al-Assad died and was succeeded by his son Bashar. In general, it is fair to say that Bashar showed far less "tact" in taking care of the "Lebanese file" and that he generally took Lebanon and its politicians for granted, an attitude that perhaps also contributed to the rise of the tensions between the two countries.

Within Lebanon, the year 2000 also saw the unilateral redeployment of the Israeli Defense Forces behind the Blue Line (Hajjar 2002). Following the withdrawal, voices from both the international community, as well as from within Lebanon, started to more openly question the purpose of Syria's presence.

Moreover, Syria's position within the international community deteriorated sharply in the aftermath of 9/11, as the country became more isolated internationally due to its ambiguous position with regards to financing and otherwise supporting terrorist organizations, as well as because of its de facto backing of insurgent activities in Iraq following the American invasion in 2003.[1]

Damascus's response to the mounting international isolation was to tighten its grip on Lebanon by cracking down on political dissent (International Crisis Group, Report 39, 2005), and by extending pro-Syrian President Emile Lahoud's term, following its official expiration in 2004 (Al-Manar Television, September 3, 2004). The latter was a decision made against Saudi and French advice to avoid meddling excessively in Lebanese internal affairs, and which led to the deterioration of Syria's relations with both countries.

In turn, this led Paris and Washington, supported by regional powers like Saudi Arabia, to press the UN Security Council to openly address the issue of the Syrian occupation of Lebanon, leading to the passing of resolution 1559 in September 2004, calling for an immediate redeployment of "foreign forces," urging the disarming of all existing militias, and asserting the importance of free elections.

Ultimately, Syria ignored the international pressure and pushed Lebanon's pro-Syrian Parliament to renew Lahoud's presidency. This caused a further deterioration in the relationship between Damascus and the Lebanese Sunni PM Rafic Hariri, who at the time was serving his second term as prime minister.

By late 2004, Syria was facing growing pressure from the international community, while in Lebanon it also faced the rise of a truly multi-confessional domestic alliance against Damascus. In this context, the assassination of PM Rafic Hariri on February 14, 2005 greatly accelerated this process by leading to mass protests organized by a new political coalition, originally including main parties like Hariri's Future Movement, the Christian Lebanese Forces, and the Free Patriotic Movement (FPM) as well as smaller groups and civil society organizations. The new "March 14 Coalition" (the broad anti-Syrian coalition,

---

1   See, for example, US Congress, Syria Accountability and Lebanese Sovereignty Restoration Act of 2003, 108th Congress, 2003, HR 1828.

named after the day of their largest anti-Syrian march) backed by the international community was primary responsible for pressuring the Syrian regime, leading to its withdrawal from Lebanon on April 26, 2005 (Salloukh 2005).

With the "Cedar Revolution" and the end of Syrian "tutelage," Lebanon concretely opened a new chapter of its history. But did the revolution really lead to a decline in Syrian influence in Lebanon?

New Lebanon, Old Syria: The Post-2005 Years

In the period preceding February 2005, Damascus was facing the toughest challenge to its power and influence within Lebanon: the rise of a solid, broad, and truly cross-sectarian anti-Syrian opposition movement. This possibility was seen as a serious strategic threat to Damascus, which had always centered its Lebanese strategy on a "divide and conquer" approach. In this sense, the assassination of Rafic Hariri could be seen as a last option to stop the rise of such political opposition by depriving the nascent movement of a strong leadership figure (Phares 2005), in the hope that without such leadership, preexisting rivalries and sectarian concerns would reemerge, leading to the demise of the opposition movement from within.

From this perspective, even thought it is fair to say that the perpetrators heavily miscalculated the backlash of the assassination, still the attack succeeded in deflating the anti-Syrian movement. Only a few months after the killing of Hariri, the former anti-Syrian coalition started to collapse under the pressure of a rift between a sector of the Christian community and the rest of the March 14 forces. The divorce between March 14 and Michel Aoun's FPM would deny the newly elected March 14 government the possibility of having an absolute majority within the Parliament and the Cabinet (Safa 2006), diminishing its capacity to truly revolutionize the Lebanese political system in a way that would be harmful to Syria (for example, by taking steps to disarm Hezbollah, or by deposing Lahoud as President).

Moreover, the parallel emergence of a solid pro-Syria opposition movement backed by Hezbollah (the "March 8" coalition) would also contribute to stall the "Cedar Revolution" and reinstate Syrian influence. After 2005, Syria began to rely even more on its local political allies. Hezbollah in particular stepped up its political activism after 2005 and, for the first time since its initial participation in electoral politics in 1992, decided to join the country's executive cabinet (Alagha 2005). An increasingly politically active Hezbollah was a favorable development for Syria, and the Assad regime made it even more a priority to strengthen its partnership with the Lebanese-Shiite group.

Therefore, only a few months following the military withdrawal of Syria, Lebanon was already starting to grasp that becoming independent of Damascus's political influence would prove a complex and daunting task.

In these months, despite facing a strong opposition, March 14 attempted to take concrete steps to put checks on Syrian control and inference in Lebanon. Practically this translated into renewed calls to discuss the disarmament of all existing militias in Lebanon (Hezbollah) and in a campaign to bring to justice those responsible for the Hariri assassination. With respect to the former, the March 14 forces lacked sufficient political backing to even begin to take steps to fully enforce UN Security Council resolution 1559; however, with respect to investigating the Hariri assassination, March 14 scored a political victory in December 2005 by passing a cabinet resolution that asked the UN to establish an ad hoc tribunal to look into the assassination of the prime minister (Harris 2011). On that occasion, the Shiite political parties, Hezbollah and Amal, organized a two-month boycott of the cabinet to protest the resolution. Regardless, the March 14 forces survived the political crisis, after providing Hezbollah with renewed assurance that the government would not attempt to disarm them (AFP, February 2, 2006).

However, the actual degree of authority and control of the elected government was again put to test in 2006: first with the July 2006 war between Hezbollah and Israel, and then with the beginning of the opposition's boycott of the Cabinet beginning in the fall of 2006.

With the "Second Lebanon War" in July 2006, the elected March 14 government was dragged into a conventional military confrontation with the most powerful army in the region, without having been in any way previously consulted or even informed. The confrontation constituted a powerful reminder of Hezbollah's military strength and of its consistent refusal to bring its "resistance" agenda under a national umbrella.

After the war, despite the official declarations praising Hezbollah's "steadfastness," there was widespread irritation among the March 14 forces regarding Hezbollah's defiance of the government. Taking advantage of the terms set forth in UNSC resolution 1701 which brought an end to the conflict and urged Lebanon to take full control of its territory while disarming its militias, numerous voices from the March 14 coalition started to ask for the group's disarmament with a renewed vigor and sense of urgency. For example, March 14 Industry Minister Pierre Amine Gemayel (assassinated a few months after giving this statement) said, "Hezbollah has to deliver its weapons to the Lebanese army, and its light weapons to the police" (AP, August 14, 2006).

However, strong from the popular support won by its "divine victory" against Israel and from a new political alliance with the FPM—which had by then fully shifted from the anti-Syrian to the pro-Syrian coalition—Hezbollah had no intention of complying with the government's requests. Instead, from the fall of 2006, the March 8 opposition forces attempted to reassert their political influence by demanding that PM Saniora create a new "national unity" cabinet with March 8 forces, and to be awarded at least one-third plus one of the cabinet seats.

In other words, starting in late 2006, the opposition began to demand veto power as a condition for participation in the Cabinet. These calls, rejected by the elected majority and by PM Saniora, would eventually lead the opposition ministers to resign from the cabinet in November 2006, dragging Lebanon into a *de facto* political paralysis that would last 18 months, until May 2008. Officially, the resignation from the cabinet and the boycott of the government originated not so much over the question of obtaining veto power in the cabinet, but rather as a measure to stop the government from approving a protocol for the UN Special Tribunal for Lebanon (STL) (Harris 2011).

From Damascus's perspective, the political crisis was useful in at least three important ways. First, it managed to stall and question the process of establishing the tribunal; second, it profoundly weakened the anti-Syrian government while *de facto* neutralizing its ability to act against Damascus; third, it showed the international community that Syria, through its strategic partnership with the opposition forces in Lebanon, was still very much calling the shots. Simply by stalling the political process and not openly intervening to mediate, Syria was making its power and influence clear by inaction. Not surprisingly, in the months following the crisis, the international community—only two years following Syrian withdrawal from Lebanon—started again to visit Damascus to discuss the Lebanese crisis (Gambill 2010).

In the meantime, as the pro-Syrian forces stalled the political process, an old tactic historically used by Syria to keep its political opponents in check resurfaced to increase the pressure on the March 14 forces: a renewed wave of political assassinations. Already in November 2006, Industry Minister Pierre Amine was shot dead in Beirut. In September 2007, only a week before the scheduled date for the first round of presidential elections, another March 14 MP, Antoine Ghanem, was killed in a truck bombing. Ghanem was the eighth anti-Syrian politician to be killed since 2004 and the sixth victim of political assassinations of March 14 members since February 2005 (Berti 2007). All in all, this meant that Damascus was feeling increasingly stronger, and thus it was also growing more defiant both within Lebanon as well as internationally.

Amid renewed assassinations and political paralysis, the situation in Lebanon in 2007 was in a downward spiral. Eventually, the escalating crisis reached its peak in May 2008, when Hezbollah reacted to the Saniora Cabinet's attempts to remove Hezbollah sympathizer Wafic Shkeir from his post of security chief at the Hariri International Airport, and to shut down the organization's communication network by turning its weapons against its Lebanese political foes (CNN, May 9, 2008).

Military power has historically been Lebanon's strongest political currency. In this case, taking the streets of west Beirut resulted in a political victory for Hezbollah. In fact, the May 2008 clashes led the parties to meet in Doha, where they signed a reconciliation agreement that *de facto* granted the March 8 forces its main demands: veto power in the cabinet, representation of Aoun's FMP, electoral reforms, and the election of a Michel Suleiman as Lebanon's next president (Doha Agreement 2008; CNN, July 11, 2008).

The Doha Agreement represented a double victory for Syria. Internationally, it helped boost the country's position and made clear to the world the power of its political alliance with the opposition forces. Within Lebanon, the situation was once again under strong Syrian influence and the tides of the Cedar Revolution had begun to turn, further eroding the strength of the March 14 coalition.

To recognize such a favorable situation and to indicate a rapprochement in Syrian-Lebanese relations, in August 2008, Damascus established full diplomatic relations with the Lebanese Republic (Aljazeera, August 13, 2008).

Indeed, it seemed that in the aftermath of the Doha Agreement, a new tendency from within the March 14 coalition started to emerge to somewhat mend relations with Damascus. Druze leader Walid Jumblatt was the first member of the coalition to indicate such an intention, eventually achieving a full "reconciliation" with Damascus and drifting away from the March 14 camp in the period following the June 2009 parliamentary elections (Sakr and Qawas 2010).

Jumblatt's exit would prove a hard blow to March 14, especially since the results of the elections had once again failed to provide the anti-Syrian forces with an absolute majority (Slackman 2010). In turn, this led the pro-Syrian bloc to once again achieve its demands, and obtain the creation of yet another "unity" Cabinet (AFP, November 11, 2009).

Just as the new Cabinet was representative of Lebanon's political reality and of the strong influence that Syria and its domestic political allies held, similarly the new government and its PM Saad Hariri recalibrated their attitude with respect to Syria to reflect the existing balance of power. Accordingly, Hariri went to Damascus in December 2009, pledging to create a "strategic partnership" with Syria in the interest of "Arabism" and "resistance against Israel" (BBC Monitoring Middle East, December 20, 2009) Similarly, the new government increased its diplomatic visits to Syria, while investing in renewed cooperation initiatives (*Daily Star*, June 25, 2010). The culmination of this trend would be PM Hariri's "apology" for having prematurely accused Damascus of having orchestrated the assassination of his father, Rafic (Aljazeera, September 6, 2010).

The statement came in the context of the ongoing mediation process between Saudi Arabia and Syria over Lebanon's response to the UN Special Tribunal (UN STL). In fact, since having been formally established in May 2007, following the Lebanese government's request for the UN Security Council unilateral endorsement of its constitutive protocol (Harris 2011), the UN Tribunal had been working on Hariri's assassination case and, as of the summer of 2010, rumors spread that the Tribunal was preparing to issue its first indictments. More specifically, reliable leaks asserted that the investigations had revealed the implication of Hezbollah, rather than Syria, in the murder, a rumor that only contributed to the rising tone of confrontation between March 14 and the opposition forces.

It is in this context of high political tension that Saudi Arabia and Syria decided to intervene in order to find a settlement between the parties and avoid the escalation of violence (Sakr 2010, Aziz 2010, al-Amin 2010). Syria's role as mediator with respect to the UN STL is especially interesting and sheds light on Syria's political victory with respect to its former "protectorate."

Syria had always been very critical of the idea of creating an ad hoc international tribunal to investigate the political assassination of PM Rafic Hariri. However, as the investigations started to point at Hezbollah as the main suspect in Hariri's murder, Damascus could start to breathe a sigh of relief and get involved as "mediator". To be sure, the indictments do not exculpate Syria. Quite the contrary: Hezbollah's involvement does by default implicate Syria, given both the strength of the relationship between the two parties and the extent to which Damascus controlled Lebanon during its "tutelage" period. However, for the time being, the regime effectively avoided international sanctions and condemnation.

In the end, probably because of the strong (and mutually exclusive) interests of the mediators, the mediation efforts did not succeed. As a consequence, Lebanon found itself again in the eye of the political storm in early 2011, when the prolonged disagreements over the UN tribunal eventually led to the official resignation from the executive cabinet of the ten ministers of the Hezbollah-led March 8 coalition and of an "independent" minister who had been appointed by President Suleiman.

In turn, this caused the collapse of the national unity government led by Saad Hariri (Daragahi and Richter 2011), and the rise of a new parliamentary majority dominated by the March 8 forces and the FPM, in alliance with Jumblatt's PSP and led by PM Najib Mikati—an independent candidate with strong and amicable ties with Damascus.

The new government—despite its official declarations pledging to stand by existing international commitments—served as a guarantee that Lebanon would not enthusiastically stand by the STL and its findings, definitely a positive development for Syria. More significantly, the fall of the March 14 government and the rise of a new pro-Syrian majority and PM brought the country back to the pre-Cedar Revolution era, strengthening the influence of Syria on Lebanese domestic politics.

In other words, less than a decade after its initial withdrawal in 2005, Damascus managed to reposition itself in Lebanon, obtaining a high degree of influence in the country's domestic politics, while de facto marginalizing its political opponents. What's more, it found a way to reach this level of "political tutelage" without having to redeploy a single tank back into Lebanon.

The return of Lebanon into Syria's political influence has been a particularly valuable asset for Damascus, especially given the ongoing internal turmoil and the mounting international pressure against the Assad regime. However, with Syria descending into a bloody civil war and with the Assad regime engaged in a survival struggle against the anti-regime opposition forces, it is probably just a question of time before the country's grip on Lebanon starts to finally fade.

The Role of the Islamic Republic of Iran in Lebanon Since 2005: Involvement Redefined

The Roots of Iranian Involvement in Lebanon: Overview

Iranian involvement in Lebanon differs from that of other foreign powers in at least one important way: no other state can claim an equally solid and long-standing—both ideologically and politically—alliance with a local political actor. The relationship between Iran and Hezbollah is in this sense a defining characteristic of Iranian policies with respect to Lebanon. While all major political parties in Lebanon depend to a certain degree on other regional and global actors for sponsorship and funding, none has an external relationship as pervasive or crucial as Hezbollah's with Iran. Similarly, no state has invested as much as Iran has invested on the Lebanese Shiite militia.

The solid and unique partnership between Hezbollah and Iran builds upon the preexisting ties between the Shiite community of Lebanon and its Iranian counterpart, a relationship that goes as far back as the sixteenth century.

In addition, the connection between the Lebanese Hezbollah and Iran is ideological, with the Lebanese Shiite organization's belief system strongly grounded in the teachings of the Iranian Revolution. What's more, Iranian interest in supporting the creation of Hezbollah in the early 1980s responded to the Islamic Republic's early drive to export Khomeini's revolution outside its own borders. To achieve this political and ideological objective, Iran looked very closely at Lebanon, where the fact that the Shiite community was the largest religious minority within the country (Armanios 2004), combined with the vacuum of power created by the civil war, offered a particularly favorable environment to attempt exporting the revolution.

Since its initial establishment, Hezbollah has become strategically important for Iran, and Iranian involvement in Lebanon has focused on protecting and promoting the Lebanese Shiite organization. Hezbollah has served as a poster child for the Iranian Revolution, while Tehran used the group's resistance against the State of Israel as a means to gain political leverage within the region, as well as to foster concepts like "Pan-Islamic" unity to gain popularity in the largely Arab and Sunni region.

In addition, Tehran's assessment of Lebanon as a proxy theatre of confrontation with Israelalso reflects another important reason behind the Islamic Republic's involvement in Lebanon. In addition to ideological and political considerations, Iran—through Hezbollah—also regards Lebanon from a security perspective. Accordingly, Hezbollah can act not only to improve the leverage of Iran with respect to the Arab–Israeli conflict, but it can also play a role in power projection and deterrence against the country's enemies.

For all these reasons, Iranian involvement in Lebanon has always centered on its partnership with Hezbollah. The Iranians were actively involved in the process of creation of the Lebanese Shiite organization. In the early 1980s, Iran had sent between 1,000 and 2,000 Revolutionary Guards to Lebanon's eastern Bekaa Valley to provide the nascent militia with logistical support and training (Hokayem 2010). This presence was maintained for several years, creating what still today is a strong bond between the Lebanese militia and Iran's revolutionary elites (Zisser 2011). Short of this logistical support and generous funding—which occurred under Syria's watch and with Damascus's explicit approval (Deeb 1988)— it is doubtful that Hezbollah would have risen so quickly to become Lebanon's most powerful militia.

Following Hezbollah's creation in 1982, the partnership between Tehran and Hezbollah continued well past the end of the civil war, due to a unique mix of personal ties, ideological proximity, and financial dependence.

Following the Taif Agreement and the beginning of the Syrian "tutelage," Iranian involvement in Lebanon was primarily channeled through its support for Hezbollah. This assistance was monitored and approved of by Damascus, which shared with Iran a common interest in promoting Hezbollah's war against Israel. At the same time, throughout the years of Syrian occupation of Lebanon, it was Damascus, not Tehran, who called the final shots as to how much leverage Hezbollah would have in its day-to-day activities. In fact, although Syria supported and defended Hezbollah's armed campaigns against Israel, it also sought to curtail all other military operations, seeking to preserve its limited hegemony of Lebanon (Jaber 1997).

In other words, the pre-2005 patterns of Iranian involvement in Lebanon can be easily analyzed through Tehran's support for Hezbollah, which acted within Lebanon in a way consistent with both Syrian and Iranian foreign policy interests. In this context, the Syrian withdrawal constituted a true watershed for the Islamic Republic's strategy with respect to Lebanon.

The Cedar Revolution and Tehran: The Post-2005 Years

The Iranians were not at all excited by the prospects of a Syrian withdrawal from Lebanon. The pullout was seen as a potential threat to Hezbollah and its weapons, as well as a way to strengthen the anti-Syrian and pro-Western domestic political forces, thus distancing Lebanon from Iran and its "Axis of Resistance."

However, at the same time, this potential danger presented the Iranians with the opportunity to take advantage of the temporary vacuum of power left by the Syrians and to exploit it to increase Tehran's influence within Lebanon. The withdrawal represented a paradigm change: until 2005, Syrian direct occupation of the country made clear who really called the shots in Lebanon, relegating Tehran to a supporting role. However, following the 2005 pullout, it became in Iran's interest to increase its involvement in Lebanon.

Indeed, Iran has been making that push, thus competing with Syria over Lebanon. This is the case even though the competition is far from confrontational, and Iran still generally coordinates and consults with Syria on Lebanese affairs, partly recognizing the "Syrian prerogative" over Lebanon..

Since 2005, Tehran's strategy in Lebanon has been simple: to support the growth of Hezbollah and its political allies, to seek to further institutionalize both Hezbollah's "resistance" within Lebanon, and to boost Iranian-Lebanese official government relations.

First, while maintaining its direct support of Hezbollah, Iran also gradually strengthened its relationship with Hezbollah's political allies within the March 8 coalition. One example was the gradual rapprochement of former anti-Syrian, anti-Iranian-turned-pro-Hezbollah FPM leader, General Michel Aoun. After solidifying his political alliance with Hezbollah and obtaining the creation of a unity government in May 2008, Aoun traveled to Tehran in October 2008. He declared that Iran was "especially helping Lebanon" (*Daily Star*, October 14, 2008), also asserting that "Iran never helped one Lebanese party against the others," not resisting the temptation to praise his new patron while taking a stab at Hariri's Future Movement's relation with Saudi Arabia.

Second, the Islamic Republic has been upgrading its role within Lebanon by investing in government-to-government official relations. Iran focused on both its diplomatic relations with Lebanon and on improving their existing economic partnership. Since 2006, bilateral trade between Iran and Lebanon has been increasing, going from $78.4 million in 2006 to roughly $180 million in 2009 (Xinhua, 2011). Although the number is not particularly high, there has been a steady growth in bilateral trade. Similarly, the governments of Lebanon and Iran have been pushing to upgrade economic ties. Recently they adopted an economic memorandum of understanding in June 2010, which paved the way for future cooperation, and decided to set joint commercial councils and a permanent government committee to monitor the growth of the economic partnership (*Tehran Times*, 2010). While upgrading economic ties, Iran and its Lebanese political allies have also been promoting the idea of increasing the level of military cooperation and assistance between the Islamic Republic and Lebanon.

The culmination of this trend of increased Iranian activism was Iranian President Mahmoud Ahmadinejad's two-day trip to Lebanon in October 2010. In this sense, the visit served to emphasize Tehran's continued interest in playing a leading role in domestic Lebanese politics, as well as to highlight its support for Hezbollah. During his visit, Ahmadinejad was indeed adamant in declaring his support for Hezbollah and in praising the group's "resistance" against Israel and the other "bullying countries" attempting to dominate the region (Berti 2010).

In turn, the message strengthened the idea that Iran aimed to portray Lebanon as part of the "Resistance Axis." In addition, Ahmadinejad's declarations in support of Hezbollah were also particularly significant, as they came only weeks before the expected release of the findings of the STL (Worth 2010). In this context, Ahmadinejad's presence in Lebanon and his declared support for Hezbollah, along with his open questioning of the international tribunal, also constituted a warning to the March 14 government to refrain from continuing their support of the STL.

Moreover, the visit came in a period when Saudi Arabia and Syria were the two most involved regional actors in the STL–Lebanese crisis, attempting to find a compromise between the parties on the issue of the UN Special Tribunal. The Iranian visit then served to make Tehran and its stance on this issue more prominent. It is therefore not surprising that, in the weeks following the president's visit, the Iranian ambassador to Lebanon met with Syrian and Saudi envoys in Lebanon to involve Iran more prominently in the Syrian-Saudi mediation efforts (*Tehran Times*, November 2, 2010). In sum, Ahmadinejad's visit represented the culmination of Iran's trend of increasing direct involvement in Lebanese political affairs.

Currently, Iranian influence in Lebanon is still going strong, especially after the rise of the Mikati government and the new Hezbollah-backed parliamentary majority. The new government has adopted a particularly friendly attitude with regards to Iran, with PM Mikati rushing to ensure Tehran that all existing bilateral agreements would be implemented urgently (Fars News Agency, June 21, 2011), and with the newly appointed foreign minister declaring that Iran holds an essential role in ensuring peace and security in the region (ibid., June 23, 2011). Even more recently, in the summer of 2011, Lebanon reached out to Iran to help the country develop its oil and gas fields (*Daily Star*, July 21, 2011).

Within Lebanon, the rise in Iranian influence has been harshly criticized from within the ranks of the March 14 forces, with former PM Saad Hariri voicing his fears about Hezbollah's role and its reliance on Lebanon "as a base to fuel internal conflicts in the Arab countries" (14March.org, March 22, 2011).

Are Hariri's fears justified? Partly. It is indeed clear that, with the present government, Hezbollah's role has been strengthened and, therefore, also Iranian influence on Lebanon is more consolidated. However, this consolidation of influence is not enough to achieve a strategic realignment of Lebanon into Iran's direct sphere of influence. Partly this depends on the pluralistic nature of Lebanese politics and on the number of other foreign actors that, together with Iran, are competing for power and influence in the tiny Mediterranean country.

In addition, although it is true that Hezbollah's rise reflects positively on the role and influence of the Islamic Republic in Lebanon, it must not be forgotten that the process that led to such a rise has been largely directed and monitored by Damascus. In the past years, Syria has reasserted its strong power in Lebanon and it has no intention to relinquish its grip on Lebanon.

This concept was clearly explained by Bashar al-Assad himself in October 2010, in an interview tellingly released only a couple of weeks after Ahmadinejad's "triumphant" visit to Lebanon. In the interview, Assad insisted on the importance of Lebanese-Syrian ties and asserted that Iranian involvement in Lebanon was centered on macro issues such as the resistance, but that the country was not concerned with the finer points of Lebanese reality. In contrast, Syria, thanks to its deep knowledge of the Lebanese context and to its decades spent in Lebanon, was better equipped than Iran to deal with the "micro level" *(Dar al-Hayat,* October 26 and 27, 2010). In other words, Assad was telling Tehran that it is all nice and well to continue supporting Hezbollah, but, when it comes to running the show in Lebanon and on working on the day-to-day functioning of the country, not a single leaf should move without Syria's approval. So far, Syria has acted act as a constraining force to the rise of Iran, although the competition between the two actors should not be overestimated, as both Tehran and Damascus share a similar outlook on most foreign policy matters, including Lebanon.

The Role of Saudi Arabia in Lebanon Since 2005: Behind the (Syrian-Iranian) Curve

The Roots of Saudi Involvement in Lebanon: Overview

Saudi Arabia's interest and involvement in Lebanon—much like in the cases of Syria and Iran—is grounded in a number of ideological, political, and geo-strategic factors. First, the regime feels a sense of kinship with the Lebanese Sunni community, a link that has been strengthened by the ongoing ties between the local Sunni community and the Kingdom—where Lebanese Sunni elites and middle-class alike have studied, worked, and developed personal and professional relations. A particularly significant example of how a shared religious identity, combined with businesses relationships and personal ties, have contributed to solidifying the bond between the Saudis and the Lebanese Sunnis is, of course, the case of the Hariri family. The ties between the Hariris and the Saudis have developed since the early 1990s and have become an important factor in explaining the dynamics of Saudi involvement in Lebanon.

Secondl, Lebanon has represented a proxy for the Saudis to deal with their biggest regional competitors, both Iran and Syria. Accordingly, the Kingdom's strategy in Lebanon has been shaped by its political and security perception of the region's challenges, and by the policies devised to tackle them. In addition—in understanding Saudi's involvement in Lebanon—it is crucial to keep in mind the Kingdom's persistent sense of its own vulnerability and its related strategic concern to preserve a favorable regional balance of power, while preventing both regional instability and the spread of revolutionary movements.

Saudi Arabia's role as an essentially reactionary regional power impacted the country's role in the Lebanese civil war, where Riyadh disregarded its natural allies—the Palestinians and the Lebanese Muslims—to offer behind-the-scenes support to the "forces of restoration" led by the Christian militias (Ajami 1977–78). Following this initial posture, the country was mostly involved in the Lebanese civil war through the Arab League, serving in the role of mediator, while letting the Syrians take the lead within Lebanon (Khalidi 1985).

In fact, during the years of the civil war and after, the Saudis did not ostracize the rise of Damascus's hegemony on Lebanon; on the contrary, they were careful not to speak against the Syrians, and even to endorse their role and presence in publicly (Thompson 2001). This reaction was in line with Riyadh's strategy with respect to Damascus, which focused on creating a working relationship with the Syrians, an objective that it sought to achieve by providing substantial financial assistance to the Assad regime ($1.6 billion annually by the end of the 1970s) (Badran 2006). In turn, this relationship—which was not based on any shared political ideology or mutual respect, but rather on Riyadh's desire to appease a potential enemy—had a direct impact on Lebanon, as the Saudi's endorsement of the Syrians becamean important source of Pan-Arab legitimacy for the Assad regime.

This Saudi-Syrian entente over Lebanon bore fruit in Taif, where the Arab League and the Saudis' mediation efforts to end the civil war led to the signing of the homonymous agreement, de facto institutionalizing Syrian presence in Lebanon (Khalot 2002).

The years of Syrian "tutelage" between 1990 and 2005 continued to show the same pattern of Saudi's tacit (and, at times, public) endorsement of Damascus's role in Syria. In addition, the Saudis assisted the post-civil war reconstruction of Lebanon, investing more money in Lebanon than any other Arab state. The Syrian economy also benefited from Saudi assistance, both by directly receiving money, as well as by taking advantage of Lebanon's development (for instance, through remittances) (Badran 2006).

This massive amount of economic assistance and public endorsement was no free lunch for the Syrians: in return, the Kingdom expected Damascus to guarantee basic Saudi interests within Lebanon and to allow for the rise of the Sunni PM Rafic Hariri. Hariri, a self-made billionaire, had found his fortune in Saudi Arabia and had developed strong personal connections to the Saudi elites (Safa 2006). The political ascent of Hariri during the 1990s was strongly backed by the Saudis who saw him as a crucial ally in Lebanon.

However, this Saudi-Syrian relationship slowly began to crumble by the end of the 1990s, in parallel with the progressive deterioration of the relationship between Damascus and Hariri during the politician's second term as PM (2000–04). By the early 2000s, Saudi Arabia slowly abandoned its traditional policy of endorsement of Syrian tutelage, and gradually began to pressure Damascus to allow for greater freedom within Lebanon. What's more, when Syria continued to ignore Saudi's calls to allow for internal reforms and to refrain from extending the presidential term of General Émile Lahoud, the Saudis decided to back the United States and France in pushing the UN Security Council to pass resolution 1559 (International Crisis Group, Report 39, 2005).

This shift in Saudi Arabia's strategy with respect to Lebanon would become even more obvious following the assassination of Saudi's traditional protégé Rafic Hariri.

Riyadh Bets on the Revolution: The Post-2005 Years

The Saudis were both infuriated and shocked by the killing of their closest Lebanese ally and they were determined to find a way to go after the perpetrators. In the short term, this meant urging the Lebanese authorities to find those behind the murder, while strongly pushing for a Syrian withdrawal from Lebanon. Clearly, these two objectives were perceived as interrelated since, despite the lack of formal accusations (Badran 2006), there was little doubt in the Saudi rulers' minds that Syria had been behind, or at least involved with, eliminating Hariri. Therefore, in the months between the Hariri assassination and the Syrian withdrawal in April 2005, Riyadh assumed a resolute stance in demanding Syrian complete withdrawal from Lebanon (Sands 2005).

Even following the withdrawal, however, the Saudis were not ready to resume their cordial relationship with Damascus: in fact, the Saudis continued to endorse the idea of political change within Lebanon, both by refusing to take steps against the establishment of the UN Independent Investigation Commission tasked to look into the Hariri murder (Badran 2006), and by strongly supporting the March 14 coalition—from the beginning very close to the Saudis.

Keeping these close ties in mind, it is possible to see how, in the period following Hariri's assassination, the Saudis continued to put pressure on Damascus to both change their ways with respect to Lebanon (that is, end their campaigns of political assassinations), and to cooperate with the ongoing UN investigations on the Hariri murder. The latter would involve, in part, not checking the March 14's hostile feelings with respect to the Assad regime. An example of this strategy was in Saad Hariri's declarations praising the preliminary results of the UN investigation, which were released in October 2005 and which implicated several high-ranking Syrian officials in the murder (ibid.). Although the Saudis did not publicly endorse the report, Saad Hariri, while on a diplomatic trip to Saudi Arabia, openly praised it and reiterated his commitment to finding all the perpetrators, suggesting that he had the Saudis' blessing (if not encouragement) to take such a stand.

At the same time, while standing behind the March 14 forces and their anti-Syrian declarations, the Saudis also remained directly engaged with Damascus: for example, they attempted to increase Damascus's cooperation with the UN (Rouman, 2005; SPA News Agency, 2005), and they sought to broker a "normalization" of relationships between Beirut and Damascus (Young 2006). The reason behind this "moderate" approach with respect to Syria was twofold:first, Riyadh has a strong distaste for revolutions and instability, and, as such, they did not want to obtain a regime change within Syria, but rather to "reform" Assad. In addition Syria's increasing international and regional isolation in the aftermath of the Hariri assassination had pushed Damascus directly into the arms of the Iranians, a development that the Saudis did not particularly welcome.

In the end, however, the Saudis' efforts and their "middle-of-the-road" approach did not succeed. The Syrians were not cornered into pledging to collaborate with the UN investigations, nor did they feel the need to give up on their growing ties with Iran while continuing to engage with Saudi Arabia; simultaneously, they maintained their aggressive strategy with respect to Lebanon. What's more, by the spring of 2006, the regional momentum to pressure Assad was beginning to fade, with both Egypt and Saudi Arabia holding "conciliatory" meetings with Damascus and with the Arab League pledging "solidarity with Syria" (Gambill 2010).

In this context, the beginning of a new round of hostilities between Hezbollah and the State of Israel in the summer of 2006 served to rekindle the Saudis' efforts, both, to support the Lebanese government and the March 14 forces, and, to contain the role and impact of Iran and Syria in Lebanon.. Therefore, the Kingdom was quite firm in its condemnation of Hezbollah, declaring that "It is necessary to make a distinction between legitimate resistance [to occupation] and irresponsible adventurism adopted by certain elements within the state" (*Daily Star*, July 15, 2006).

The March 14 government was extremely appreciative of the Saudis' position (Diyab 2006), especially in the aftermath of the passing of UNSC resolution 1701, which promised to facilitate the government's attempts to rein in Hezbollah and reestablish control of southern Lebanon. However, the momentum for eroding the legitimacy of Hezbollah, along with its Syrian and Iranian patrons, never materialized in Lebanon, as by the fall of 2006, the pro-Syria opposition began the political boycott of the Saniora government, precipitating Lebanon into 18 months of political paralysis.

The attitude of Saudi Arabia in this period was one of renewed activism: the Saudis had in fact been stepping up their role in Lebanon since August 2006, following the Syrian president's speech, which characterized those rulers who has criticized the "resistance" in Lebanon as "half men" (Blanford 2007). On the one hand, this activism translated into renewed support for the government and into renewed economic assistance to the country (Khuri 2007). On the other hand, the Saudis attempted to increase their direct dealings with both the Iranians and the Syrians, with the objective of breaking the political impasse caused by the political boycott orchestrated by the Hezbollah-led March 8 coalition.

Ultimately, the negotiations went nowhere, leading to a deterioration of the relations between Syria and Saudi Arabia, and prompting the Saudis to pledge to organize a boycott of the Arab League's meeting scheduled to be held in Damascus in March 2008, short of Syrian collaboration on ending the Lebanese crisis (Gambill 2010). This move was also the result of a joint US-Saudi push to end the Lebanese crisis in March 2008, by attempting to get the Syrians to agree elect a new president for Lebanon (Wright 2008).

However, once again, the failure to obtain a true mobilization against the Syrian strategy in Lebanon at the regional level, combined with the solid grip Damascus (and Tehran, through its local ally, Hezbollah) had on Lebanon's political destiny, ensured that the Saudis returned to Riyadh empty-handed.

In this context, Hezbollah's temporary takeover of West Beirut in May 2008 and the subsequent ratification of the Doha Agreement served as powerful reminders of where the power really rested.Following the Doha Agreement, the Saudis decided it was time to redefine their strategy with respect to Lebanon and to abandon their previous strategy aimed at isolating and pressuring the Syrians. Implemented since 2005, it seemed that the efforts to curtail Damascus's influence in Lebanon had not been successful. They had failed to lead to a regional mobilization against Assad, they had only resulted in strengthening the Syrian-Iranian axis and the role of Tehran in Lebanon.

To reverse this trend, the post-Doha Saudi strategy was to engage the Syrians, trying to bring them closer to Riyadh and, in doing so, taking a stab at their main regional enemy, Iran. In this context, the Saudis gradually started to invest in their relationship with the Assad regime—a move that would also lead to the gradual rapprochement between the Syrians and prominent members of the March 14 coalition.

These reconciliation efforts started to become especially prominent in the months following Israel's war in Gaza (January 2009) (Young 2010), and led to increased contact with the Syrians, the Lebanese opposition forces, and Hezbollah (SPA News Agency, May 20, 2009). The peak of this reconciliation process occured in October 2009, with King Abdullah's trip to Damascus (Barnes-Dacey 2009), a visit that also led to the issuing of a joint Saudi-Syrian statement calling on Lebanon to break its domestic political impasse over the creation of an executive cabinet (*Arab News*, October 9, 2009). Not surprisingly, only a few weeks after this declaration—which revealed that Damascus and Riyadh had managed to find an agreement over the future composition of the Lebanese executive cabinet— new PM Saad Hariri announced the formation of the cabinet, five months after the June 2009 parliamentary elections.

The Syrian-Saudi cooperation seemed mutually convenient: on the one hand, the Saudis obtained the resumption of normal political life within Lebanon, boosting both internal stability as well as the role of the March 14 forces, the country's closet local political allies. On the other hand, the deal was even more advantageous for the Syrians, as it allowed them to remain at the center of the Lebanese political stage, while de facto obtaining Saudi recognition of their "Lebanese prerogative." What's more, Syria never had to disengage with Iran or Hezbollah in order to enjoy the Saudi rapprochement, enjoying the best of both worlds.

In this context, Syrian-Saudi relations continued on this same track in 2010, first with the two countries' cooperation during the March 2010 elections in Iraq (Salem 2010), and then through the Syrian-Saudi mediation efforts over the STL indictments (Blanford 2010).

Reportedly, the Saudis were trying to broker a behind-the-scene deal that would have allowed the tribunal to continue to function, in exchange for the PM's assistance in exonerating Hezbollah as an organization (Gambill 2010). It is in this context that PM Hariri allegedly agreed to issue the infamous "Syrian apology." By the end of 2010, rumors emerged regarding a Saudi-Syrian "paper" that would have guaranteed the continuation of the Hariri government, in exchange for the formal cessation of any cooperation between Lebanon and the STL, along with a formal request to halt the judiciary process and with an insurance of the PM's public backing of Hezbollah (*Al-Diyar*, December 22, 2010). If reached, this deal would have been a decisive victory for the Syrian-Iranian axis and a very modest accomplishment for the Saudis.

However, in the end, the Syrian-Saudi deal never saw the light of day, in part because of direct US pressure on both the Saudis and the March 14 forces to continue in their complete commitment to the STL (*Jaam-e Jam*, January 26, 2011). With the fall of Saad Hariri as PM and the rise of the Mikati-Hezbollah, the Saudis would see Damascus's and Tehran's influence on Lebanon soar—a worrisome development for Riyadh. This is true despite the preexisting ties between Mikati and Riyadh, and even if it is unlikely that the new government could have been approved short of minimal guarantees to the Saudis.

In sum, when looking at the patterns of Saudi involvement in the post-Rafic Hariri Lebanon, it appears that with the progressive demise of the political power and momentum created by the Cedar Revolution, the prospects for establishing stronger Saudi influence—at the expenses of Syria and Iran—grow thinner.

In the future, however, the role and impact of both Saudi Arabia and its regional adversaries in Lebanon are very much undecided: both the ongoing civil war in Syria and the potential implications of the STL indictments on Hezbollah leave the Saudis and its domestic allies with the hope that the tide will once again turn in Lebanese domestic politics.

Conclusion: Lebanon's Murky Political Future, a Reflection of its Murky Past

Internally divided along sectarian lines and with an inherently weak government, Lebanon has over the past decades been a surrogate for regional and international confrontation. As such, virtually every regional (and, to a lesser degree, international) power has developed some stakes in Lebanon.

First and foremost, this list is headed by Syria. Looking at Lebanon through the lens of the concept of "Greater Syria," and treating Lebanese domestic and foreign policy as a matter of national concern, the Assad regime has always asserted a special prerogative over Lebanon. Although many analysts had interpreted the end of the Syrian "tutelage" in 2005 as a sign of the imminent end of Syrian control over Lebanon, the account of the role and influence exercised by Damascus in the post-Rafic Hariri Lebanon tells a radically different story. Since 2005, Damascus was able to thrive and to reposition itself at the center of the Lebanese political arena by playing on the internal divisions among the anti-Syrian movement, and by capitalizing on their political alliance with the Hezbollah-led March 8 forces. Before the beginning of the "Syrian Spring" in 2011, Damascus's influence on Lebanon was stronger than ever, thanks to the rise to power of the Hezbollah-backed Mikati government and to the political marginalization of the political forces that had orchestrated the anti-Syrian revolution. Following the beginning of the Syrian crisis and the gradual descending of the country into a civil war, the Syrian grip on Lebanon is now somewhat shaken.

However, even though Syrian power within Lebanon remained strong after 2005, it is still true that the end of Syrian limited hegemony and "tutelage" did somewhat reshuffle the cards in Lebanese politics, paving the way for the rise of new foreign powers. This is certainly the case of the Islamic Republic of Iran. Tehran had always been invested in Lebanon through its strategic partnership with Hezbollah. However, when the Syrian tanks withdrew in 2005, the Iranians perceived a possible challenge to the role and power of their local protégé, Hezbollah, and reacted by stepping up their direct involvement in Lebanese affairs.

Ideally, the Islamic Republic would like to swing Lebanon away from its western alliances, and to bring it closer to the so-called "Axis of Resistance" formed with neighboring Syria. However, this battle is far from over, as other powers have been also at work within Lebanon since 2005 in an attempt to counter the rise of the Iranian-Syrian alliance.

In this context, Saudi Arabia has been investing heavily in Lebanese domestic politics, partly because of the connections between the Kingdom and both the Lebanese Sunni community and the Hariri family, and partly in an effort to oppose the rise of the "Shiite crescent." In this context, Saudi Arabia shifted from a traditionally friendly policy with respect to the Assad regime and its "tutelage" of Lebanon to one of progressive confrontation between 2003 and 2005, leading the country to assume an important role in pushing the Syrians out of Lebanon following the assassination of Rafic Hariri. Following the withdrawal, however, Saudi involvement in Lebanon has failed to prevent the domestic rise of Syria and Iran. Between 2005 and 2008, the Saudis sought to isolate Damascus and limit its influence, while refraining from aggressively pursuing these objectives, fearing to push the Syrians further into the hands of the Iranians. In the end, this middle-of-the-road approach did not succeed, as it failed to compel Damascus to mend its ways with respect to Lebanon, while allowing the Iranian-Syrian alliance to grow. In the months following the 2008 Doha Agreement, Saudi Arabia shifted its overall strategy and began a rapprochement with the Assad regime, again hoping to establish its influence on Lebanon by working a deal with the Syrians, also with the aim of excluding Tehran.

Currently, following the collapse of the Saudi-Syrian negotiations over the STL in late 2010 and the rise of the Mikati government, it appears clear that even if the Saudis are still a key power-broker in the Lebanese political arena, they have still not managed to curtail Iranian influence within Lebanon.

This does not, however, mean that Lebanon has officially transitioned towards the "Resistance Axis" and that it has completely turned its back on its other allies. To this day, the country continues to have tight economic and political relations with Saudi Arabia, and it appears keen to continue its relation with the US.

In turn, this means that Lebanon is being pushed simultaneously in two opposite directions by two powerful and antagonistic political blocs. Although the Syrian-Iranian bloc has the upper hand at the moment, it lacks the capacity to implement such a dramatic political change, short of the risk of igniting a renewed internal conflict.

At the moment, the future of Lebanon looks rather precarious, especially as the political fate of the country is linked, once again, to dynamics that reside entirely beyond its realm of control: respectively, the developments of the STL trial and the ongoing unrest within Syria.

Following the first release of indictments against the suspected perpetrators and organizers of the Hariri assassination on June 30, 2011, Lebanon and its government have been walking on eggshells. Although the issuance of the indictments against Hezbollah members has, for the time being, failed to ignite internal strife, still the level of tensions, especially between the Sunni and Shiite communities, is extremely high. In addition to carrying a potential for renewed internal strife, the STL also risks further eroding the relationship between Lebanon and its western allies, threatening to bring the country even closer to the "Resistance Axis."

What's more, the civil war raging in Syria has further exacerbated the pre-existing political and sectarian Sunni-Shiite cleavage within Lebanon, with the Sunni community largely backing the opposition forces in Syria and the Shiite community by and large supporting Assad.

In the future, a possible collapse of the Assad regime would probably be an important blow against Hezbollah and its political allies. Within Lebanon, this could also lead to an internal reshuffle of power and to a renewed moment of strength of the March 14 coalition.

References

2004. "Lebanese Parliament Votes To Extend President's Term." Al-Manar Television, September 3. Available from LexisNexis. [accessed: September 19, 2011].

2005. "King says Saudi mediation led to UN-Syria deal." SPA News Agency, November 28. Available from LexisNexis [accessed: September 19, 2011].

2006. "Shiite Parties Call Off Lebanon Cabinet Boycott." Agence France Press, February 2. Available at <http://www.lebanonwire.com/0602LN/06020205LWAF.asp> [accessed: September 19, 2011].

2006."Arab states take dim view of 'adventurism' by Hizbullah." Daily Star, July 15. Available at <http://www.dailystar.com.lb/News/Politics/Jul/15/Arab-states-take-dim-view-of-adventurism-by-Hizbullah.ashx#ixzz1TCP75OBb> [accessed: September 19, 2011].

2006. "Lebanese Official: Hezbollah Must Surrender Weapons." Associated Press Worldstream, August 14. Available from LexisNexis [accessed: September 19, 2011].

2008. "Hezbollah militants take over West Beirut." CNN, May 9. Available at <http://edition.cnn.com/2008/WORLD/meast/05/09/beirut.violence/index.html≥ [accessed: September 19, 2011].

2008. *Doha Agreement*. Available at <http://www.nowlebanon.com/NewsArchiveDetails.aspx?ID=44023> [accessed: September 19, 2011].

2008. "Lebanon announces unity government." CNN World, July 1. Available from LexisNexis. [accessed: September 19, 2011].

2008. "Lebanon, Syria agree to full ties." Aljazeera English, August 13. Available at: <http://english.aljazeera.net/news/middleeast/2008/08/2008813338596455.html> [accessed: September 19, 2011].

2008. "Aoun Credits Iran With 'Helping Lebanon Achieve National Unity.'" *Daily Star,* October 14, 2008. Available from LexisNexis [accessed: September 19, 2011].

2009. "Saudi Ambassador to Lebanon meets with deputy chairman of Hezbollah." SPA News Agency, May 30. Available from LexisNexis [accessed: September 19, 2011].

2009."Without National Consensus New Cabinet Will Achieve Nothing." Agence France Presse, November 11. Available from LexisNexis [accessed: September 19, 2011].

2009. "Saudi Arabia, Syria call for unity government in Lebanon." Arab News website, October 9. Available from LexisNexis [accessed: September 19, 2011].

2009."Without National Consensus New Cabinet Will Achieve Nothing." Agence France Presse, November 11. Available from LexisNexis. [accessed: September 19, 2011].

2009. "MP Jumblatt Says Lebanon's Destiny 'To Be On Syria's Side'." Al-Manar TV, November 14. Available from LexisNexis [accessed: September 19, 2011].

2009."Syrian leader, Lebanese premier discuss ways to strengthen two countries' ties." BBC Monitoring Middle East, December 20. Available from LexisNexis [accessed: September 19, 2011].

2010. "Iran, Lebanon Sign economic MOU." *Tehran Times*, June 3. Available at <http://www.tehrantimes.com/index_View.asp?code=220676> [accessed: September 19, 2011].

2010. "Lebanon, Syria Ink Strategy For Monitoring Border." *Daily Star*, June 25, Available at <http://www.dailystar.com.lb/News/Politics/Jun/25/Lebanon-Syria-ink-strategy-for-monitoring-border.ashx> [accessed: September 19, 2011].

2010. "Syria, Lebanon Joint Statement Stresses Importance Of Realizing Arab Solidarity." Syrian News Agency SANA, July 19, 2010. Available from LexisNexis [accessed: September 19, 2011].

2010. "Lebanon PM Retracts Syria Charge." Aljazeera English, September 6, 2010. Available at <http://english.aljazeera.net/news/middleeast/2010/09/201096122131619695.html> [accessed: September 19, 2011].

2010. "Interview (Part I and II)." *Dar al-Hayat*, October 26 and 27. Available at____<http://www.daralhayat.com/internationalarticle/195882>; <http://international.daralhayat.com/internationalarticle/196213> [accessed: September 19, 2011].

2010. "Syria, Saudi, Iran Envoys bid to ease Lebanon Tension." *Tehran Times*, November 2. Available at <http://www.tehrantimes.com/index_View.asp?code=229792> [accessed: September 19, 2011].

2010. "Al-Hariri says he agreed to abolish the STL for the sake of the country." *Al-Diyar*, December 22. Available from LexisNexis [accessed: September 19, 2011].

2011. "Iran paper discusses Syrian, Saudi, Turkish efforts to solve Lebanese crisis." *Jaam-e Jam*, January 26, 2011. Available from LexisNexis [accessed: September 19, 2011].

2011. "Lebanese caretaker PM slams Hezbollah's arsenal." Xinhua, March 12. Available at <http://news.xinhuanet.com/english2010/world/2011-03/12/c_13773936.htm> [accessed: September 19, 2011].

2011. *March 14 Statement,* March 22, 2011. Available at <www.14march.org> [accessed: September 19, 2011].

2011. "Lebanese PM Underscores Implementation of Tehran-Beirut Agreements." Fars News Agency, June 21. Available at <http://english.farsnews.net/newstext. php?nn=9003310708> [accessed: September 19, 2011].

2011."Lebanese FM Underlines Expansion of All-Out Ties with Iran." Fars News Agency, June 23. Available at <http://english.farsnews.net/newstext. php?nn=9004020156> [accessed: September 19, 2011].

2011."Lebanese cabinet okays energy agreement with Iran." *Daily Star*, July 21. Available from LexisNexis [accessed: September 19, 2011].

Ajami, F. 1977–78. "Stress in the Arab Triangle." *Foreign Policy* (29): 90–108.

Alagha, J. 2005. "Hizballah after the Syrian Withdrawal." *Middle East Report* (237):34–9.

al-Amin, I. 2010. "Saudi Ambassador: Tribunal In The Hands Of The Security Council." *Asharq al-Awsat,* October 2. Available from MidEast Wire [accessed: September 19, 2011].

Armanios, F. 2004. "Islam: Sunnis and Shiites." *Congressional Research Service,* 23 February.

Aziz, J. 2010. "Talk About The Tribunal Between [Beirut's] Suburbs And Damascus." *Al-Akhbar*, June 15. Available from MidEast Wire [accessed: September 19, 2011].

Badran, T. 2006 "Saudi-Syrian Relations after Hariri." *Middle East Monitor* 1(1). Available at <http://www.mideastmonitor.org/issues/0602/0602_2.htm> [accessed: September 19, 2011].

Barnes-Dacey, J. "Fearful of Iran's Influence, Saudi King reaches out to Syria." *Christian Science Monitor*, October 7. Available from LexisNexis [accessed: September 19, 2011].

Berti, B. 2010. "Ahmadinejad in Beirut: Reasserting the Islamic Republic's Influence in Lebanon." *INSS Insight* (217), October 20. Available at <http:// www.inss.org.il/publications.php?cat=25&incat=&read=4494> [accessed: September 19, 2011].

Berti, B. 2007. "Political Fragmentation Hinders Lebanon's Stability." *Asia Times*, October 10. Available at <http://www.lebanonwire. com/0710MLN/07101408PINR.asp> [accessed: September 19, 2011].

Blanford, N. 2010. "Rare Arab Summit to Forestall Possible Hezbollah Unrest in Lebanon." *The Christian Science Monitor*, July 30. Available from LexisNexis [accessed: September 19, 2011].

Blanford, N. 2007. "Is Iran Driving New Saudi Diplomacy?" *Christian Science Monitor*, January 16. Available from LexisNexis [accessed: September 19, 2011].

Daragahi, B, and Richter, P. 2011. "Lebanon's Government Collapses Eleven Cabinet Ministers Quit Because Of A Dispute Over The Assassination Tribunal." *Los Angeles Times*, January 13. Available from LexisNexis [accessed: September 19, 2011].

Dawisha, A. 1984. "The Motives of Syrian Involvement in Lebanon." *Middle East Journal* 38(2): 228–36.

Deeb, M. 1988. "Shia Movements in Lebanon: Their Formation, Ideology, Social Basis, and Links with Iran and Syria." *Third World Quarterly* 10(2): 683–98.

Diyab, Y. 2006. "Lebanese minister lauds Saudi support, comments on Syria ties, UN resolution." *Al-Sharq al-Awsat*, August 29. Available from LexisNexis [accessed: September 19, 2011].

Gambill, G. 2010. "Syria's Triumph in Lebanon: Au Revoir, Les Ententes." *MERIA* 14(4). Available at <http://www.gloria-center.org/meria/2010/12/gambill.html> [accessed: September 19, 2011].

Gates, C. 1998. *The Merchant Republic of Lebanon: Rise of an Open Economy.* Oxford and London: Centre for Lebanese Studies and I.B. Tauris.

Harris, W. 2011. "Lebanon's Day in Court. The Controversial Life of the Hariri Tribunal." *Foreign Affairs*, June 30. Available at <http://www.foreignaffairs.com/articles/67971/william-harris/lebanons-day-in-court?page=show> [accessed: September 19, 2011].

Harris, W. 1985. "Syria in Lebanon." *MERIP Reports* 134: 9–14.

Hajjar, S.G. 2002. "Hizballah: Terrorism, National Liberation, Or Menace?" Strategic Studies Institute, US Army War College. Available at <www.strategicstudiesinstitute.army.mil/pdffiles/pub184.pdf> [accessed: September 19, 2011].

Hokayem, E. 2010. "The Iran Primer: Iran and Lebanon." United States Institute of Peace, October 18. Available at <http://www.iiss.org/whats-new/iiss-experts-commentary/the-iran-primer-iran-and-lebanon/?locale=en>   [accessed: September 19, 2011].

International Crisis Group. 2005. "Syria After Lebanon, Lebanon After Syria." *Middle East Report* 39, April 12. Available at <http://www.crisisgroup.org/en/regions/middle-east-north-africa/iraq-syria-lebanon/syria/039-syria-after-lebanon-lebanon-after-syria.aspx> [accessed: September 19, 2011].

Jaber, H. 1997. *Hezbollah: Born with a Vengeance.* London: Fourth Estate Ltd.

Khalidi, R.I. 1985. "Lebanon in the Context of Regional Politics: Palestinian and Syrian Involvement in the Lebanese Crisis." *Third World Quarterly* 7(3): 495–514.

Khalot, S. 2002. *Civil and Uncivil Violence in Lebanon.* New York: Columbia University Press.

Khuri, G. 2007. "Saudi, Lebanese ministers comment on aid to Lebanon." Al-Arabiyya TV, January 26. Available from LexisNexis [accessed: September 19, 2011].

Phares, W. 2002. "After the Hariri Assassination: Syria, Lebanon, and U.S. Policy." Foundation for Defense of Democracies, March 2. Available at <http://www.

defenddemocracy.org/index.php?option=com_content&task=view&id=11774
920&Itemid=102> [accessed: September 19, 2011].

Rouman, R. 2005. "Syria Will Let U.N. Question 5 Officials; Deal Ends Stalemate
in Hariri Probe." *Washington Post*, November 26. Available from LexisNexis
[accessed: September 19, 2011].

Safa, O. 2006. "Lebanon Springs Forward." *Journal of Democracy* 17 (1): 22–37.

Sakr, K. 2010. "Syrian Sources: Assad, Abdullah Agree With Lebanese Sides
Over Tribunal." *Al-Quds al-Arabi*, August 3. Available from MidEast Wire
[accessed: September 19, 2011].

Sakr, E. and Qawas, N. 2010. "Jumblatt Plans Syria Visit, Denounces UNSCR
1559." *Daily Star*, January 4. Available at <http://www.dailystar.com.lb/
News/Politics/Jan/04/Jumblatt-plans-Syria-visit-denounces-UNSCR-1559.
ashx#axzz20Dcboarh> [accessed: September 19, 2011].

Salem, P. 2010. "Lebanon's Fall?" Carnegie Middle East Center, November 18.
Available at < http://carnegie-mec.org/publications/?fa=41964> [accessed:
July 10, 2012].

Salloukh, B. 2005 "Syria and Lebanon: A Brotherhood Transformed." *Middle East
Report* 236: 14–21.

Sands, D.R. 2005. "Saudi Arabia Demands Syria Ouster." *Washington Times*,
March 4. Available from LexisNexis [accessed: September 19, 2011].

Slackman, M. 2009. "U.S.-Backed Alliance Wins in Lebanon." *New York
Times*, June 7. Available at_<http://www.nytimes.com/2009/06/08/world/
middleeast/08lebanon.html?_r=1> [accessed: September 19, 2011].

The Taif Agreement. 1989. Available at <http://www.mideastinfo.com/documents/
taif.htm> [accessed: September 19, 2011].

Thompson, E. 2002. "Will Syria Have to withdraw from Lebanon." *Middle East
Journal* 56(1). Available at <http://www.highbeam.com/doc/1P3-105196832.
html> [accessed: September 19, 2011].

Wright, R. 2008. "U.S.-Saudi Effort Seeks to End Syrian Interference in Lebanon."
Washington Post, March 1. Available from LexisNexis [accessed: September
19, 2011].

Worth, R.F. 2010. "Iran's Leader Cements Ties on State Visit to Lebanon." *New
York Times*, October 14. Available at <http://www.nytimes.com/2010/10/14/
world/middleeast/14lebanon.html> [accessed: July 10, 2012].

Young, M. 2010. *The Ghosts of Martyrs Square. An Eyewitness Account of
Lebanon's Life Struggle*. London and New York: Simon & Schuster.

—— 2006. "What's Gotten into You Michel Aoun?" *Daily Star*, January 26.
Available from LexisNexis [accessed: September 19, 2011].

Zisser, E. 2011. "Iranian Involvement in Lebanon." *Military and Strategic Affairs*
3(1): 3–16.

Chapter 5

Challenging the Hashemites:
The Muslim Brotherhood and the Islamic
Action Front in Jordan

Kürşad Turan

Introduction

The Middle East has long been a region in turmoil. The sources of this instability can be traced back to developments at both international and domestic levels. Internationally, we can speak of interventions by non-regional actors in search of influence and natural resources. These interventions traditionally changed the power balances in the region and led to more authoritarian regimes that are somewhat more predictable in their behavior and can be more easily manipulated. It also made it harder to reach political stability at state level. Domestically, very few countries experienced democratic regimes and even those limited experiments failed to last long enough to make a significant impact. As a result, regardless of the label they adopt, the majority of political systems in the region remained patrimonial, which is defined by Reinhard Bendix as state structures functioning as "an extension of the ruler's household in which the relation between the ruler and his officials remains on the basis of paternal authority and filial dependence" (Bill and Springborg 2000: 112).

In order to have a better understanding of the political instability in the region, it is important to become familiar with the political structure, because in patrimonial systems only a relatively small group of people have indirect access to power, and recruitment and advancement are not based on merit, but on closeness to the ruler. This emphasis on personalism is an attempt to guarantee the loyalty of political elites to the source of that power, the ruler of the country. As a result, the political elites that run the country are often quite small groups relative to the country's population, and access to these groups is very limited for ordinary citizens. This inability to obtain power or become a relevant political actor is one of the main reasons why, if change does take place, it ends up being a complete regime change, often achieved through violent methods.

Since they gradually gained their independence after World War I, democratic experiments often prematurely ended in violent coups that established some form of authoritarian system along the lines of traditional patrimonial regimes. Very few countries in the region escaped this cycle and managed to establish stable political systems. The Hashemite Kingdom of Jordan is one of these countries. It was established in 1921 as one of the mandate regimes that enjoyed very little domestic support and, at least initially, completely relied on external support for its survival. Like many countries at the time, the Emirate of Transjordan was the result of Great Britain and France's efforts to shape the post-Ottoman Middle East. While many of these regimes were gone by the 1950s, the Hashemite Dynasty in Jordan managed to survive.[1]

Jordan's success lies in the early years of the Emirate/Kingdom. There were two factors that allowed Hashemite rule to take root in Transjordan and forge a national identity that brought together various groups in the country. First, British support was crucial against both the internal and external threats that the Hashemite dynasty faced early on. Britain's presence not only provided the time Emir Abdullah needed to strengthen his rule, but also established a state structure that, for the most part, still stands. The political structure and the elites it relied on were the result of these early efforts. The second factor was the political elite structure, established by Emir Abdullah and improved by King Hussein, which was based on a large coalition that brought together factions of Jordanian society that felt the need to band together in the face of common threats. Even though the threats they faced changed over time as a result of regional developments, this alliance managed to stay together.

Today, however, Jordan is facing new challenges that are significantly different than past experiences; whether the Hashemite Kingdom will survive in its current form remains to be seen. In this chapter, I will first look at the Hashemite regime in Jordan and how it developed the ruling elite coalition over time. Then I turn my attention to the Jordanian Muslim Brotherhood and its political wing, the Islamic Action Front, focusing especially on how over time they shifted from a loyal opposition group to a contender. Finally, I will focus on the latest developments and why the Muslim Brotherhood (MB) and the Islamic Action Front (IAF) represent a unique challenge to the Hashemite dynasty, with a realistic chance of breaking up the elite coalition that has been together for almost a century.

The Jordanian Ruling Elite

Jordan has been ruled by the Hashemite Dynasty since its inception in 1921. This monarchy is a excellent example for patriarchal regimes in the region. Its center is occupied by the Hashemite family surrounded by various allies. Over time, the family relied on two sources in order to maintain its hold on power. Internationally, British support was key for the weak and imported dynasty that faced opposition from many fronts from the beginning. Britain not only provided security, but also created the state structure which, to a large extent, is still intact.

---

1   The other three efforts to establish Hashemite dynasties in Syria (1920), Iraq (1921–58), and Hijaz (1916–24) rapidly failed.

This close relationship lasted until the late 1950s when, in an attempt to appease Arab Nationalist regimes in the region, British presence and influence in the country was limited. Soon afterward, Britain was replaced by the United States as the Jordanian state's main supporter, which still applies today. Domestically, the Hashemite regime relied heavily on a patronage system that brought together a mixture of ethnic and security units, including Bedouin tribes, Circassians, Christians, the military, and the intelligence services.

By the end of World War I, there were three Hashemite regimes established in the Middle East. While Sharif Hussein, who had played a key role in the Arab revolt against the Ottoman Empire, established his rule in Hijaz, his two sons Faisal and Abdullah had become the rulers of Syria and Transjordan respectively. Faisal's time in Syria was cut short by French authorities and he was later sent to Iraq to become king. Abdullah's rule in Transjordan began as a compromise between the British and the Hashemite family to keep them from attacking Syria to reestablish Faisal as king. Abdullah was announced as the Emir of the newly established territory of Transjordan in 1921; however, not being from Transjordan, the Hashemites were perceived "as 'refugees' from the Hijaz precariously perched on shaky thrones erected by British imperialism" (Milton-Edwards and Hinchcliffe 1999: 28–9). At that time, Transjordan had a population of approximately 250,000 people, half of which were from nomadic Bedouin tribes (Susser 2000). The population was mostly homogenous consisting of Sunni Arabs, with small minorities of Circassians and Christians. These minority groups welcomed Abdullah as a central authority who could provide security against the threat posed by the Bedouin tribes (ibid.). Naturally, this support by itself would not be enough to sustain Abdullah's regime, and without active British involvement, Abdullah's rule would probably have been as short-lived as Faisal's in Syria. During the early years, the country was predominantly ruled by the British who controlled the foreign relations and finances of Transjordan, while at the same time helping to establish a state structure. With British assistance, Emir Abdullah was able to survive two threats to his authority: Bedouin tribes and Arab nationalists. One advantage the regime had at the time was that these two opposition groups could not join together as a single front because they represented two significantly different world-views, with differing plans for the country. While Abdullah militarily defeated the tribes, he also included them in the ruling elite through marriages, offers of land, government positions, and tax exemptions. The British incorporated the military force of these tribes into the British-created and led Arab Legion, not only eliminating a potential threat, but also creating a military structure directly loyal to the ruling family. Abdullah's policy toward the East Bank Bedouins was essentially based on highlighting "the extraordinary role of the Bedouin tribes in the development of the state and [Abdullah] has deliberately promoted Jordan's tribal heritage as a 'symbol of Jordan's distinctive national identity'" (ibid.: 94).

Against the Arab nationalists, the state had to adopt a dual policy. During the early years of state, despite their non-Transjordanian origins, Arab nationalists were included in Transjordan's bureaucracy because they represented the better-educated portion of the population and were needed to run the country. Later on, when the regime managed to improve the education levels of its supporters, they were pushed out to be replaced by Transjordanians.

By the end of Abdullah's rule, the ruling elite that consisted of the East Bank Bedouin tribes, various minority groups including the Circassians and Christians, the military, the intelligence structure, was in place. Throughout the following decades, the regime faced two serious threats from Arab nationalists and Palestinians, and neither of these was able to weaken the elite coalition. This was due to the fact that all members of the coalition felt almost equally threatened by these challenges, and these challenges served as a tool that bound them further together.[2]

The most recent threat to Hashemite rule appears to be the Jordanian Muslim Brotherhood and its political party, the Islamic Action Front. This, however, represents a different type of challenge. Unlike the Arab nationalist movement, it does not pose a major threat to the way of life of the predominantly conservative Bedouin tribes. Also, unlike the Palestinian challenge that resulted in Black September, it is not posed by an ethnically separate unit. As a result, it not only has the potential to divide the ruling elite inside the country, but its claim to power is also supported by the regional wave that brought down a number of authoritarian regimes.

The Jordanian Muslim Brotherhood

The Jordanian Muslim Brotherhood (JMB) is one of many branches of the organization that has spread not only to the Middle East, but to a majority of Muslim countries. In Jordan, the Muslim Brotherhood has been a legal organization since the rule of King Abdullah. Its original role was to provide support to the regime in the form of a loyal opposition. Since 1979, following the Iranian Islamic Revolution, the JMB gradually began to act like a real opposition party, seeking power and increasingly challenging the regime. The JMB's evolution was a gradual move from the social to the political realm only after it succeeded in establishing a constituency for itself through its extensive social programs, a strategy we often see under semi-authoritarian regimes. The fact that they provide the existing regime with some level of legitimacy by accepting the rules of the political game as determined by the regime, in addition to a commitment to democratic methods displayed by participation in elections, makes such organizations more acceptable to ruling elites and the JMB took full advantage of this (Ottaway and Hamzawy 2008: 9).

Although an Islamic organization, one must distinguish Muslim Brotherhood (MB) chapters from jihadist organizations. As Rubin (2007: 2) points out, there are three main differences between these two types of organizations. First, even

---

2   During King Hussein's rule there was a military coup attempt by the Arab nationalists officers in 1957, but it failed as a result of the tribal elements in the military remaining loyal to the King.

though these two strands are not enemies, they represent two different ideologies and methods competing for the control of state power and, more importantly, the support of the masses. While the MB usually seeks opportunities to participate in the political process (despite the system being biased against it), jihadist groups reject the political system as being illegitimate. The second difference is their targets. In most cases, jihadists target the "far enemy"—described as Israel and the West in general—while MB-type organizations essentially target their own governments. Finally, regarding their methods, jihadists tend to focus on armed struggle, but the MB is tactically more flexible, using social services and education to indoctrinate the masses and showing restraint in order to escape state repression. These strategies make MB-like groups more visible and politically more active.

Initially, all chapters of the MB considered themselves branches of the same Egyptian organization. The only exception to this was the semi-autonomous character of the Syrian chapter (Bar 1998: 9). One example of this unity was the Egyptian, Syrian, and Transjordanian chapters' participation in the War of 1948 against Israel with a military force of 10,000 men (ibid.: 11). Today, despite their shared ideology and general structure, these organizations do not act collectively, but parallel to each other (Rubin 2007: 3). Even though they support one another in principle, in practice what determines their policies and strategies are the domestic conditions of the country they are established in. Even the organizational structure of each branch is different from one another. The Jordanian Brotherhood had adopted a structure based on the Egyptian example, but more appropriate to the needs of a much smaller country (Bar 1998). According to Rubin, there are two main reasons for this separation. First, the conditions in each country are different. Each country's group faces varying degrees of government restrictions, not leaving them much flexibility in choosing their methods. While the Jordanian MB is very cautious in domestic politics, the Syrian MB clearly positions itself as anti-regime, and the Egyptian MB claims support for democracy and further democratization (Rubin 2007). Secondly, the countries in which they are established tolerate their presence to a certain degree most of the time. A high level of international cooperation between the branches would lead the governments to perceive them as more of a threat and increase the level of repression they faced. In order to avoid this, the organizations prefer establishing bilateral relations rather than multilateral ones.[3]

Despite their varying stands in domestic politics, all the Muslim Brotherhoods share the same position on an international issue: the Palestinian question. They

---

3   Rubin's example of the relationship between various MB branches and Hamas is important: "Hamas in Gaza Strip is related to the Egyptian Brotherhood, while Hamas in the West Bank has its links to the Jordanian Brotherhood. Furthermore, to make matters even more complex, the Hamas external leadership is located in Damascus, where the Syrian Brotherhood is outlawed, and its patron is the regime that persecutes the Brotherhood" (Rubin 2007: 4–5).

have consistently called for a unified Islamic Arab world that will support the Palestinian cause (Amr 1990).

In Jordan, the regime and the MB were close allies when the perceived threat came from leftist ideologies, but now that the Islamist ideology appeared to be the main threat for the regime, the former allies found themselves to be rivals. The period of adjustment to this new reality still continued, the JMB still carefully avoiding any open confrontations with the regime other than carefully worded statements. Susser (2000: 108) argues that the period of peaceful coexistence was due to the imbalance of power between the two actors that heavily favored the regime. However, such balances were not necessarily sustainable over the long run, especially in the Middle East, and were heavily influenced by external factors. The JMB's case fits this generalization and developments during the 1980s played an important role in their change.

The Pre-1989 Muslim Brotherhood

The Jordanian Muslim Brotherhood was first legalized by King Abdullah following the country's independence in 1946, making the organization the oldest political opposition group in Jordan. Following the end of the War of 1948 and Jordan's occupation of the West Bank, Transjordanian and Palestinian branches of the Brotherhood merged, leading to the strong representation of Palestinians in the organization, which still continues. The group's special treatment was based on two characteristics the group possessed: their role as "the regime's counterweight" (Robinson 1998: 401), and the origins of their leadership. The regime used the JMB as a counterweight against leftist, Nasserite, and even fundamentalist Islamist (Islamic Liberation Party – *Hizb al-Tahrir-al Islami*) groups which were perceived as more immediate threats. In addition, the organization's leaders tended to come from "well-established political families in Jordan" (ibid.), and were not believed to pose a revolutionary threat to ruling elites. By 1955, the majority of the JMB's members were from the upper-middle classes and numbered around 6,000 (excluding the youth organizations), organized in 19 branches (Bar 1998: 15).[4] Gradually expanding its field of operation, the JMB first created a range of charitable activities brought together under the Islamic Center Society in 1965 (Brown 2006: 5). This is considered as the organization's first involvement in politics and the expansion came after long arguments between the two groups within the organization. While the liberal wing emphasized religion over politics, others argued that the organization should become more politically oriented. The dispute was settled following the repression of the Egyptian MB by the government; in order to avoid a similar fate, the majority of the Jordanian branch members decided to engage more actively involved in politics. Bar (1998:

---

4   Bar (1998: 16) lists these branches: in the East Bank (Amman, Irbid, Salt, Zarqa, Jarash, Karak, and the refugee camps of Karama and Jabal Hussein), and in the West Bank (Jerusalem, Hebron, Nablus, Jenin, Tulkarem, and the refugee camps in Jericho).

17) cites the movement's constitution which announced in Article Two that it works for "the realization of the aims for which Islam has come to earth." In their efforts to become a politically significant actor, they tried to attract members from the religious establishment, participated in elections for various professional associations, and published a number of periodicals, facing legal resistance along the way (Brown 2006: 5). Professional organizations were key in the process of politicization. Even though the JMB had rejected any ties with these organizations in the past, claiming that they were leftist, the group eventually realized that in an environment where political parties were banned and political activity in general was severely limited such organizations served as the main political outlet. These efforts paid off and by 1985, in addition to controlling a large portion of professional organizations, the organization had also developed a strong student group in two of Jordan's largest universities—Yarmuk University in Irbid and Jordanian University in Amman—where previously the dominant student groups were leftists, Palestinian and Arab nationalists (Bar 1998).

Despite becoming increasingly political, the JMB made a clear effort not to criticize the government too openly, remaining neutral on many issues and avoiding government crackdowns. Susser (2000: 109) claims that the MB's acceptance of the rules of the political game was the result of the experiences of 1957 and 1970, and the regime's brutal action against its opponents. Although its members and leaders were imprisoned at times, their moderate stance allowed the MB to continue its operations, unlike other opposition groups. This mild opposition, however, did not mean that the organization shared the regime's position on all issues. Their slogan against American aid in 1957 ("No reconciliation [with Israel], no dollar, no atheism, and no imperialism") showed that the Palestinian conflict was not the only issue where they disagreed with the government (Brown 2006: 5).

Despite its favorable status, the strength of the MB was somewhat limited due to the divisions within the organization. Robinson calls these two main groups social Islamists and political Islamists. He argues that not only the agendas but also the profiles of these two groups were quite distinct:

> Social Islamists are often East Bankers, are more likely to have had formal religious training, tend to push for changes centering primarily on social issues (such as banning alcohol from the kingdom and segregating the sexes at schools) generally support Hashemite rule, and urge close relations with the crown ... political Islamists in Jordan tend to be more interested in larger political issues ... and use a discourse often associated the left: Western and Zionist imperialism, social justice, regime corruption, unequal distribution of wealth, and the like. Political Islamists are disproportionately Palestinian in origin and are often independent in political affiliation. Virtually none are members of the *ulama*; rather, they tend to be college-educated in technical fields ... Political Islamists are much more likely to be critical of the regime, and are often critical of the Muslim Brotherhood's close relationship with it. (Robinson 1998: 403)

The long-term failure of the moderates to reach the organization's goals strengthened the hand of the radical wing, leading "to more rigid or conservative stances and are often repelled by appeals to flexibility or reform" (Ottaway and Hamzawy 2008: 17).

In the political arena, the JMB took advantage of the liberalization process that followed King Hussein's accession to throne in 1952. However, due to the rising Nasserite Pan-Arabism and American efforts to establish the Baghdad Pact as a defense pact against the Soviet Union, the political opening did not last long. The JMB decided not to participate in the 1954 elections and actively protested against the Baghdad Pact and the US's growing influence over Jordan. These led to the arrest of many Brotherhood leaders and a temporary worsening of relations with the regime. Because the leftist threat continued to be the main concern of the regime, within two years they had to reevaluate their position against the Brotherhood and the JMB was allowed to renew its activities, deciding to participate in the 1956 election by nominating independents. Their decision was based on the fact that these would be the freest elections up until that point and that *Hizb al-Tahrir*, the MB's main competition, had also decided to participate (Bar 1998: 26). Despite gaining just four seats, the MB became the second largest group in the Parliament.

Throughout the 1960s, while *Hizb al-Tahrir* chose to challenge the regime by participating in two failed *coups d'état*, the JMB, on the other hand, remained neutral and did not even support Palestinian organizations against the regime. This loyalty was rewarded by the government with the appointment of Ishaq al-Farhan, a sympathizer of the Brotherhood, as the Minister of Education for five consecutive governments (ibid.: 32).

The importance of the Muslim Brotherhood as a political actor began to increase during the late 1970s and early 1980s, parallel to the developments within and around Jordan. According to Al-Khazendar (1997: 137–8), there were a number of factors that facilitated the rise of the Jordanian Muslim Brotherhood. First, the role Islam played in Jordanian politics was more significant than many other countries in the region. Even though the regime was not and did not claim to be Islamic in any way, the fact that the Hashemites often based the legitimacy of their rule on their descent from the Prophet Muhammad made it justifiable for the JMB and other groups to bring religion into politics. Secondly, and more generally, the failure of Arab nationalism to offer a solution to existing problems or a democratic environment led people to seek alternatives, and religion was at the top of the list because it appealed to the majority of the population, regardless of their level of education. Third, the success of Islamist movements in countries like Iran created the belief that Islam could be a viable political ideology. Despite its Shiite origins, the Iranian Revolution was seen as a victory for Islam, even among the Sunni population of many countries in the region. Along the same lines, the invasion of Afghanistan by the Soviet Union gave the organization a new cause to rally around. Fourth was the Arab failure to combat Israel, which created the perception that new regimes were needed to restore Arab pride with successes against Israel on the side of Palestinians. The Israeli-Egyptian peace process, especially, was opposed by all branches of the MB and King Hussein's moderate position gave the impression that Jordan could follow a similar path and join the peace process, giving the JMB another opposition point. Fifth, the high levels of economic growth partly caused by the Lebanese civil war shifted economic activity to Jordan; this led to high inflation rates and increasing inequality between the rich and the poor. These economic problems, combined with the government's inability to provide for lower-income groups, increased the importance of the Brotherhood's social services. Sixth, and perhaps most important, was the King's suspension of Parliament in 1976, severely reducing the acceptable area for political activity and leaving politics to clubs and professional organizations. These developments shifted the nature of the relationship between the government and the MB for the worse.

During the early 1980s and in line with its traditional support for Iraq, Jordan began to support the Syrian Muslim Brotherhood in order to weaken Hafez Asssad's regime in Syria, which was supporting Iran against Iraq (Al-Khazendar 1997: 144). This support for the Syrian MB helped improve relations between the Jordanian regime and the JMB until the Jordanian and Syrian regimes became closer around the mid-1980s and a new wave of political repression swept across Jordan. Despite being one of the groups repressed by the regime, the Brotherhood did not respond with protests (ibid.: 144–5).

By the end of the 1980s, a new democratization process began with the reopening of the Parliament. Since 1967, when the King had closed down the Parliament, eight seats had become vacant and were up for election. Six of these eight seats were reserved for Muslims and the other two for Christians. Islamist candidates managed to win three out of the six Muslim seats. Even though the regime saw this as a rising trend and a major threat, their attempts to limit it proved to be unsuccessful in the municipal elections of 1986. The elections came after a confrontation between the regime and the Muslim Brotherhood over the demands made by the JMB to make the Jordanian monarchy "wholly Islamic" and legislation to be based on the principles of Islam (Lust-Okar 2004: 168).

The Palestinian Intifada and the emergence of Hamas created problems for the Jordanian Brotherhood. Many of the leaders of the MB were active in Hamas, were instrumental in the drafting of Hamas's covenant, and provided government access to West Bank Hamas leaders (Bar 1998: 40). Even though they did not perceive it as a problem at the time, this pro-Hamas stance directly contradicted with the Brotherhood's traditional policy of not confronting the Jordanian Monarchy because Hamas's covenant clearly rejected the idea that anybody could lay claim to any portion of Palestinian land, which King Hussein did at the time regarding the West Bank. In addition, Bar also argues that the members of the Brotherhood was also played an important role in Hamas's decision "to turn to 'armed struggle'", which was against the King's rejection of the use of force (ibid.: 41). At the same time, the Brotherhood opposed King Hussein's disengagement from the West Bank in 1988 and the PLO's declaration of independence in the West Bank and Gaza, even though Hamas supported both (ibid.).

Throughout the process of confrontation,

> ... the Government continued publicly to proclaim its own loyalty to the traditional culture of Islam, while calling for modernity and rejecting religious extremism. Nevertheless. The Muslim Brotherhood continued to be the more radically Islamic force with a particular ability to monopolize the Islamic appeal and consequently exert greater religious influence and power than the Government ... The competition between the Government and the Muslim Brotherhood thus involved the appeal of Islam, particularly in the educational institutions, the media, and the mosques. (Al-Khazendar 1997: 148–9)

The Liberalization Process

The last parliament, elected before the War of 1967, consisted of the representatives of the East and West Banks. By the time the parliament reopened in 1989, the West Bank was under Israeli occupation and unable to send representatives. The situation had changed after the King decided to sever ties with the West Bank in 1988. This decision triggered a wave of dissent which was met with an opposing wave of repression, including the arrests of left-wing opposition leaders, and changes in the editorial boards of major newspapers as they shifted their positions to more closely reflect the government's views. In addition to limitations on political activity, there were also tensions regarding "charges of corruption, limited freedom of speech, the under-representation of the urban majority in the NCC, and the failure of national legislation to conform to Islam" (Lust-Okar 2004: 168).

The regime also faced an economic crisis that reduced the country's per capita GNP from $2,000 in mid-1980s to under $1,500 in 1989 (Robinson 1998: 390). Combined with the dropping levels of remittances from Jordanians working abroad and aid received from the Gulf States,[5] the country's economy, already on shaky ground, took a major hit and forced the government to accept IMF adjustment plans (Lust-Okar 2004: 169). Because this would meant significant cuts in subsidies and welfare programs, and an increase in the cost of living, the government initially decided to keep the deal a secret; however, once these policies were adopted, Jordan experienced uprisings that lasted three days. Protests began in the south of the country and quickly spread to the capital. The most worrying aspect of these riots was that they threatened the very coalition the regime was based upon; clashes between the military and the Bedouin tribes forced the King to implement a liberalization process that would at least respond to some of the

---

5   The initial drop in remittances was the result of the decrease in oil prices and reduced the amount from $1 billion annually to $23 million in 1989. With the beginning of the Gulf War, the remittances rose again to $500 million in 1990 and $450 million in 1991 (Robinson, 1998: 390). Direct aid received from Gulf States varied from $550 million to $1.3 billion between 1980 and 1989. In 1990, that number dropped to $393 million and in 1991 to $164 million.

protestors' demands. The King announced that full elections would take place and the corruption charges would be investigated.

Milton-Edwards (1993: 193–4) sees the decision to democratize as a combination of external and internal factors. Externally, there was pressure on the King to democratize in exchange for financial assistance and, because Jordan lacked the resources to get out of the financial crisis by itself, Hussein needed to address these demands in order to secure new loans. Domestically, the riots had shown the regime the need for some political change; in order to continue their rule and regain the legitimacy they had lost, the elites needed to adopt a democratization process while still maintaining control. As a result—though the riots were mainly about rising prices, with only limited demands for further democracy—a democratization process began.

The sudden decision to hold elections, in an environment where political parties were still banned, did not give much time for opposition groups to organize, while helping groups that were already organized. In Jordan, this meant that only two groups—the JMB and the Bedouin tribes—were prepared.

The electoral process was handled extremely clumsily. Martial law was still in effect, political parties were still banned, and it was unclear who could run for a parliamentary seat. The announcement that all candidates would be allowed to run, regardless of their political views, did not come until only two weeks before the election, reducing the legal 25-day campaigning period to 15 days and making it very difficult for the majority of candidates to run an effective campaign (Amr, 1990).

The Brotherhood saw these elections as an opportunity to increase their political power and create some significant change in Jordan. In order to make a difference, candidates needed to represent a bloc, but this was very hard to achieve in the absence of political parties. The JMB was further aided by its social network which was already in place and had become more important for the population following the economic crisis; the JMB's past experiences in participating in elections with independent candidates also helped. They adopted "Islam is the solution" as their slogan, organizing their campaign around their already existing network of mosques, charity organizations, professional associations, and universities (Milton-Edwards 1993: 195).

Other groups were not as fortunate. As a result of decades of state pressure, leftist groups did not have an organized structure in place. Considering the short time period between the announcement and elections, they spent most of their time struggling to organize and failed to run an effective campaign. Traditionalists and tribal groups were shaken up by the riots that had originated in regions that traditionally supported them. Aware that they were the ones that stood most to lose, their main goal was to reestablish their dominance in those regions. Instead of trying to win the support of urban areas and Palestinians, they focused on maintaining the support they already had.

Out of the 80 seats available, nine were reserved for Christians, two for Circassians, and one to Circassians and Chechens, leaving 68 seats for Arab Muslim candidates. These seats were spread over 20 electoral districts, each with two to nine seats. The Brotherhood entered the elections through a list of 26 independent candidates; 20 won the election. Another twelve Islamist candidates also managed to enter the parliament. This gave the Islamists 32 seats, while centrists and tribal candidates won 35, leaving the leftists with only 13 seats (Robinson 1998: 392).[6]

The parliament had to deal with four major issues: the IMF structural adjustment program, the political parties law, the press and publications law, and the push for lifting the martial law (ibid.: 393). Though the Islamist Bloc came into the parliament confident that they could create significant change, in most cases they lacked the experience to be effective. Developments in the Persian Gulf in 1991 and their disagreements with the King regarding Jordan's position further limited their ability to be effective. Despite Jordan's announcement of its neutrality in the conflict, a wide variety of groups in the newly elected parliament came together under the name National Front to support Saddam Hussein. The regime's refusal to cooperate with the alliance against Iraq resulted in a major increase in public support, while internationally the country was punished financially, especially regarding the support coming from Gulf States (Milton-Edwards 1993) (see Table 5.1).

Table 5.1   The Jordanian Muslim Brotherhood's electoral performance

Year	Number of seats up for election	Seats won by the MB
1954	40	4
1957	40	4
1963	40	2
1967	60	2
1984*	8	3
1989	80	22**

* This election was to fill the eight seats in the reopened parliament that had become vacant since 1967.

** The Muslim Brotherhood had only 29 candidates running.

6   There appears to be disagreement about the seats won by the Islamists and the Muslim Brotherhood. According to Brynen (1998: 75), Islamist candidates won "roughly 33 seats (22 of these going to candidates associated with the Muslim Brotherhood)." This is probably the result of the candidates' inability to identify themselves as representatives of political parties.

In 1992, the parliament finally authorized the formation of political parties. The appearance of new political parties meant that the JMB could face more competition from the center and the left. However, the development of political parties in Jordan remained very slow and the JMB continued to enjoy its advantage. Due to two attributes of the law (Robinson 1998: 395), it also meant that the Brotherhood would be subject to new limitations and be treated in the same way as other political parties. First, it was forbidden for political parties to receive financial support from outside; because the JMB was predominantly financed by Gulf State sources, this meant that the organization's resources would be severely limited. Secondly, the law made arrangements that if Palestinian citizenship ever became an option, Palestinians in Jordan would have to make a choice between Jordanian and Palestinian citizenship; if they chose the latter, they would be excluded from Jordanian politics. Both of these arrangements were interpreted as the regime's attempts to limit the JMB's influence. In order to overcome these limitations, the JMB opted for the creation of a new political party that would be a separate entity, but still function as the organization's political wing. This would also keep the Brotherhood safe from any regime pressure aimed at political parties.

The Islamic Action Front

The Islamic Action Front (IAF) was formed as an umbrella political party in 1992 to represent the Muslim Brotherhood's political wing, as well as some of the independent Islamists. The party reflected the same divisions we saw in the JMB. Following its establishment in 1992, the first and temporary Shura Council, elected for one year, mainly consisted of political Islamists who were replaced one year later by social Islamists for a four-year term (Robinson 1998: 403–4). A second dimension of the division was the struggle for influence between Palestinians and East Bankers. While Palestinians saw the advancement of the Palestinian cause as the main goal of the political party, East Bankers aimed at achieving political and social change in Jordan (Ottaway and Hamzawy 2008: 17–18).

Before the split occurred, during the 1993 elections, the secretary general of the IAF, Ishaq al-Farhan, as well as one-third of the Executive Bureau and the 120-member Shura Council were of Palestinian origin. Out of the 16 IAF members in the parliament, eight were Palestinian too. This level of Palestinian representation was due to religious views being the main criterion for membership, not ethnic background. The Brotherhood was one of very few places Palestinians could freely get involved in politics inside the Kingdom.

Prior to the 1993 elections, the regime made another attempt to engineer the parliament by changing electoral laws. This was considered to be necessary because King Hussein was planning to normalize Jordan's relations with Israel and adopt a second set of IMF austerity measures, and both developments would require a friendly parliament. The two measures adopted by the regime were a new electoral system based on "one-person, one-vote," and reorganized electoral districts. The adoption of the "one-person, one-vote principle" was especially crucial because up until that point voters had two votes to cast and they could use one of their votes based on their tribal affiliations and still cast a vote based on their ideological preference. The JMB was the group that benefited most from this arrangement. With only a single vote to cast, voters would have to make a choice and that, in most cases, meant that the IAF would lose votes to tribal candidates. The IAF and 16 other opposition parties united against the planned changes, but after long discussions on whether they should boycott the election, they eventually decided not to directly oppose the regime and announced that they would participate. The results show that, despite having more candidates, the IAF gained fewer seats. Despite this drop in seats, considering the difficulties they had to overcome, the Front performed better than expected. Robinson (1998: 399–400) attributes this relative success to three factors. First, due to slow development of political parties, the IAF was still the best organized non-governmental organization in Jordan and they relied on their social services to gain the support in poorer areas. Secondly, Islamic candidates were seen as "pious, selfless, and incorruptible," compared to other politicians. Finally, the Palestinian presence in the Front's leadership helped them overcome the traditional "Palestinian electoral apathy."

The peace process between Israel, the Palestinians, and Jordan caused major opposition from Islamist groups as well as the leftists against Jordanian government and led the regime to take necessary precautions to make sure that domestic political developments did not threaten the process. This meant the end of liberalization, and new restrictions were placed on the press and political parties. These restrictions led the IAF and other opposition parties to join together to demand changes in the electoral system prior to the 1997 election. When the regime refused to give in, the IAF boycotted the election. This, however, did not achieve much other than leaving the IAF outside the parliament. During the 2003 election, the IAF returned to the political field and performed better than they did in 1993 despite the biased electoral system, prompting the regime continued to see the movement as the major threat. During Israel's invasion of Lebanon in 2006, the disagreements became increasingly clear. On the one hand, the IAF criticized Arab regimes for being passive against Israeli aggression and "declared, 'It is now time for the *umma* ... to cease supporting the enemy by restricting [public] freedoms and repressing opposition'" (Hamzawy and Bishara 2006: 13). Government officials, on the other hand, accused the JMB and the IAF of putting their foreign alliances before Jordan's national interests (ibid.: 11). This conflict showed to some members that it was becoming increasingly hard to remain in the regime's good graces and strengthened the hand of the hawks within the movement.

In 2007, due to a new set of restrictions, including the redrawing of districts in order to increase the advantage of the rural tribal areas, the IAF performed badly, only gaining six seats. The Brotherhood's problems were not limited to an uneven political field. The organization also faced an internal crisis triggered by three developments (Al-Farawati 2008). First, Hamas's decision to form the Palestinian Muslim Brotherhood meant that the Jordanian branch would no longer be able

Table 5.2   **The Islamic Action Front's electoral performance**

Year	Number of seats up for election	Number of candidates	Seats won by the IAF
1993	80	36	16
1997	80	Boycotted the election	
2003	110	30	18*
2007	110	22	6
2010	120	Boycotted the election	

* One of these seats came from the seats reserved for women. In addition to these 18 seats, six former members of the IAF ran and won elections in this election.

to represent Palestinians, would lose some of its membership to the new chapter, and Jordan's Palestinian population's support for the JMB and the IAF would decrease. Secondly, the IAF's failure in the election led to the decision to dissolve the Shura Council, meaning an intensification of the struggle between the hawks and doves. Finally, the regime's pressure, and the group's inability to agree on a policy against this pressure, further damaged organizational unity.

The parliament was dissolved in 2009 for a new election, but the election was postponed by the King to allow a new electoral law to be drafted. Naturally, the new law further complicated the electoral system, making it harder for the opposition to succeed. There were two points of contention. First was the creation of sub-districts that further divided 45 electoral zones Jordan had up to that point. Each voter would have one vote and even though candidates stood in one of the sub-district, voters could cast their vote for any candidate in their electoral zone regardless of the sub-district. This arrangement made it more difficult to track votes, and opened the way for electoral misconduct. In addition, the number of seats in the parliament increased from 110 to 120. A majority of these seats were given to rural electoral zones where the population density was much lower than urban areas, boosting tribal representation in the parliament.

The IAF criticized these arrangements and once again decided to boycott the election. The IAF's efforts paid off to a degree and electoral participation was the lowest since the parliament had reopened in 1989, down to 53 percent from 58.9 percent in the previous election with almost record lows in urban areas (Hazaimeh

2010).[7] While this showed the level of support the organization had, it did not achieve much in changing the regime's position (see Table 5.2 below).

By remaining outside the parliament, the IAF once again turned within itself to renew its leadership and continued to criticize the regime over various policies. The challenge for both sides came soon after the elections in the form of a widespread wave of opposition in the Middle East, often called the "Arab Spring." The protests that spread to almost every country in the region gave the Brotherhood its best chance in a long time to challenge the regime and claim a portion of the political power it sought for so long. The Hashemite regime, on the other hand, faced one of its most serious challengers with an ailing economy and a region that was becoming less and less stable.

The Arab Spring and Jordan

Compared to countries like Tunisia, Egypt, Syria, Bahrain, and Yemen, Jordanians' experience with the Arab Spring has been mild so far, prompting many observers to claim that the Hashemite regime was under no immediate danger. The view was based on two factors: Jordanian protests have been mainly about economic problems,[8] and despite its shortcomings, the Jordanian political system is relatively more free than the majority of other countries.

The role of the JMB during protests has been somewhat different from the Muslim Brotherhood chapters in Egypt and Syria. In Egypt, the Brotherhood's leadership had chosen not to get involved in the protests until it became clear that the Mubarak regime was about to fall, while younger members of the organization were among the participants. In Syria, on the other hand, the MB has been active against the regime and actively sought to mobilize the people in order to bring the regime down. The JMB adopted a middle ground by acting with other opposition groups in organizing protests, but not openly challenging the regime. This was because none of the major opposition groups in Jordan pushed for a regime change, limiting their demands to political and economic reform.

On January 26, 2011, the JMB called Jordanians to protest against Prime Minster Samir Rifai's economic policies and the political circumstances of the country, carefully avoiding direct criticism of the Hashemite dynasty (see "Thousands protest in Jordan"). These initial protests led by the JMB, leftist groups, and trade unions resulted in the appointment of Marouf al-Bakhit as prime minister. The announcement declared that "Marouf al-Bakhit had the task of 'taking practical, swift and tangible steps to launch a real political reform process, in line with

---

7   Only 1,255,024 of 2,373,579 eligible voters participated. The turnout was 34.4 percent in Amman and 36 percent in Zarqa (Hazaimeh 2010).

8   Jordan was facing a budget deficit of $2 billion and inflation had risen by 1.5 percent to 6.1 percent in December 2010. Unemployment was estimated to be around 12 percent, with poverty around 25 percent (see "Thousands protest in Jordan").

the king's version of comprehensive reform, modernization and development'" (Kadri and Bronner 2011). The King also asked for a "comprehensive assessment ... to correct the mistakes of the past" and a "revision of laws governing politics and public freedoms" (see "Jordan's king fires Cabinet amid protests"). In order to show that the regime was serious about reform, the King first announced a $125 million subsidies package that included basic goods, fuel, and a pay increase for civil servants, followed by setting up a group of fifty people to discuss the controversial electoral law and other political reforms; the group was given a three-month deadline to come up with an agreement. At the same time, in order to allow protesters vent their frustrations, the regime also made the necessary changes to allow more freedom of expression.

The appointment of a new prime minister failed to end the protests and, when reforms were not adopted fast enough, the IAF and 19 other opposition parties formed a coalition and continued their calls for economic and political reform. Al-Bakhit's statement that both leftists and Islamists might be in the new government was quickly rejected by the IAF's announcement that the organization was seeking real reform. Because they represent the largest opposition bloc, the government actively sought the JMB/IAF's involvement, only to be rejected. This risky strategy may leave the JMB/IAF isolated if the regime succeeds in reaching a compromise with remaining opposition groups.

Starting in March 2011, the protesters began to clash with the regime's supporters. Many of these clashes were limited, with the exception of Salafi protests that were more violent, but separate from leftist and JMB protests. There was even an attack on King Abdullah II's motorcade, which was later denied (see "Jordan: Protesters lob stones at King Abdullah II"). As a result of increasing dissent and slow reform process, some members of the royal-appointed political reform committee quit. Finally, in June, the protesters achieved some of their goals when Abdullah II announced that he would relinquish his right to appoint cabinets and that future cabinets would be formed by elected parliamentary majorities (Gavlak, June 12, 2011).

Despite certain positive signs, Parliament forced al-Bakhit's government to resign on October 17, 2011, for not implementing the political reform package fast enough; he was replaced by Awn Shawkat al-Khasawneh, a former judge of the International Court of Justice. One of the new prime minister's first announcements was that Jordan would no longer tolerate rigged elections and he guaranteed that an independent organization in charge of municipal and parliamentary elections would be established (Gavlak, November 4, 2011).

Throughout this process, the main concern for the regime was to keep the ruling elite coalition together. Even though they had been the main group in the ruling elites for a very long time, it was clear to everybody that the Bedouin tribes were unhappy about the recent developments, especially the economic hardships they were experiencing. In addition, during his 12-year reign King Abdullah II had failed to achieve his father King Hussein's popularity, especially with the Bedouin tribes. In January, the King promised "tens of millions of dollars he did not have to improve [the tribes'] situation," and it was not clear whether he would still enjoy their support when he failed to deliver (Bronner 2011).

The regime's concerns that they may not be able to hold their traditional coalition together in the face of increasing tensions make it more likely that there will be certain attempts to reform. Even the JMB seems to acknowledge that there may be certain political reforms in the short run, but they do not believe these will be enough. Up until 2012, each time the regime announced reforms the demands seemed to increase, meaning that we will continue to observe a bargaining process between the political center and major opposition groups.

Conclusion

As a resource-poor, small country, Jordan relied heavily on external sources and its strategic position to survive. Despite facing a number of challenges that its neighbors also dealt with, the country's Hashemite dynasty proved to be one of the longest lasting regimes in a region that is not known for its stability. The main reason for the regime's longevity was the political elite coalition it built and the dynasty's ability to keep this coalition together in the long run. However, the most recent challenge to the regime, namely the Jordanian Muslim Brotherhood and its political wing the Islamic Action Front, pose a more serious threat than the regime has faced so far.

This is due to four advantages the JMB/IAF enjoys over other opposition movements. The first advantage is the fact that the movement is not based on ethnicity or ideology, but on religion. In an ethnically and ideologically divided country, where the large majority of the population is Sunni Muslims, this widens the group's appeal and maximizes the number of potential supporters. It also helps bring together individuals from previously divided groups such as the Palestinians and Bedouin tribes from the East Bank. Secondly, with increasing levels of urbanization, traditional tribal ties tend to weaken and open the way for alternative allegiances. The JMB fills this vacuum effectively by providing an easily understood ideology that is based on a common identity these masses already share, making them feel like they belong. Third, JMB, with the help of foreign sources, provides education, healthcare, and other social services to the poor. This, in a country where state subsidies are reduced regularly and poverty is increasing, creates the impression that the organization is achieving something that the state cannot. Finally, the organizational structure of the JMB, as well as the IAF, puts them at stark contrast with the rest of the political establishment, not just in Jordan, but throughout the Middle East. As Brown (2006: 3) explains, the JMB embraces "more diverse ideological currents than almost any of its sister Islamist organizations, it has suffered schisms and divisive internal debates only on short-term tactical questions." In addition, the JMB/IAF did not produce a charismatic leader, and none of their leaders died in office; they either completed their terms or were forced out through elections, and their internal procedures are more democratic than other parties in the region. These characteristics create the perception of a selfless and incorruptible group in a political environment where politicians are generally viewed as greedy and corrupt.

Furthermore, the government's attempts to limit the organization's political power have backfired in the long run. The constant redrawing of electoral districts to shift the representation advantage from urban areas to rural tribal areas, and changing electoral laws before each election support the perception that the political system is corrupt. When the JMB/IAF criticize these arrangements, but still manage not to openly challenge the regime, they appear to be persecuted by the political elites.

Despite these advantages the JMB/IAF appear to enjoy, it is safe to assume that the regime is under no immediate danger of being replaced during the Arab Spring. While it is true that Jordan has experienced its fair share of protests and that even some of the traditional supporters of the regime joined in these protests, the divided nature of Jordanian politics and society seems to be an advantage for the regime's future.

First of all, one should keep in mind that at the center of the protests are demands regarding economic problems and political reforms. So far the opposition did not challenge the regime itself, but demanded that it is reformed to allow more freedoms and democracy. As long as the King is responsive to these demands and manages to find the resources needed to stabilize the Jordanian economy, there is no reason for people to challenge his rule.

Another advantage for the regime is the divided nature of the opposition. Salafist groups, for example, appear to be more extreme than the rest and organize their own protests. Moderate Islamists (such as the JMB) and leftists cooperate and are more peaceful and effective in attracting the government's attention. Despite their coalition, these groups have different plans for the country and share very few of each other's goals. For example, the JMB's insistence on the implementation of *shari'a* (Islamic law), a ban on the consumption of alcohol, and conservative dress standards are not acceptable to leftist groups. This means it could be possible for the regime to satisfy their common demands without giving up much.

There is also the issue of Palestinians, who are estimated to comprise 60 percent of the population, in addition to 1.2 million registered as refugees in a country of approximately 6 million people. The heavy Palestinian representation in the JMB/IAF creates worries among some groups "that if Palestinians are allowed greater role in the country's politics, they could drag it into the Israeli-Palestinian conflict against Jordan's best interests" (El-Shamayleh 2011).

Finally, there is likely to be international concern over the Hashemite dynasty being replaced by a new regime that is likely to be led by the Muslim Brotherhood. Following the experiences of Egypt and Syria where the Brotherhood chapters stand to gain most from regime change, Jordan's pro-Western role is more needed than ever. This may prompt various countries to give the King the economic support he needs in order to reduce dissent.

Overall it appears unlikely that the Hashemite regime will fall victim to opposition movements like many regimes in the region did. The long-term well-being of the regime rests on its ability to satisfy the opposition's demands in two areas. Politically, it will have to reduce the role of the King and change its political systems to allow more representation, which is something the regime showed some willingness to do. Economically, the regime will have to reduce unemployment, inflation, and poverty levels, which is something it does not appear to be capable of by itself. It appears, once again, the regime's survival will rely on a combination of domestic balancing and external support.

References

Al-Farawati, O. (2008). "Troubled Waters." *Al-Ahram Weekly Online* (883, February 7–13). Retrieved from <http://weekly.ahram.org.eg/2008/883/re8. htm>.

Al Jazeera. (2011, January 28). "Thousands protest in Jordan." Retrieved from <http://aljazeera.com/news/middleeast/2011/01/2011128125157509196. html>.

Al-Khazendar, S. (1997). *Jordan and the Palestine question: The role of Islamic and left forces in foreign policy-making.* Reading, UK: Ithaca Press.

Amr, W. (1990, January). "Do Fundamentalist Victories in Jordan Elections Threaten Liberalization?" Retrieved from <http://www.wrmea.com/ component/content/article/123/790-do-fundamentalist-victories-in-jordanian-elections-threaten-liberalization.html>.

Bar, S. (1998). *The Muslim Brotherhood in Jordan.* Tel Aviv: The Moshe Dayan Center for Middle Eastern and African Studies.

BBC (2011, June 13). "Jordan: Protesters lob stones at King Abdullah II." Retrieved from <http://www.bbc.co.uk/news/world-middle-east-13751299>.

Bill, J. and Springborg R. (2000). Politics in the Middle East. New York, NY: Longman.

Bronner, E. (2011). "Jordan Faces a Rising Tide of Unrest, but Few expect a Revolt." *New York Times*, February 4. Retrieved from <http://www.nytimes. com/2011/02/05/world/middleeast/05jordan.html?pagewanted=all>.

Brown, N.J. (2006). "Jordan and Its Islamic Movement: the Limits of Inclusion?" *Carnegie Papers: Middle East Series* (November). Washington, DC: Carnegie Endowment for International Peace.

Brynen, R. (1998). "The Politics of Monarchical Liberalism: Jordan." In B Korany et al. (eds), *Political Liberalization and Democratization in the Arab World: Volume 2 Comparative Experiences.* Boulder, CO: Lynne Rienner Publishers.

El-Shamayleh, N. (2011). "What lies beneath Jordanian calls for reform." *Al Jazeera English*, July 21. Retrieved from <http://blogs.aljazeera.net/middle-east/2011/07/21/what-lies-beneath-jordanian-calls-reform>.

Gavlak, D. (2011). "Jordan's King Abdullah vows to allow elected cabinets." *BBC*, June 12. Retrieved from <http://www.bbc.co.uk/news/world-middle-east-13744640>.

—— (2011). "Jordan searches for answers to Arab Spring demands." *BBC*, November 4. Retrieved from <http://www.bbc.co.uk/news/world-middle-east-15579864>.

Halaby, J. (2011). "Jordan's king fires Cabinet amid protests." *Arab News*, February 1. Retrieved from <http://www.aolnews.com/2011/02/01/jordans-king-sacks-government-in-wake-of-protests/>.

Hamzawy, A., and Bishara, D. (2006). "Islamist Movements in the Arab World and the 2006 Lebanon War." *Carnegie Papers: Middle East Series*. Washington, DC: Carnegie Endowment for International Peace.

Hazaimeh, H. (2010). "Over 1.25 million vote in 16th parliamentary election." *Jordan Times*, November 10. Retrieved from <http://www.jordanembassyus.org/new/newsarchive/2010/11102010002.htm>.

Kadri, R., and Bronner, E. (2011). "Jordan Protesters Set Up Camp in Amman." *New York Times*, March 24. Retrieved from <http://www.nytimes.com/2011/03/25/world/middleeast/25jordan.html>.

Lust-Okar, E. (2004). "Divided They Rule: The Management and Manipulation of Political Opposition." *Comparative Politics* 36(2): 159–79.

Milton-Edwards, B. (1993). "Façade Democracy and Jordan." *British Journal of Middle Eastern Studies* 20(2): 191–203.

—— and Hinchcliffe, P. (1999). "Abdullah's Jordan: New King, Old Problems." *Middle East Report* Winter 213: 28–31.

Ottaway, M., and Hamzawy, A. (2008). "Islamists in Politics: The Dynamics of Participation." *Carnegie Papers* 98 (November). Washington, DC: Carnegie Endowment for International Peace.

Robinson, G.E. (1998). "Defensive Democratization in Jordan." *International Journal of Middle East Studies*, 30(3): 387–410.

Rubin, B. (2007). "Comparing Three Muslim Brotherhoods: Syria, Jordan, Egypt." *The Middle East Review of International Relations* 11(2). Retrieved from <http://meria.idc.ac.il/journal/2007/issue2/jv11no2a8.html>.

Susser, A. (1999). "The Jordanian Monarchy: The Hashemite Success Story." In J. Kostiner (ed.), *Middle East Monarchies: The Challenges of Modernity*. Boulder, CO: Lynne Rienner Publishers.

Chapter 6

The Micro-foundations of Religious Party Moderation: Religious Party Supporters and Ideological Changes[1]

Sultan Tepe

Can democratic inclusion change religious parties despite their deep commitments to their religious doctrines? Is electoral competition a cure for the radicalism of religious parties, or do countries risk arresting their democratic processes by including religious parties into their electoral systems? In other words, does electoral competition temper the radicalism of religious parties, or induce them to adopt more extremist positions? Does the inclusion of religious parties in the electoral process strengthen or deplete democratic capital in general and that of the Middle East in particular, and how? As religious parties establish themselves as pivotal actors in a wide variety of countries from India to Japan, these questions have become critical to our understanding of party politics. Despite the increasing number of studies, two prevailing models have emerged to explain how religious parties affect their respective democracies. The first religious doctrine-centered framework rests on the presumption that religious parties' main loyalties are to their religious doctrine. Analyses in this genre ask whether the ideas and institutions endorsed in a given religious doctrine are compatible with democratic practices (for example, Tibi 1996, Kramer 1996) and suggest that religious parties' ideologies are often tenacious and not amenable to democratic changes. Such studies often contend that religious parties are likely to maintain their uncompromising positions informed by their respective religious doctrines, even when they accept the main rules of democracy. Allowing religious parties to participate in the electoral system, therefore, amounts to tolerating undemocratic parties for the sake of democracy and thereby endangers the very future of democracy.

While the insight of the first framework has influenced (or shaped) many analyses, an increasingly vocal second genre views religious parties as novel agents that forge a localized understanding of democracy. As a result, in this alternative approach, the inclusion of religious parties is crucial in producing a home-grown version of democratic principles and in opening up the constrained public sphere of

1   An early draft of this paper was presented at the "Moderation and Immoderation of Religious Political Parties in Democratic Politics Workshop," organized by Princeton University in Eichstätt, Germany (June 16–18, 2011).

these countries (for example, Kamil 2001, White 2002). Underlying this argument is the assumption that democracy takes root only once it grounds itself in local religious-cultural values. More importantly, all participants in a democracy, once they are engaged in electoral competition, one way or another change and come to accept not only the procedures but also the principles of democracy.[2] This highly popular argument, commonly called the "inclusion-moderation model," rests on the assertion that democratic bargaining and strategic actions induced by external actors and institutions, not ideological commitments, compel religious parties to become tamed agents of democracy.[3] Democracy can happen without democrats, and democratic ideologies are often not the main ingredient, but a byproduct of democratic electoral competitions.

A quick review of the literature on religious parties reveals that, among competing perspectives, the inclusion-moderation thesis has gained a significant analytical purchase over the last few years and guides the assessments of many researchers and practitioners (for example, Kalyvas 2000, Tezcur 2010, Somer 2011). Despite its increasing appeal, the inclusion-moderation approach falls short in many areas. For instance, the model privileges the transformative power of political context and negotiations among important political actors and thus implicitly treats moderation as an automatic or self-reinforcing process. Perhaps due to their deterministic structures, what is often glossed over in these accounts is the intricate nature of the very process of moderation and its mixed outcomes. Likewise, due to the inclusion-moderation thesis's emphasis on the party elite, one of the less studied aspects of religious party moderation has been the role of religious party constituencies. As such, the existing literature emphasizes the overall structure of the political system (for example, whether the religious parties are excluded or included in electoral competition) and party elite (for example, whether the elite are open to negotiations with other elite) (for example, Kalyvas 1996, Schwedler 2006, Browers 2009). Such studies assume that the elite either closely follow the positions of their party constituencies, or that both the elite and their constituents' positions are bounded by the injunctions of their religious doctrine, and thus are the same. In either case, the role of religious party supporters does not constitute an important component of their assessments.

In order to contribute to the debates on the vexing question of whether and how religious parties moderate their positions, this analysis brings to the fore the neglected actors of religious party literature: religious party supporters. It

---

2   Carrie Rosefsky Wickham's analysis of Islamist parties in Egypt, Jordan, and Kuwait offers one of the rare exceptions. For Wickham, "moderate" Islamists are simplified as those who accept the procedural elements of participating in elections without questioning their vision of what shape a future Islamic state might take. For more details, see Barsalou (2005). In another study that sheds light on the complexity of moderation, Stathis N. Kalyvas (1998) shows that democratic bargaining and strategic action—not ideological commitments—forced religious parties to become agents of democracy in Belgium.

3   For a critical review of the inclusion-moderation thesis, see Schwedler (2006).

seeks to offer one of the first systematic, empirically grounded accounts of the interaction between the religious party elite and their party constituencies. To this end, it explores one of the most drastic changes in two religious parties' positions in Turkey and Israel. As explained below, despite their distinct religious doctrines, religious parties have been shaping the political currents in Israel and Turkey's competitive electoral systems. Taking a closer look at Israel's Shas Party and Turkey's Justice and Development Party (JDP) and their increasingly pivotal role in their respective politics, the following discussion focuses on the crucial transformations where the parties drastically changed their positions. Such comparative assessment seeks to develop a thorough account of the micro-foundations of ideological and behavioral changes.

More specifically, in Israel's case, one of the country's most controversial and powerful religious parties, the Shas Party, and its party elite's support for the peace process constituted a drastic breakaway from the traditional ultra-orthodox parties' positions. Assessing such a shift enables us to question why and under what circumstances a religious party alters its political dicta. Turkey's Islamic parties' approval of EU membership, after a long period of staunch opposition, offers another excellent case to question if and how religious parties' supporters respond to such changes. The subsequent discussion of these unparalleled changes tries to place the religious constituencies within their country context as well as trace their reactions to the policy changes initiated by their respective party elite. What makes these shifts remarkable is that they do not only capture a simple policy change but also pose a major challenge to these parties' religious ideologies. Accordingly, the first section below introduces the case selection. The following two sections explain how Israel's Shas Party and Turkey's JDP altered their positions on two domestically and internationally salient issues—namely, the peace process and European Union membership. The final section offers an inductive model of the role of party constituency in religious party moderation. The discussions show that the changes to religious party ideologies are not the result of haphazard adjustments, nor are they inconsequential. Instead these changes occur under certain circumstances, particularly when first, the political context is conducive to political change (for example, the positive learning from an agreement); secondly, a new position can be justified through use of religious rationale without undermining the party ideology's internal consistency, and finally, religious party supporters acquiesce to, or sanction, the proposed change.

Religious Parties and Case Selection

Around two hundred books on the subject of religious parties can be found in the US Library of Congress. A closer look at these books indicates that more than 150 of these books were written after the mid-1990s. This remarkable increase in the publication of studies on religious parties is not an isolated trend. In fact, the spike reflects the increasing use of "religious party" and "moderation" in our daily political lexicon since the end of the Cold War. Notwithstanding the global pervasiveness of the terms, the existing studies on them often center their analyses solely on Islamic parties. Despite their remarkable successes, the increasing appeal of religious parties in non-Islamic contexts such as India, Japan, or Israel are classified as the unexpected rise of fringe parties. In the same vein, more often than not the existing arguments of religious parties draw on single case studies (for example, Willis 1995, Tugal 2009, Brownlee 2010). While the scarce attempts at comparative studies present very insightful findings, for the most part these studies focus on intra-faith comparison, such as comparing the policies of religious parties in Jordan, Yemen (for example, Schwedler 2006), Iran, or Turkey (say, Tezcur 2010), Egypt and Turkey (Gumuscu 2010). Likewise, moderation and extremism are seen as the only two modes of behavior of religious parties. Religious parties' acceptance of electoral rules and their conciliatory positions towards secular institutions are often taken as an indicator of their moderation. Such studies often fail to take into account that the changes to these parties' electoral strategies do not necessarily enable them to recognize, join, and negotiate with once-excluded political actors. More importantly, moderation is a *process* that can yield different results. For instance, Turkey's first wave of Islamist parties under the leadership of Necmeddin Erbakan adopted an increasingly confrontational language despite their full acceptance of electoral rules. Likewise, the Israeli Mafdal Party's initially moderate religious ideology has become less tolerant of religious ethnic difference.

Given the empirical and theoretical limitations of the studies on religious parties, this analysis offers a cross-religious comparison of parties that vie for political power in two different, competitive electoral systems, Israel and Turkey. While Israel and Turkey both have electoral systems that promote proportional representation, each follows different rules that result in different party configurations. The Israeli electoral system seeks to accommodate all political parties and factions in the parliament by setting a very low national threshold, namely 2 percent, for parliamentary representation. In Turkey, on the other hand, a threshold of 10 percent seeks to dissuade small parties and promotes political stability.[4] The relatively less restrictive law of political parties, combined with the exceptionally low national threshold, allows Israeli parties to cover a much wider ideological spectrum than their Turkish counterparts. Gaining entry to the Knesset requires approximately 25,138 votes which, in effect, enables any political association of a religious group to run as a party.[5] In contrast to Israel's "easy entrance policy," the Turkish electoral regime comes across as highly selective. The party competition in Turkey lacks the diversity of religious parties common in

---

4   In order to prevent the political instability that marked the 1970s, in 1983 the Turkish Parliament began requiring that parties win at least 10 percent of the total popular vote to gain seats in parliament.

5   The threshold was increased from 1 percent of the total popular vote to 1.5 percent in 1992, and to 2 percent in 2004.

the Israeli system because of its prohibition against parties that promote an ethnic and religious agenda (see Figure 6.1).

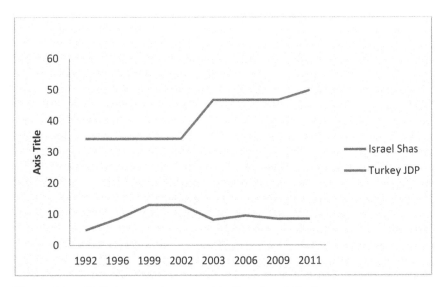

Figure 6.1   Religious party support in Israel and Turkey

What is paradoxical is that despite their different electoral rules, both the Israeli and the Turkish political systems are characterized by intense party competition. In the 2009 Israeli national election, 43 parties competed for about 4 million votes.[6] Regardless of the obstacles facing small parties and their constituencies in Turkey, a surprisingly high number of parties (a total of 19) were on the ballot in the 2011 national election. In both Israel's and Turkey's vibrant political spheres, the Shas Party and the Justice Development Party play a pivotal role. Since its entry into Israeli politics, Shas consistently maintained its power, while Turkey's Justice and Development Party has acquired unprecedented electoral success by gaining more than 47 percent of the votes in the 2011 elections. In Israel's political sphere, the Shas Party represents the orthodox, Sephardi community (that is, the Jewry of Middle Eastern, African and Asian backgrounds), and its ideology challenges not only secular but also religious parties and has become a prevalent topic for various research (Peled 1998, Yutchman-Yaar 2000). Likewise, Turkey's Justice and Development Party presents itself as that country's new conservative democratic party. It blends religious and liberal political ideas, and seeks to advance the rights of religious groups and shield them from state regulation (Tepe 2005, Onis 2007, Somer 2007, Yavuz 2010).

---

6   For a more detailed discussion of Israel's fragmented system, see Sandler and Mollov (2001).

Ideological Transformation of Religious Parties

The European Union and the Islamic Paradigm Shift in Turkey

In his 1980 parliamentary speech, the leader of both Turkey's Islamic movement and the first genre of Islamic parties, Necmeddin Erbakan described Turkey's efforts to be part of the European Custom Union as a blind step towards "willingly placing the national sovereignty in the hands of western countries." Erbakan was also the political mentor of the JDP's leader Tayyip Erdogan, depicted his anti-EU position as a form of spiritual and trade warfare. For Erbakan, joining the EU would mean allowing European countries to control Turkey's lands and businesses.[7] Erbakan's parliamentary speech in 1980 reflected the position of the Erbakan-led National View Party and the early position of JDP leader Erdogan, which contended that the Islamic world needs Turkish leadership to take advantage of its global position and awakening. Participating in the EU's political union, in Erbakan's view, would separate Turkey from the Islamic world and institutionalize its subordination to the West. Despite the ostensible negotiations between the EU and Turkey behind closed doors, Erbakan argued, the EU refused to seriously consider the Turkish application on the grounds that an Islamic country could not be a part of this Christian group. Given Turkey's exclusion, and its historical and religious capital, its efforts to form a union of Islamic countries with a common currency (the Islamic Dinnar) would be the real solution for Turkey's economic problems.[8]

Paradoxically, notwithstanding Turkey's first wave of political Islamic movements' unequivocal objections to the country's efforts to join the European Union in 2000, Erbakan declared the National View movement's wishes to revisit its stance on the EU. As the Erbakan-led movement found itself at a crossroads, the defection of a group of leaders led by Tayyip Recep Erdogan to form a new party resulted in the establishment of the country's first mass, pro-Islamic party: the Justice and Development Party. Despite Turkish Islamists' critical position on the EU, the JDP not only became a strong advocate of Turkey's candidacy bid, but also ensured that its policies would help the country to secure full membership in the EU. While this significant change in position occurred at the elite level, if and how these shifts were accepted by the broader party constituency and the constituents' reactions to such changes received scant attention. The public reactions to Turkey's quest for EU membership have often been studied in general terms to explore Turks' reactions to the prolonged membership bid (Carkoglu 2004, Senyuva 2009). However, understanding these responses requires a systematic review of the positions and reactions of the supporters of today's Prosperity Party, the most influential representative of Turkey's first wave of Islamists and the supporters of

---

    7   Necmeddin Erbakan, speech delivered at the Turkish Parliament on Foreign Policy, April 26 1980, Ankara.

    8   Necmeddin Erbakan, speech delivered at the Turkish Radio and Television, 1992.

the National Action Party that seeks to synthesize Turkish nationalism and Islam as well as the supporters of the Justice and Development Party.

A review of six major public opinion studies—including the 2001 and 2007 World Values Survey, the 2001 Trust Survey (conducted by Ali Carkoglu), the 2005 Turkey Religious Party Support Survey (conducted by the author), and the 1996 and 1999 surveys conducted by Turkey's Social Research Foundation— provides us with the empirical foundation to better understand how the pro-Islamic party supporters reacted to the political positions *vis-à-vis* the EU. In order to better trace the evolution (or development) of these changes, this section focus on three parties: the Prosperity Party, the National Action Party (NAP), and the JDP's supporters. The Prosperity Party currently represents the Erbakan-led National View movement. Although widely ignored by scholars, the National Action Party constitutes one of the most important political movements in Turkey, as it blends Turkish nationalism and Islam in its ideology into what can be called "Turkish Islamic Idealism." As explained above, the JDP was first formed as a splinter of the Erbakan-led National View movement, yet described its guiding principles as part of a brand new ideology: conservative democracy. A review of the general characteristics of these three groups of party supporters enable us to question how they positioned themselves *vis-à-vis* the EU membership bid issue and how they reacted to the changing elite position.

A quick review of the results shows that despite the Turkish political system's efforts to eliminate religious and ethnic fault-lines as the foundation of party competition, Turkey's pro-Islamic party constituency revealed distinctive characteristics and differed from other party supporters by their religious identification. For instance, the survey results from 2001—shortly *before* the JDP was established—indicate that Virtue Party supporters (the name of the party under Erbakan's leadership from 1998 and 2001) differed from the rest, as 98 percent of its supporters rated their religiosity as 5 or more (on a 0–10 religiosity scale), which exhibits a striking difference from the rest of the population (see Figure 6.2). This astonishingly high rate was followed by those of NAP's supporters: 95 percent rated their religiosity as 5 or more.

After the emergence of the Justice and Development Party, Turkey's pro-Islamic parties formed an increasingly fragmented block. The JDP became the preeminent pro-Islamic party, while the National Action Party maintained its presence as the country's *national* religious party. The Prosperity Party maintained its political presence, but witnessed a drastic decline in support. This fragmented picture poses the question of if and how these parties' supporters differed in their most commonly shared characteristic, that is, religiosity. According to the 2005 survey (see Figure 6.3), more than 50 percent of the Prosperity Party's supporters identified themselves as "very religious"—or observant of all of the requirements of Islam. Likewise, *all* of the party's supporters rated themselves 5 or higher on a 10-point scale, where 0 indicated "not religious" and 10 indicated "very religious." While 96 percent of the JDP's supporters and 86 percent of NAP's rated themselves 5 or more on a 0–10 religiosity scale, their self-identified religiosity spanned a

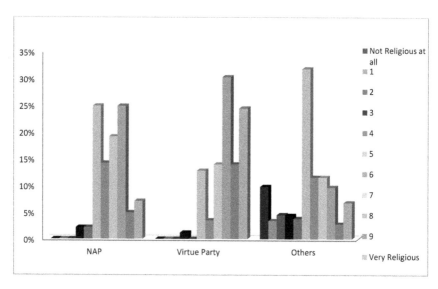

Figure 6.2   Self-identified religiosity, 2001

Source: The 2001 Trust Survey

broader spectrum, revealing a significant level of variation. The consistently high level of religiosity among the JDP constituency after 2001 suggests that although the JDP emerged as a brand new catch-all party, declaring itself a "conservative-democratic" party, it also managed to appeal to the values of the constituency of its predecessor, the Virtue Party. While the JDP supporters' profile is not drastically different from those of its predecessors and is exhibited mostly among those who identify themselves as observant, the religious terms in its national discourse have become highly muted.

Although the JDP appears to have inherited most of its predecessors' supporters, the party broke away from its predecessor's ideology in many ways. The JDP refrained from using overt Islamic references, and declared its full commitment to a range of liberal economic policies; yet it also promised to expand the government's role in social policies (Onis 2010). Attesting to these changes, shortly after the party came to power, the JDP leadership launched a massive campaign to secure a positive review of Turkey's application to EU candidacy. Given the common roots of the Prosperity and JDP parties, to what extent the JDP supporters embraced the party leaders' novel positions does not offer a straightforward answer. A comparison of survey results from 1999, 2001, 2005, and 2007 shows that the fragmentation of the pro-Islamic parties was echoed in the assessments of the religious party supporters. A review of the 2001 survey results shows that more than one-third (34 percent) of NAP's supporters and 42 percent of the Prosperity Party's supporters expressed strong mistrust in the EU. On a 0–10 scale, where 0 indicates "I do not trust at all" and 10 indicates "I trust completely,"

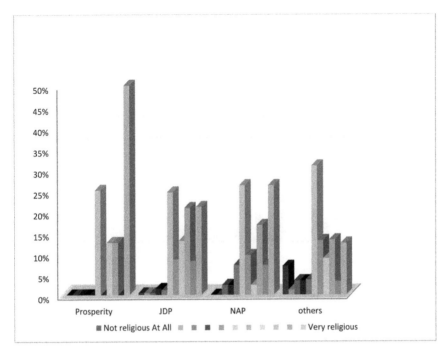

Figure 6.3   Self-identified religiosity, 2005

Sources: Tepe 2005 Religious Party Support Survey.

a majority of the Prosperity and the National Action parties' supporters rated their position as 0, 1, or 2 (see Figure 6.4).

Assessments of the public opinion surveys reveal that *after* the JDP elite officially committed themselves to pursue EU membership divisions within the broader community of religious party supporters widened. Erbakan-led Prosperity Party supporters expressed an overwhelming mistrust in the EU. With a drastic increase, 87 percent of the Prosperity supporters rated their trust as 0 on a 0–10 scale, where 0 signified "complete mistrust" and 10 signified "complete trust." What is striking is that 22 percent of the JDP supporters shared the Prosperity Party supporters' degree of mistrust and rated their position as one of extreme mistrust (with most rating their positions as 0, 1, or 2). Yet 32 percent rated their position as "highly trust" or "completely trust" (rating themselves as 8, 9, or 10 on the 0–10 scale, where 10 indicates complete trust), a rate higher than the supporters of other parties. Forty-one percent of NAP's supporters exhibited an extremely critical position and declared that the EU "cannot be trusted." Therefore, although Erbakan first revisited his position on the EU (perhaps due to the competition with the JDP), Erbakan's new position did not resonate with the National View Party supporters. Nevertheless, despite the JDP's newly adopted support for the EU, its supporters covered the entire spectrum of positions—from extreme mistrust to complete trust.

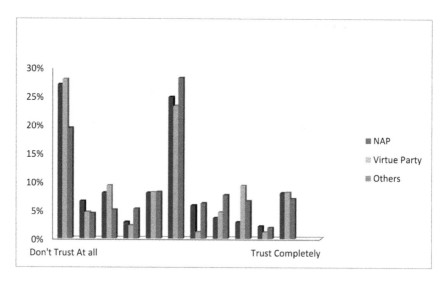

Figure 6.4   Trust in the EU, 2001

Source: The 2001 Trust Data.

It is important to note that after the successful adoption of the EU-required reforms in the early 2000s, Turkish public opinion in general became more critical of the EU, due to the delays in the full-membership negotiations. Despite this critical public stance, the survey results indicate that the JDP constituency's support of the EU remained at its highest level, along with the supporters of Turkey's Kurdish-based Democratic Society Party. Interestingly enough, the EU membership brought the JDP and Kurdish party constituencies together in their enthusiastic support for the EU's commitment to expand religious and ethnic rights in member countries (see Figure 6.5).

The trends cited above indicate that the shifts in the positions of the political elite do not translate into coherent ideological blocks and repositioning among the supporters. Perhaps due to the legacy of the Turkish Islamists' long-term opposition to the EU, one can find a rather fragmented picture among the pro-Islamic party supporters. The results show that the supporters of the Prosperity Party loyal to Turkey's first Islamic party's leader Erbakan did not change their positions on the EU, despite Erbakan's own more supportive position. In fact, not only did Erbakan become more supportive of the EU, he also petitioned the European Court of Human Rights (ECHR) to review Turkey's Constitutional Court's decision to close down his party, the Welfare Party. His appeal asserted that the decision violated the principle of freedom of expression and that the closure of political parties was anti-democratic. By bringing his case before a European court, Erbakan granted a de facto legitimacy to European institutions.

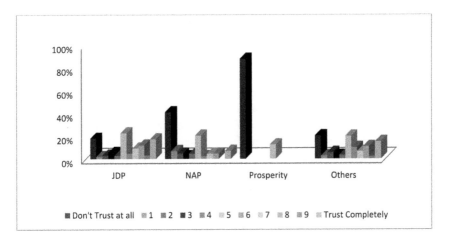

Figure 6.5   Trust in the EU, 2005

Source: The Tepe 2005 Religious Party Support Survey.

Notwithstanding such overt support, the Erbakan-led party supporters remained highly suspicious and critical of the EU.

In fact, the party leadership eventually toned down its sharp criticism and advanced a novel position, later adopted by the JDP and incorporated into its stance on the EU. In the words of Erbakan, the National View Party's positions *vis-à-vis* the EU had been consistent and had not changed. As such, for Erbakan, "It is not the party but the Union that altered its position."[9] In contrast to its initial adversarial perspective, the EU came to recognize the futility of its approach and corrected its course: "The Union now offers a new framework where human rights, multiculturalism and free competition are promoted thus it no longer contradicts the party's positions" (Erbakan 1999).[10]

As discussed in more detail below, Erbakan's new position followed the experience of the Custom Union where the National View Party supporters became the main beneficiaries of trade policies. Despite the presence of such a conducive political-economic environment, it is important to note that the supporters are often exposed to more complex and sometimes dual discourses than outside observers. As such, in spite of his increasing support, Erbakan's support to the EU came with many caveats. For instance, he remained critical of the EU's excessive use of its political power to subdue Turkey's own policies. Thus the Prosperity Party supporters' critical position *vis-à-vis* the EU can be seen as a reaction to the leadership's dual messages. However, taking the Erbakan-initiated new perspective on the EU to a new level,

---

9   Necmeddin Erbakan, "Why did we oppose the European Union and why we support it now?" speech delivered at TEKDER association, Saadet Partisi: Istanbul, 1999
10   Ibid.

the JDP addressed the EU in its party program, thus adopting a clear position. The party's program states that the party will maintain and advance its relationship with the EU for the sake of Turkey's economic and national interests.[11] The party program cites specific policies such as the protection of savings accounts and the introduction of new initiatives to adopt EU standards to prevent corruption. In line with its initial anti-corruption policy, the party also promises to join the European Council's Union of States Against Corruption. The issue of EU membership is also mentioned briefly in the "Foreign Relations" section, along with other regional cooperative efforts. Thus, while Erbakan's discourse on the EU blended cultural, political, and economic arguments, and had many caveats, the JDP adopted a clear social-utilitarian approach and explained its support of the EU as a means of advancing its political agenda of economic liberalism and of limiting state involvement in cultural and religious affairs.

Perhaps due to the JDP's utilitarian approach, a closer look at these public opinion surveys clearly shows that, despite their initial rejection of the EU, the JDP supporters' positions exhibit a more multifaceted picture. It is possible to attribute the reasons behind such change to a range of factors, such as the JDP's ability to form ad hoc election coalitions, thus promoting the party's ability to attract people from various ideological stances. One open-ended question in the 2005 questionnaire allows us to review how the JDP's supporters explain their own position on the EU and their rationale in their own terms. In fact, the findings of the 2005 survey shows that the pro-Islamic party respondents positions form a collage of new and resilient positions. For instance, the supporters of the Prosperity Party closely cluster around a religiously grounded rejectionist position. In many of the open-ended answers to the survey, the Prosperity Party supporters share the belief that "The EU's real intention is to exploit Turkey," and "Even though the membership benefits the country economically it will exploit the country culturally." The NAP supporters, on the other hand, state that "the EU in essence is a coalition of Christian countries and thus has no real intention to include Turkey"; as a result, "the EU-required policies disadvantage the citizens and weaken Islam."

Likewise, despite the JDP's support of the EU, Erbakan's initial position continues to resonate with some of the party supporters as they state "the EU is an inherently anti-Islamic organization and thus is likely to corrode Turkish culture." Nevertheless, a majority of the JDP supporters state that "the EU will open up new investment areas and thus help to alleviate unemployment," "provide the citizens with the rights to free passage in the union," "will increase Turkey's trade capacity," and "the cultural sacrifices will be surpassed from the benefits to our children." Perhaps one of the most interesting rationales offered by the JDP's supporters is that "the EU negotiations are carried out by trusted people and thus the process and outcome also need to be supported." Such explanations indicate that the JDP leadership has been successful in shaping their supporters' positions. Nevertheless, the JDP supporters do not lend a uniform support to the party's

---

11   The Justice and Development Party Program, Ankara, 2002.

policies. Yet the party supporters' increasing confidence in the EU, despite the declining trust of other parties, show that the JDP supporters increasingly rally round their leadership's positions. Increasing bifurcation among the Prosperity Party and the JDP supporters' positions also indicate that the religious party supporters' views can be rather tenacious.

Intransigent Peace and the Sephardi-Haredi Perspective Change in Israel

In Israel's multidimensional electoral arena, where more than forty parties vie for political power, it is not easy to categorize parties. However, as indicated by Gideon Doron, "the only dimension where significant differences between Left and Right really exist is the orientation toward various aspects of the Israeli–Palestinian conflict" (Doron 2005). That is, the left is more willing to make territorial concessions, while the right holds a more rigid and mistrusting position toward the intentions of the Arabs. In fact, conventionally, the right-wing parties opposed the peace negotiations that involved territorial concessions, while the left-leaning parties appeared more open to "land for peace" formulae. Israel's ultra-orthodox parties defy these fault-lines, as their theological positions did not allow them to grant legitimacy to the Israeli state and subsequently to its negotiations. According to Israel's ultra-orthodox parties (for example, Agudat Israel and Ha Degel Torah), the Jewish state's reestablishment is a divine promise, not a human project, thus the current Israeli state which is the outcome of man-made Zionist ideology cannot be recognized. Therefore, due to their theological positions, Israel's ultra-orthodox parties remained silent on the political negotiations of the Israeli state, including negotiations on the peace process.

The Shas Party entered the Israeli political scene as an off-shoot of Agudat Israel, the country's most ultra-orthodox party. Agudat Israel's main motto— "restoring the crown to its old place"—meant both the reestablishment of the Sephardi groups' lost glory, and the expansion of the Torah community (Lehmann and Siebzehner 2006). Given its roots, many people expected the party to remain within the orthodox tradition and not take a position on the peace process, or oppose a "land for peace" formula. This lies in contrast to the expectations on which the Shas Party based its policies, that is, on its spiritual leader Ovadia Yosef's interpretation of *Pikuach Nefesh*—the principle that privileges the protection of Jewish life over the protection of land. Given the rather stringent fault-lines among different ideological blocs, the Shas Party's position was meant to endorse "land for peace" formulae. This endorsement of territorial compromises in return for peace has been one of the most revolutionary positions taken by an Israeli religious party. For many, this shift indicated that the party wanted to fashion itself as a coalition partner to the left-wing, pro-peace parties. Therefore, for many observers, the party's position on the territories was merely strategic and paradoxically anti-religious. For others, the Sephardic religious tradition is not territorial but community centered, thus such concessions do not affect the party supporters' beliefs. Regardless of the Shas Party's reasons for endorsing the territorial compromises, this change in position unsettled Israel's political landscape. The Shas Party's acceptance of territorial compromises, even though it was stated as a contingent commitment, pits the Shas Party elite against the Nationalist Religious Party elite, who fiercely opposed any territorial concessions and any restriction in the expansion of settlements. What has been missing in these discussions and observations is an assessment of whether or not the party supporters—beyond the elite leadership—endorsed such change or if such policy change alienated some of the party's constituency.

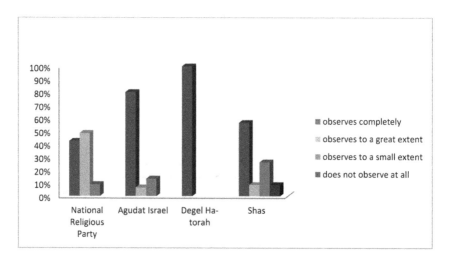

Figure 6.6   Self-identified religiosity, 1992

Source: The 1992 Israel National Elections Data.

An assessment of the reaction of the Shas Party's supporters to the party's religiously controversial position first requires a brief description of the party supporters' overall religious standing. Despite Shas's popular image as an ultra-religious party, the personal identification of the party supporters consistently shows that the party attracted voters from a diverse cross-section of the religious public.

As the above self-identifications indicate, since the rise of religious parties in Israel, supporters of these parties were not comprised solely of individuals that completely observe Jewish tradition and Halachic law. Instead, perhaps due to its strong nationalist appeal, Mafdal attracts supporters with differing degrees of religiosity. Likewise, contrary to its designation as "ultra-orthodox"—perhaps due to its ethnic appeal and lenient positions on religious issues—Shas attracts supporters from among different religious views: 58.8 percent of the supporters identify themselves as thoroughly observant of Jewish tradition, yet 17.6 percent report their observation as limited or absent. A closer look at the religiosity of Israel's parties indicate that, just like their Turkish counterparts—with the

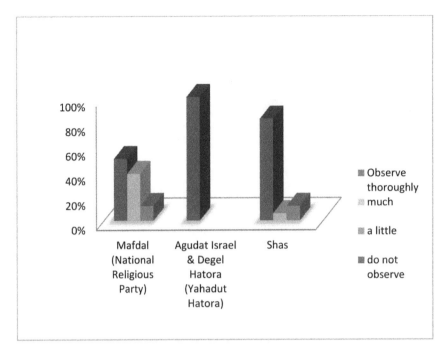

Figure 6.7   Self-identified religiosity, 1996

Source: The 1996 Israel National Elections Data.

exception of the supporters of Yahadut Hatora—religious party supporters exhibit surprisingly different degrees of religiosity, which elicit a broad range of reactions to the changes introduced by the party leadership (see Figures 6.6–8).

It is important to note that, as explained in detail below, Shas's position on "land for peace" hinges on the condition that such concessions would result in the preservation of Jewish life (see Figure 6.9). Perhaps in part because of the party's nuanced position, when Shas supporters are given the broad question of whether territories should be returned in exchange for peace, their reactions varied. However, within the religious bloc, Shas's supporters appear to be the most willing in accepting such traditionally religiously challenged compromises among other religious party constituencies.

The variations in religiosity and practices among Shas's supporters thus pose the question of what instigates these individuals to support the party. When this question was directly addressed to respondents in the 1992 Israeli election survey, the results show that the party's specific issue positions are not the main reasons why some Israelis support Shas. While Mafdal supporters draw on the party's potential to be a part of government, none of the Shas supporters report this as the main reason for supporting the party. Mafdal supporters' overall identification with the party and its *ideology* appear to be the most important determinant of those who support the party.

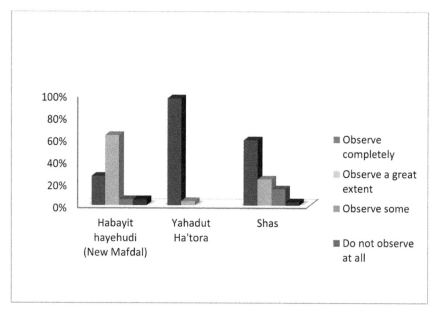

Figure 6.8   Self-identified religiosity, 2009

Source: The 2009 Israeli National Election Data.

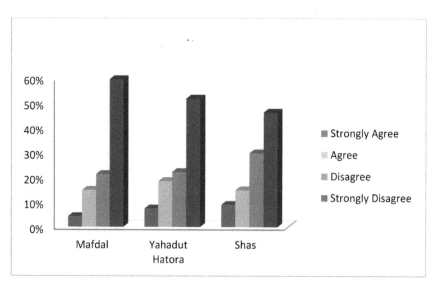

Figure 6.9   Territory for peace, 2006

Source: The 2006 Israeli National Election Data.

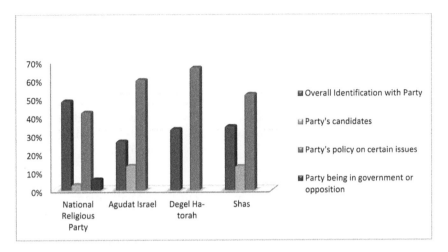

Figure 6.10   Reason to vote, 1992

Source: 1992 Israel National Election Survey.

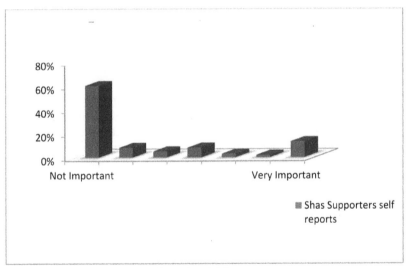

Figure 6.11   Shas support and territorial issues

Source: Tepe, 2003 Shas Survey.

More than one-third of Shas supporters report that they endorse the party due to their overall identification with the party. Despite the strong pull of the party's overall profile (35 percent), it is the specific issue positions that affect the support of around 50 percent of Shas supporters (see Figure 6.10).

The importance of the party's issue position poses the question of whether the party's position on the territories is one of the main reasons why constituents turn to (or away from) the party. In fact, many accounts of the Shas Party assert that the party's elite positions are detached from the party's popular base, and that the party supporters are more hawkish than their own leadership (Willis 1998). Despite these popular accounts, according to party constituents' own assessments, the party's position on the peace process is not a defining factor. In fact, 60.2 percent of Shas supporters do not deem the issue as critical to their endorsement of the party. These findings suggest that the leadership's drastic move did not have electoral repercussions. Instead, the supporters' views were and remain diverse enough to accommodate such a policy change (see Figure 6.11).

Modeling the Role of Constituency in Religious Party Moderation

The studies of religious party moderation often neglect the role of religious party supporters and treat them as a homogenous block of ideological voters. Although religious party supporters' political decisions and the mechanisms through which they are made form a complex structure, religious partisans are often depicted as political actors who seek to increase the role of religion in the public sphere at any political cost. However, the relationship between the religious party constituency and the party elite in general, and the ideological articulations of party leadership and the responses of the electorate in specific, form a rather dynamic relational matrix. In order to better assess the role of religious party supporters in their parties' transformations, it is important to note that party support and party relations are shaped by a range of political and religious factors. Many of these factors take a unique form in their respective polities and need to be approached as such. For instance, although party supporters' donations and active participation in primaries play an important role in many countries, a different relationship exists between political parties and their members in countries where the public financing of political parties and primaries is rare. In the Israeli system, all parties are supported by state funds and enjoy free access to media outlets for electoral campaigning. Likewise, in Turkey, political parties also derive their main income from public funds. The level of funding is based on the proportion of votes the party obtained in previous elections; this system favors large and influential parties over smaller ones. In contrast to political parties facing different constraints, religious parties in Israel and Turkey are not directly financially dependent on their members for financing elections.

Although many depictions of religious parties present their supporters as a captive audience, or as homogeneous, a closer review of the popular bases of religious parties reveal that these parties often attract people with various orientations. Even on the spectrum of religiosity, one of the core characteristics of the religious party supporters, religious partisans span a wide spectrum. These variant positions suggest that the religious party elite's relation to their constituency is not monolithic. Therefore the common arguments that assert religious parties are completely (in)dependent from their supporters may offer conclusions that are highly misleading. As exemplified in the case of Turkey's JDP and Israel's Shas Party, religious parties tend to have large memberships. They rely on the labor and capital contributions of their members to provide for the parties' labor-intensive educational and social service networks and door-to-door election campaigns. Despite their critical role in sustaining the party organizations, party members are often given only a limited or symbolic role in the party organization, particularly in decision making and ideological repositioning. While their specific organizational forms may vary, religious parties in general maintain rather hierarchical party organizations wherein a small number of leaders decide on the parties' electoral candidates and policies. For instance, in Israel, the Shas Party's decision-making body, the Council of Torah Sages, hand picks the party's candidates for local and parliamentary elections. As exemplified by the recent formal dismissal of a Shas Party member of the Knesset, Chaim Amsellem, the party leadership can and often does oust dissidents (Mandel 2010).

Despite the strong control of the party elite, religious parties have been very successful in building a large intermediary leadership and nationwide membership. Nevertheless, these intermediary levels of leadership that tie local interests to the party organizations and larger memberships do not translate into members' direct and greater influence on party decisions. As such, although Turkey's JDP membership currently exceeds 4 million (10 percent of the existing electorate), a limited number of delegates (1,345) selects the party chairman. Attesting to the charismatic nature of religious party leadership, the JDP's leader was reelected twice, securing 1,342 votes out of a total of 1,343 delegates whose selection is closely screened by the party leadership.[12] Although some parties, like the Mafdal in Israel and the NAP in Turkey, differ from others with their competitive internal elections, such elections have a limited impact in promoting internal democracy. While such elections allow for leadership change, the factions that lose dominance within the party often form a new party and leave the elected leadership with full control of the party's agenda.

However, it is also important to note that religious party supporters punish or reward the changes in their parties' position at the voting booth. For example, in Israel, due to the un-conciliatory position of Mafdal, the level of defection of its supporters reached such a level that the party became a small faction of today's Jewish Home Party. In contrast, the Shas Party's conciliatory position (regardless of sporadic exclusivist remarks), allowed the party to maintain its political base in Israel's highly volatile system. Such dynamic relations between the religious party's elite and supporters indicate that simplistic deductive accounts—which assert that as political parties grow the membership exerts more influence in shaping the parties' policies and compels parties to endorse more moderate policies—do not hold. Yet on the other hand, the party supporters review and react to their parties' issue positions and not all the changes allow religious parties to

---

12   "JDP's Party Congress," *Haber Vitrini*, November 12, 2006 and *Sabah*, October 3, 2009.

expand their popular base. In other words, religious parties cannot randomly adopt politically expedient positions and expect the approval of their supporters. Any change needs to meet some important criteria such as the presence of conducive political context, as well as clearly -substantiated religious justification. Therefore, ironically, due to the lack of internal democracy and the importance of grass-roots supporters for these parties' electoral fortunes, the success of religious parties hinges on the leaderships' ability to present positions and policies that ensure their members' loyalty by maintaining the coherence of their ideologies, promoting the role of religion and sustaining their national, social, and religious networks. These multiple demands amount to a dynamic framework for religious parties' decisions; their ideology and the electoral support of their followers play a critical role in defining the direction and outcome of party changes and moderation.

Although the religious party literature focuses on the role of religious party supporters in the party organization, it is the party's overall ideology and consistency in issue positions that play a key role in defining the relationships between the religious party supporters and the party elite (Browers 2009). As the above examples illustrate, the (dis)approval of changes of party ideologies plays a pivotal role in shaping the *presence*, *scope* and *direction* of the party's overall transformation. Had Shas not supported the territorial concessions, and if such a shift was punished by its electorate, the historic coalition between Labor and Shas in 1999 would have not occurred and Shas would have not maintained its support. Likewise, had the JDP not adopted an EU-friendly approach and had such a position not been endorsed by the Islamic circles, hundreds of Turkey's political and administrative reforms would have not been adopted. However, as indicated above, changes to the religious party ideologies are not the result of haphazard adjustments, nor are they inconsequential. Instead these changes occur under certain circumstances, particularly when (i) religious parties view their political context as conducive to change, and (ii) party leaders are able to justify the party's position through the use of religious rationale without undermining the party ideology's internal consistency.

Conducive political contexts can exist due to the specific structure of electoral competition—for example, Israel's competitive system that often makes large, influential parties rely on small parties to form coalitions and endow them with extensive political benefits—or due to the presence of new ideological positions that promise policy-related and electoral advances and can be accommodated within the party-endorsed religious framework. The lack of internal party democracy thus relegates party members and other supporters to an indirect yet critical role and as such they often punish their parties at the polls if the parties do not offer ideologically consistent positions and deliver on their policy promises. Therefore religious parties' ideological change involves delicate calculations while the viability of such changes ultimately depends on the party leadership's capacity to present new positions in a religiously acceptable and consistent way.

To better analyze the examples discussed in the first section, it is important to note that changes in party positions are not a result of swift, politically convenient decisions. Neither do such changes always amount to ideological moderation. Ultimately, the endorsement of territorial compromises by the Shas Party in Israel rests on some critical elements: although Shas's position on the territories became popular in the 1990s, the party leadership also upheld a similar principle in the late 1970s. The party's overtly open stance on the acceptability of territorial compromise occurred within the conducive context of coalition building with left-leaning parties. Despite the other sectarian religious parties' rejection of such compromise, Shas's position also introduced an elaborate religious justification and presented its stance not as an absolute but as a religiously rooted yet contingent position. Given Yosef's prior use of the same principal, the new policy position was not seen as a politically expedient adjustment. As such, the Shas Party's position on the territories draws on its spiritual leader Rabbi Ovaida Yosef's Halachic ruling. According to Yosef, the Halachic principle of *Pikuach Nefesh* ("saving lives") holds primacy over other commitments (except murder, idolatry, and adultery). In other words, the principle of *Pikuach Nefesh states* that saving lives needs to be given priority over other commandments, such as the settling of the land of Israel. As a result, the Shas Party does not categorically dismiss any agreement that includes territorial compromise, as one is permitted, or even obligated, to make such sacrifices if they act to protect members of the Jewish community.

As the above analysis shows, Shas supporters are receptive to such messages for many reasons. As their own self-assessments indicate, Shas supporters do not come strictly from the religious bloc. Instead, the party appeals to a small number of secular and a large group of religiously traditional individuals who observe Jewish traditions selectively. This uniquely broad support base for an "ultra-orthodox party," as well as the unparalleled ability of Shas's spiritual leader Ovadia Yosef to justify unconventional decisions within the Halachic tradition, distinguished the party within the religious bloc. One can also argue that the adoption of such conciliatory positions also allows the party to attract religious constituencies who endorse less hawkish positions *vis-à-vis* peace negotiations. What made the decision highly effective is that, although it equipped the party with more political power (for example, enabling it to form a coalition with the left-leaning parties), the issue did not raise great objections among the party supporters. In fact, with their mixed levels of religiosity, followers of Shas did not contest the rabbinical rulings but actually welcomed the capacity of the ruling to afford a broader ideological area for the party to navigate.

Given that in general the question of territories is not one of the most critical issues to the party's supporters, the leadership's ideological opening was not especially politically costly. Instead, increasingly strong identification with the party and the importance given to the Shas Party's spiritual leadership suggests that the party elite had the unique ability to adopt new positions. Given the conditional nature of *Pikuach Nefesh*, the party leadership had to clarify its position in the face of newly emerging territorial questions. For instance, the leadership opposed the Gaza disengagement of 2005 on the grounds that the engagement did not pass the test of protecting the Jewish lives. The unilateral disengagement, for Shas's leadership, lacked commitment from the Palestinian authorities. Yet the leadership also opposed the call for a referendum to decide on the status of Gaza. The party decided that such a vote would be very divisive and would undermine the Jewish community. The application of such innovative decisions with Halachic justifications allows the party to maintain its electoral success and helps the leaders to reach out to new supporters, especially from traditional, religiously conservative groups.[13]

It is important to note that Mafdal, the national religious party, opposed the use of *Pikuach Nefesh* by Shas in defining its positions on the territories. As a result, the ideological transformation of the NRP included a drastic ideological shift towards a less moderate ideological position as territorial questions dominated the government's agenda. The political questions posed by the changing political environment led to the adoption of a set of new ideological positions that increasingly emphasized the sacredness of territories, thereby refusing to recognize any actors that endorse territorial compromises. Therefore, it is not surprising that the 2003 survey shows that Shas attracts supporters from Mafdal as well as Likud, the center-right party.

As explained in the above review, the way in which Turkey's National View Party altered their position on the question of European Union membership offers another heuristic venue to understand the role of religious party constituency in the transformation of religious party positions, and how some changes open the door to ideological moderation. As widely reported by the leadership's statements, the National View Party originally refused to support Turkey's bid to join the European Union, describing it as "a Christian club" that sought to dominate Turkey's market, and declaring it a deceitful agent with which to negotiate. Yet in the late 1990s, Erbakan drew attention to the EU's efforts to enhance multiculturalism and human rights. Within the framework of this new discourse, the National View Party would be compelled to negotiate more rights for Islam.

Similar ideological articulations delivered by the party's leadership shows how the party attributes its change to the European Union's own transformation. Such accounts contend that the EU has evolved from an exclusively "Christian club" with the desire to dominate other countries' economic markets to one "that recognizes the importance of [the National View Party's religious core values] of serving humans, multiculturalism and coexistence." (Erbakan, 1999; for an extensive discussion of such transformation, see Duran 2006). Only such shifts, the leadership argued, enabled the party to evoke the Islamic principle that "the believers should negotiate with all parties when such negotiation promotes the well-being of the larger community" (ibid.). A review of the JDP's political messages show that the party built its pro-EU position on Erbakan's discourse. In his 2004 speech, Erdogan argued that Turkey's

---

13   "Traditional" is a term used in Israeli politics to distinguish very orthodox religious publics, who observe all religious rules, from religious groups who selectively observe religion.

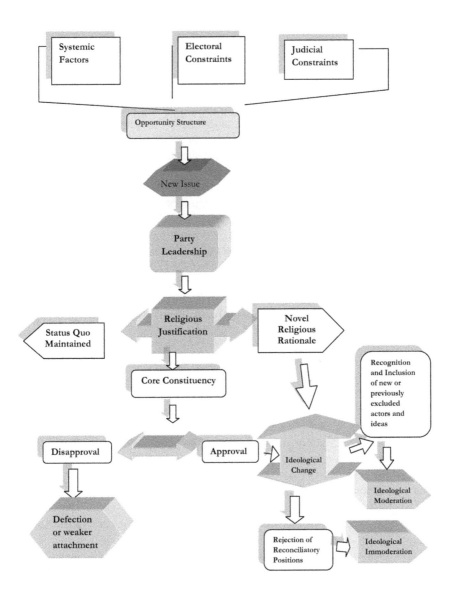

Figure 6.12 A party supporter-based model of ideological moderation

membership will be the main test for the EU's global aspirations: "If the EU seeks to represent three religious traditions to complete its vision then Turkey needs to be there to fulfill this aspiration. Otherwise excluding Turkey will undermine the EU's meaning and depth."[14]

---

14   Recep Tayyip Erdogan, party address, *Yenisafak*, May 5, 2004.

When placed within the broad perspective of its opportunity structure, the changes to the Prosperity Party and later the JDP's adoption of a new pro-EU position occurred within the conducive political environment marked, *inter alia*, by (i) the parties' flourishing political fortunes among Turkish immigrants living in EU countries, (ii) the parties' establishment of themselves s a viable force capable of controlling Parliament following the Welfare Party's remarkable success in the 1994 local elections, and (iii) the results of policy implementations that confirmed participating in the European Custom Union of 1996 would not undermine but rather benefit small and state-independent, private entrepreneurs, which constitute one of the core support groups of religious parties in Turkey. Nonetheless, *only after* the party leadership had carefully justified the change ideologically did the Prosperity Party and later the JDP alter their rejectionist policies, and start to treat the EU as a credible actor and its policies as religiously acceptable.

Although the JDP successfully justified its position on the EU, the party's attempt to make adultery a punishable crime illustrated a different process. Breaching their differences, both the JDP and the Prosperity Party leaders contended that the issue was a cultural and religious issue that needed to be accommodated within the EU's multicultural, multi-religious society.[15] The leadership argued that the law was not only rooted in an Islamic norm, but it would also advance the position of women by making adultery a crime based on official complaints. Although the leadership argued that the law intended to protect family values and protect women from deception, according to many women's groups the existing adultery law was used disproportionately against women; the proposed criminalization of adultery would encourage "honor killings" and force women to lose custody of their children, only exacerbating already poor treatment of women in the courts. Despite the party leadership's unified position on the issue, a strong reaction from non-governmental organizations forced the party to withdraw its proposal and make a commitment not to reintroduce it. Likewise the Shas Party quickly corrected the leadership's call not to negotiate with the Arabs and use force only when its supporters and the international community condemned such remarks and calls for such policies.

When the role of party supporters' positions is taken into account, a rather complex process of moderation emerges (see Figure 6.12 above).

Ideological changes occur when the context is conducive—that is, the religious party supporters seem receptive, the political payoffs are significant, and religious justification is not tenuous. It is important to note that the propitious environment per se cannot instigate a new position or lead to an ideological transformation. For instance, national religious parties in Israel and Turkey demonstrate that, despite their electorally advantageous positions, neither party sought to fully accommodate the demands of religiously unorthodox groups within their policies. Nevertheless, a political setting conducive to position change (for example, the opportunity to form coalitions to address ethnic and religious demands) serves as *a*

---

15   *Yenisafak*, September 8, 2004.

necessary condition to instigate a policy change. Not all of the policy changes led to moderation or inclusive views. In both countries, while both parties successfully recognized the main institutions and agents of their polity as credible political actors, the emergence of new issues that challenged the national and territorial integrity (that is, the question of expansion of territories in the contested areas in Israel and the demands of ethnic Kurds in Turkey) led to their increasingly exclusionary views. In other words, the emergence of new issues that would have led these parties to renew their positions and/or recognize and negotiate with new actors instead reinforced the leaderships' strict commitment to religious-ethnically exclusive views. Such changes in the Israeli case led to the disintegration of Mafdal. As a result, although a changing context might instigate an ideological change, it does not determine the nature of the change.

Subsequent revisions in response to newly emerging questions or new opportunity structures rest on the ability of religious parties to adopt novel ideological positions and successfully respond to reactions of party supporters. Had Ovadia Yosef not evoked the principle of *Pikuach Nefesh*, Shas's support for territorial compromises would have lacked religious legitimacy. Likewise, in Turkey, Erbakan's ability to relate its changing approach to the EU with the Quranic principle that "the believers should negotiate with all parties when such negotiation promotes the well-being of the larger community" appealed to those who contend that the political arena should be guided by Quranic principles.[16] Without the justification offered by Erbakan, the JDP's policies would have lacked much-needed Islamic credibility.

The ideological changes that are not endorsed by the party supporters cannot be sustained. Successful changes confirm the importance of the composition of the party supporters, as well as the presence of a critical mass who will be open to the party elite's new messages. The soundness of the religious justification, the consistency of the political message, and the religious positions of the supporters determine whether the changes in ideological positions will be embraced in the long term. As the drastic changes in the Shas Party's and JDP's positions indicate, religious parties' ideologies are more amenable to changes than the existing literature suggest. However, such changes do not occur as a response to the demands of main political actors. Instead, such changes are a result of the interactions of the views of the party elite, the dictums of religious ideologies, and the expectations of religious party constituencies. Continuous exclusion of some actors and views (for example, Russian immigrants in Israel, and Alevis in Turkey) indicates that the policy changes appear most intractable when constituencies refuse to recognize the positions that challenge the religious doctrine from within (for example, accepting the religious practices of ultra-orthodox Alevis or reform groups). Albeit it is also in these same issue areas that the ability of religious parties to develop more inclusive positions presents a promising venue in which these parties can help expand their countries' respective democracies.

---

16   Ibid.

References

Adams, James et al. 2006. "Are Niche Parties Fundamentally Different?" *American Journal of Political Science* 50(3).

Adly, Amr 2010. "Unorthodox Liberalism, Democracy, and Post-Liberal Distributional Coalitions." *Turkish Studies* 11(2).

Akbulut, Olgun and Usal, Zeynep. 2008. "Parental Religious Rights." *International Journal on Minority Rights* 15(4).

Arat, Yesim, 2010. "Religion, Politics, and Gender Equality in Turkey" *Third World Quarterly* 31(6): 869-884.

Arian, A. 2005. *Politics in Israel: Second Republic*. Washington, DC: Congressional Quarterly Press.

Arikan, B. and Cinar, A. 2002. "The Nationalist Action Party." *Turkish Studies* 3(1).

Ayan, Pelin. 2010. "Authoritarian Party Structures in Turkey." *Turkish Studies* 11(2).

Bardakoglu, A. 2004. "The Structure of the Directorate of Religious Affairs." *Turkish Policy Quarterly* 1(4).

Barsalou, J. 2005. "Islamists at the Ballot Box." *US Institute of Peace, Special Report 144* July.

Bendor, A. 1997. "Are There Any Limits to Justiciability?" *Indiana International & Comparative Law Review* 7(1).

Bick, E. 2004. "A Party in Decline: Shas in Israel's 2003 Elections." *Israel Affairs* 10(4).

Blondel, Jean. 1968. *"Party Systems and Patterns of Government,"* *Canadian Journal of Political Science*, vol.1.

Browers, Michaelle L., *Political Ideology in the Arab world: Accommodation and Transformation*, New York: Cambridge University Press, 2009

Brownlee Jason, 2010 "Unrequited Moderation: Credible Commitments and State Repression in Egypt." *Studies in Comparative International Development* December.

Brumberg, D. 2001. "Dissonant Politics in Iran and Indonesia." *Political Science Quarterly* 116(3).

Bugra, A. 2010. "Conservatives and Women." *Radikal* November 14.

Bunce, Valerie and Wolchik, Sharon. 2009. "Getting Real About 'Real Causes.'" *Journal of Democracy* 20(1).

Carkoglu, Ali. 2004. "Societal Perceptions of Turkey's EU Membership: Causes and consequences of Support for EU Membership." In Mehmet Ugur ve Nergis Canefe (ed.), *Turkey and European Integration*, London and New York: Routledge.

Cohen, A. and Susser, B. 2000. *Israel and the Politics of Jewish Identity*. Baltimore, MD: Johns Hopkins University Press.

Collier, D. and Adcock, R. 1999. "Democracy and Dichotomies." *Annual Review of Political Science* 2.

Demiralp, Seda. 2009. "The Rise of Islamic Capital." *Journal of Comparative Politics* 41(2).

Demker, Marie. 1997. "Changing Party Ideology." *Party Politics* 3(3).

Diamond, L. 2002. "Thinking about Hybrid Regimes." *Journal of Democracy* 13(2).

Don-Yehiya, E. 2000. "Conflict Management of Religious Issues." In Hazan, R.Y. (ed.), *Parties, Elections and Cleavages.* London: Frank Cass.

Doron, Gideon. 2005. "Right as Opposed to Wrong as Opposed to Left: The Spatial Location of 'Right Parties' on the Israeli Political Map." *Israel Studies* (10)3.

Duran, Burhanettin. 2006. "JDP and Foreign Policy as an Agent of Transformation." In Hakan Yavuz (ed.), *The Emergence of A New Turkey* Salt Lake City: University of Utah Press, 2006.

Erbakan, Necmeddin. 1999. "Why Did We Oppose the European Union and Why We Support It Now?" speech delivered at TEKDER association, Saadet Partisi, Istanbul.

Esengun, L. 2000, June. Interview. Istanbul, the author.

Fredrika Shavit v. *Rishon Lezion Jewish Burial Society.* 1999. Higher Court Decision 6024/97. 6,7.

The Grand Unity Party Program. 1993. Accessed September 6, 2010 <www.bbp.org.tr>.

Gross, A.M. 1998. "The Politics of Rights in Israeli Constitutional Law." *Israel Studies* 3(2).

Guida, Michelangelo. 2010. "The New Islamists' Understanding of Democracy in Turkey." *Turkish Studies*, 11(3).

Gunther, Richard and Diamond, Larry. 2003. "Species of Political Parties." *Party Politics* 9(2).

——, Montero, Jose Ramon and Linz, Juan (eds). 2002. *Political Parties.* New York: Oxford University Press.

Heilman, S.C. 1991. "Religious Fundamentalism and Religious Jews." In M. Marty and R. Appleby (eds), *Fundamentalisms Observed.* Chicago, IL: University of Chicago Press.

Heper, M. and Toktas, S. 2003. "Islam, Modernity, and Democracy." *The Muslim World* 93(2).

Hirschberg, P. 1999. *The World of Shas.* The American Jewish Committee Publications.

Horowitz, D. 2006. "Constitutional Courts." *Journal of Democracy* 14(4).

Jeffay, Nathan. 2010. "Shas Breaks Old Taboo, Joins Zionists." *Forward*, February 23.

Jelen, T.G. and Wilcox, C. 2002. *Religion and Politics in Comparative Perspective.* Cambridge: Cambridge University Press.

Kalaycioglu, E. 1999. "Elections and Party Preferences in Turkey." *Comparative Political Studies* 27(3).

Kalyvas, S.N. 1996. *The Rise of Christian Democracy in Europe.* Ithaca, NY: Cornell University Press.

——. 1998. "Democracy and Religious Politics: Evidence from Belgium." *Comparative Political Studies* 31(3).

——. 2000. "Commitment Problems in Emerging Democracies: The Case of Religious Parties." *Comparative Politics* 32(4).

Katz, Richard S. and Mair, Peter. 1995. "Changing Models of Party Organization." *Party Politics* 1(1).

Kogacioglu, D. 2004. "Progress, Unity, and Democracy." *Law & Society Review* 38(3).

Kopelowitz, E. and Diamond, M. 1998. "Religion That Strengthens Democracy," *Theory and Society* 27.

Kook, Rebecca, Harris, Michael, and Doron, Gideon. 1998 "In the name of G-D and our Rabbi: The Politics of the Ultra Orthodox in Israel." *Israel Affairs* 5(1).

Kramer, M. 1996. *Arab Awakening and Islamic Revival.* New Brunswick, NJ: Transaction Publishers.

Landau, D. 1997. "Incoming Religious Affairs Minister Opposes Pluralism." *Jewish Telegraphic Agency* August 29.

Laver, Michael J. and Budge, Ian. 1986. "Office Seeking and Policy Pursuit in Coalition Theory." *Legislative Studies Quarterly* 11(4).

Laver, Michael J. and Schofield, Norman. 1990. *Multiparty Government.* Oxford: Oxford University Press.

Lehmann, David and Siebzehner, Batia. 2006. *Remaking Israeli Judaism: The Challenge of Shas.* New York: Oxford University Press, 2006.

Lijphart, Arend. 1993. *Electoral Systems and Party Systems in Twenty-Seven Democracies.* Oxford: Oxford University Press.

Lustick, I. 1988. *For the Land and the Lord.* New York: Council on Foreign Relations Press.

Mandel, Jonah. 2010. "Ovadia Yosef slams maverick Shas MK Amsalem," *Jerusalem Post* November 21.

Marx, E. 2003. "Starting a Revolution in the NRP." *Forward* September 19.

Mayo, H.B. 1962. "How can we Justify Democracy?"*The American Political Science Review* 56(3) September.

Muller, Wolfgang and Kaare, Strøm (eds). 1999. *Policy, Office, or Votes?* Cambridge: Cambridge University Press

Nasr, S.V.R. 2005. "The Rise of 'Muslim Democracy.'" *Journal of Democracy* 16(2).

Onis, Z. 2001. "Political Islam at the Crossroads." *Contemporary Politics* 7(4).

Peled, Y. 1998. "The Enigma of Shas." *Ethnic and Racial Studies* 21.

Plattner, M. 2004. "The Quality of Democracy: A Skeptical Afterword." *Journal of Democracy* 15(4).

Przeworski, Adam. 1991. *Democracy and the Market.* New York: Cambridge University Press.

Rahat, Gideon et al. 2008. "Democracy and Political Parties" *Party Politics* 14(6).

Ranney, A. and Kendall, W. 1951. "Democracy: Confusion and Agreement." *The Western Political Quarterly* 4(3).

Ravitzky, A. 1996. *Messianism, Zionism and Jewish Religious Radicalism.* Chicago, IL: University of Chicago Press.

Sadowski, Y. 2006. "Political Islam." *Annual Review of Political Science* 9.

Sakallioglu, U.C. 2008. *Secular and Islamic Politics in Turkey.* London: Routledge.

Sandler, S. 1999. "The Religious-Secular Divide in Israeli Politics." *Middle East Policy* 6(4).

Sandler, S. 2004. "A New Turning Point in the Political History of the Jewish State?" *Israel Affairs* 10(4).

Sartori, Giovanni. 1966. "Opposition and Control Problems and Prospects." *Government and Opposition*1(2).

Schwedler, Jillian. 2006. *Faith in Moderation.* New York: Cambridge University Press.

Schweid, E. 1985. "Jewish Messianism." *The Jerusalem Quarterly* 36.

Seawright, Jason and Gerring, John. 2008. "Case-selection Techniques." *Political Research Quarterly* 61(2).

Senyuva, Ozgehan. 2009. "Public opinion of Turkey and European Union 2001–2008: expectations, requests, and apprehensions." *Uluslararasi Iliskiler/ International Relations* 6(22).

Serrano, Alan. 2000. *Comparative European Party Systems.* London and New York: Garland Publishing.

Shenhav, Sharon. 2006. "Choosing Religious Court Judges in Israel." *Jewish Political Studies Review* 18.

Somer, Murat and Liaras, Evangelos. 2010. "Turkey's New Kurdish Opening." *Middle East Policy* 17(2).

Soydan, M.A. 1994. *The Reality of Welfare.* Ankara: Birey.

Stimson, James et al. 1995. "Dynamic Representation." *American Political Science Review* 89(3).

Strom, Kaare. 1990. "A Behavioral Theory of Competitive Political Parties." *American Journal of Political Science* 34(2).

——. 1992. "Democracy as Political Competition." *American Behavioral Scientist* 35(4/5).

Tepe, Sultan. 2008. *Beyond Sacred and Secular: Politics of Religion in Israel and Turkey.* Stanford, CA: Stanford University Press.

Tezcur, Murat, *Muslim Reformers in Iran and Turkey: The Paradox of Moderation,* Austin: University of Texas, 2010.

Tibi, B. 1996. *The Challenge of Fundamentalism.* Berkeley: University of California Press.

Tsebelis, George. 1995. "Decision Making in Political Systems." *British Journal of Political Science* 25(3).

Yavuz, Hakan. 2006. *The Emergence of a New Turkey.* Salt Lake City: The University of Utah Press.

Wickham, Carrie. 2002. *Mobilizing Islam.* New York: Columbia University Press.

Willis, A. 1992. "Redefining Religious Zionism: Shas' Ethno-Politics." *Israel Studies Bulletin* 8(2).

Chapter 7

The Politics of Religious Education in Turkey

Yusuf Sarfati

This chapter discusses how religious education provided by *Imam Hatip* schools (state-run vocational religious schools) became a site of contestation between two different types of elites with contending ideologies. This contestation on the meaning and purpose of religious education is not a conflict between tradition and modernity, but rather a struggle between two competing political projects of modernity. During the state formation period, the Republican elites reduced religious education to being a tool of the new Republic by subsuming all forms of religious instruction under the authority of the secularist state. The aim of the Republican elites was to co-opt religion and to use a reformed version of Islam to draw support for their project of westernization. Beginning in the 1970s, the Islamists, and later the post-Islamists, challenged the Republicans' project by politicizing state-funded religious education. The latter's aim was not to challenge the state's control over religion, but rather to use the state's cultural and material resources for their own political agenda. The analysis of ideology construction in and around state-run religious schools discussed in this chapter provides insights for theoretical debates in social movement theory and institutionalism.

Introduction

> Throughout my life I have proudly kept in my heart that I am a graduate of an
> *Imam Hatip* school. God permitting, I will keep this honor and pride of being
> a member of the *Imam Hatip* community until my last breath. (Erdoğan İmam
> Hatipliler Kurultayında Konuştu, 2010).

These words were uttered by the Turkish Prime Minister Recep Tayyip Erdoğan in his speech in the sixth general assembly of the Alumni Association of *Imam Hatip* Schools last year. Similar to Erdoğan, several of his ministers and members of Parliament from his post-Islamist Justice and Development Party (JDP) are graduates of *Imam Hatip* schools, state-run vocational religious schools that provide education in both religious and secular subjects.

Unlike the JDP politicians' sympathetic view of these educational institutions, secularist politicians and institutions—such as the army and high judiciary—

portray these schools as the backbone of political Islam and a major threat to Turkey's secular regime. The greatest restrictions on religious education were imposed after the infamous postmodern coup on February 28, 1997. The National Security Council's decisions, which basically were a memorandum given to the elected government of Necmettin Erbakan by the army, demanded the closing of the middle-school sections of the *Imam Hatip* schools by passing the Eight Year Compulsory Education Law,[1] as well as placing significant restrictions on *Imam Hatip* graduates in university entrance examinations. With the implementation of these February 28 Decisions, the number of students studying in the *Imam Hatip* schools decreased significantly. Although the governing JDP attempted to change the status of these schools by passing a new bill in the Grand National Assembly (GNA), these efforts were thwarted by the veto of the president. Very recently, the General Staff announced that any student who had continued on to an *Imam Hatip* school at any point during their education would be disqualified from applying to military schools ("İmam Hatipliye Kapı Kapandı" 2011).

As these political developments show, the status of religious schools has become a hotly debated and polarizing political issue. This chapter tries to answer several questions surrounding this debate. The first stems from a seemingly empirical puzzle: why did the status of *Imam Hatip* schools become a point of such intense political conflict, even when neither the secularists nor the Islamists challenged the state's control over religious education? Secondly, what are the micro-mechanisms of ideology construction operating in and around religious education? Finally, how do ideas that are constructed in state-run religious schools translate to political power?

In the first part of this chapter, I argue that the Islamist National Outlook Movement (NOM), which was formed in 1970, implemented a strategy based on the politicization of state-run religious education rather than on the privatization of religious education. This strategy entailed both increasing state funding for religious education through participation in governments, and changing the public's perception of *Imam Hatip* schools from vocational schools to "alternatives to secular education" by reinterpreting the meaning of state religious schools. A closer look at the Islamists' and post-Islamists' views on religious education show that they voice strong support for the continuation of the state's control over religious education, which is similar to secularist politicians. Hence, their aim is not to carve a space for religious education outside the state, but rather use the state's control over cultural resources for their own political projects.

---

1   Before the change of the Basic Law on National Education in 1997, compulsory elementary education was only five years, while post-elementary education was six years (seven years if a foreign language was studied). The first three years were known as middle school (*ortaokul*), and the three years that followed were known as high school (*lise*). By making elementary education eight years in length, the new law incorporated the middle school into elementary education, causing an automatic elimination of the middle-school sections of the *Imam Hatip* schools.

In the second part of this chapter, I use the insights of the Social Movement Theory (SMT) on framing processes to illustrate how these schools appealed to the sociocultural grievances of the peripheral segments of the Turkish society that go back to the state-formation period. In addition to providing social provisions for the poor, several frames were formed in these schools that empowered the "cultural others" of the Turkish society. A closer analysis of these framing processes would allow us to understand how grievances are translated to political power through ideology construction within political institutions. Finally, I discuss how the social networks that formed around *Imam Hatip* schools carried those frames to larger audiences.

Ideas, Institutions, and Political Change

Analyzing the politics of religious education in Turkey can provide insights on the theoretical debate in comparative politics regarding the role of institutions and ideas in shaping political outcomes. Institutionalists—both the historical institutionalist variant (Hall and Taylor 1996) and the rational choice variant (Levi 1997)—maintain that political institutions constrain the behavior of political actors by providing incentives. Hence, political actors follow the rules, or regularized practices with rule-like qualities, of their institutional context and respond to the incentives produced by these rules while making their political decisions. While these insights of the institutionalists are important for understanding the effect of the institutional context on the political actors' decisions, this school of thought is not attentive to the role of meaning-making in politics. On the other hand, ideational theories emphasize the importance of ideas and discourses on political outcomes. For instance, political actors may strategically manipulate cultural norms to gain the loyalties of certain groups in their society (Laitin and Wildawsky 1988). Cultural symbols, norms, and rituals can provide a "tool kit" of habits, skills, or styles from which political entrepreneurs can design strategic action (Swidler 1986). Framing literature in SMT also addresses the importance of ideas and meaning creation in politics. A frame is defined as "a schemata of interpretation that enable individuals to locate, perceive, identify, and label occurrences within their life space and the world at large" (Snow et al. 1986: 464). As agents of signification, political entrepreneurs must articulate and disseminate frames of understanding that resonate with (potential) constituents (Wicktorowicz 2004: 15). These frames help to diagnose problems and attribute responsibility, as well as "suggest action pathways to remedy problems" (Zald 1996: 265).

While the ideational approach has its strengths in bringing in the role of ideas into political analysis, this school of thought heavily relies on the analyses of written texts or speeches of political actors and neglects the importance of institutional context in which ideas operate. As a response to the limitations of the institutional and ideational approaches, some scholars developed a new line of analysis, namely discursive institutionalism. This approach is attentive to ideational content and discursive dynamics, as well as the institutional context. Discursive institutionalists explain political change "by reference to agents' ideas about how they layer, reinterpret, or subvert institutions" (Schmidt 2008: 8).

In this analysis of politics of religious education in Turkey, I adopt a discursive institutionalist approach. I argue that ideas interact with political institutions in complex ways, and this interaction affects political outcomes. Islamist politicians' reinterpretation of the vocational schools as alternatives to secular schools had an important impact in changing the political dynamics between the religious and secularist parties in Turkey. Moreover, the state-run *Imam Hatip* schools provide a suitable institutional context for religious entrepreneurs to construct and disseminate their own ideological agendas. By colonizing the state, these entrepreneurs gain access to spaces through which they can propagate their ideological worldview to larger audiences by producing and disseminating certain frames. As Wuthnow (1989) aptly states, "Within these [institutional] contexts, the producers of culture gain access to necessary resources, come into contact with their audiences, and confront the limitations posed by the competitors and persons in authority."

In the context of the *Imam Hatip* institutions, I identify three main frames— namely injustice, empowerment, and prognostic frames—that were used by religious entrepreneurs to appeal to potential constituents, especially among the culturally marginalized. Injustice frames identify the victims in a societal setting, emphasize their victimization and attribute blame to certain sociopolitical actors (Gamson et al. 1982). In the Turkish case, the secular state is depicted as the agent of forceful modernization against the wills of a pious population, as represented by the students of *Imam Hatip* schools. Empowerment frames provide the students and potential constituents with cognitive tools to overcome their victimhood and construct a positive collective feeling around pious Muslim identity. *Imam Hatip* schools empower their students by emphasizing the pride in one's religiosity and pious lifestyle. The creation and affirmation of a pious Muslim identity appeal to the segments of Turkish society who had been defined as the "cultural other" by the Republican elites. Finally, prognostic frames propose a solution to the diagnosed problem (Benford and Snow 2000: 616–17). Those frames emphasize the significance of religious instruction provided in these schools in overcoming the social and political ills of Turkish society. Through the creation of these frames, state-run religious schools became sites where official secularist ideology was challenged, counter-hegemonic discourses were formed, and counter-elites were educated. These frames have also been disseminated to larger audiences through social networks formed around *Imam Hatip* schools.

Hence, the analysis of *Imam Hatip* schools provides an important example for understanding the production and dissemination of frames/ideas because producers, consumers, and subjects of cultural artifacts interact in and around these institutions. Students, principles, religious activists, journalists, and politicians are the main actors of ideology construction. They are the creators, disseminators, and recipients of the framing processes. By analyzing these state-funded schools as sites of ideological construction, I attempt to illustrate how ideas interact with their institutional context and how this interaction translates cultural grievances to political action. Before delving into a discussion of these processes, it is important to understand the sources of the cultural grievances in Turkey.

State Formation and the Creation of Sociocultural Grievances

When the modern Republic of Turkey was formed in 1923, the Republican elites, who came from the military and bureaucratic classes of the Ottoman Empire, engaged in top-down political and cultural reforms. Cultural reforms, such as the new 'Dress Code' mandating the replacement of the traditional fez with the western-style hat in all public offices, or the replacement of the Arabic alphabet with the Latin alphabet, primarily aimed to construct a modern national identity for the citizens of the newly formed Republic. For the Republican elites, modernity meant an adaptation of western cultural practices. Yet the reforms were not restricted to the cultural arena. Mustafa Kemal Atatürk's Republican People's Party (RPP) also implemented political reforms, such as the abolition of the religious courts, abolition of the institution of the Caliphate, and an outlawing of all religious orders. These reforms aimed to get rid of Islam's influence in the social and public institutions since religion was seen as a powerful alternative to the legitimacy of the Republican modernization project. Nonetheless, the Republican elites were careful not to attack Islam directly. According to the official ideology of the RPP, Islam was fully compatible with the ideas of progress and science, but a superstitious version of Islam that had been disseminated through existing religious institutions and by religious figures needed to be eradicated. Therefore, Republicans promoted a reformed and strictly state-controlled version of Islam, propagated by the newly formed Directorate of Religious Affairs, while claiming to fight against the traditional religious institutions. They insisted on relegating religion to individuals' minds and replacing tradition's role in the public and social spheres with the guidance of science.

Yet, the transformation of the Islamic way of life to a westernized one did not exactly materialize, and the inculcation of the Republican ideals of secular nationalism, progress, and positivism did not penetrate all of Turkish society, especially in the rural areas far from the big cities. The cultural idioms associated with Islam survived in the daily lives of the masses (Mardin 1993: 372–3), and Islamic consciousness remained the foundation of communal identity among large segments of society (Yavuz 2003: 55). Accordingly, a duality between the more traditional, Islamic masses residing in the villages and the secular, westernized elites residing in the big cities was created. This division, which came to be known as the 'center-periphery cleavage' became one of the most important divisions in Turkish social and political life in the years to come (Mardin 1973).

The economic policies of the Republican elites also produced stark socioeconomic inequalities between the center and the periphery. During the Great Depression, the Turkish state, like its counterparts in most of Europe, implemented a state-led industrialization program, known as *etatism*. In the decade 1929–39, the import of consumer goods was thwarted, while the import of intermediary goods was made easier in order to create infant industries (Barlas 1998). These policies led to major industrialization in the big cities. The state bureaucracy, which controlled a large part of economic activity, emerged as the main beneficiary of these policies (Keyder 2000: 147). For instance, in 1931–1940, 72.4 percent of all new firms were established by state bureaucrats (ibid.: 149).

On the other hand, these industrialization efforts heavily taxed and exploited the agricultural sector (ibid.: 150). During World War II, the government bought crops such as wheat, sugar beets, and cotton from small farmers at under the market price and sold them at a higher profit after processing them (Boratav 2003: 335). In 1944, the passage of the Soil Products' Tax (*Toprak Mahsülleri Vergisi*), a flat tax of 10 percent on all gross agricultural products, created a very heavy burden for poor and small-scale farmers. At the end of the war, the agricultural sector, which constituted over four-fifths of the Turkish economy, had many economic grievances against the state (Gürsel 1999: 142). Hence, by undertaking extensive state-led economic initiatives, the young Turkish state managed to transform socioeconomic life in the big cities. Yet, at the end of World War II, the periphery was not only culturally and politically marginalized, but also economically disadvantaged and dependent on the center.

This center-periphery cleavage has been transformed, with increasing rural-urban migration starting with Turkey's transition to a multi-party democracy after the end of World War II. With the help of the Marshall Plan, mechanization of agriculture became pervasive, and this led to a decreasing need for agricultural labor. By taking advantage of the new democratic era and liberal political opening, the unemployed villagers started to immigrate to the major cities in great numbers (Yalçıntan and Erbaş 2003: 92–3). This rural-urban migration characterized the movement of the periphery to the center; by the end of 2007, over 70 percent of the Turkish population lived in cities, compared to only one-quarter in 1945. Nevertheless, the state did not have sufficient resources to make any infrastructural plans to integrate newcomers into the cities. Therefore, most of the rural immigrants started to live in shanties called *gecekondu* (literally, 'put up by night'). The first *gecekondu* neighborhoods were built on the outskirts of the cities, although today many of them are also close to city centers due to the expansion of the cities. These settlements were characterized by poverty, a large number of young residents, and many infrastructural problems, such as lack of sewerage, transportation, paved roads, clean water, electricity, and so on (ibid.: 99–100). Most *gecekondu* dwellers worked in the informal economy with no social security. Moreover, the urbanites blamed the *gecekondu* inhabitants for ruralizing the city, coarsening sophisticated urban manners, and increasing criminal activity. They saw the existence of growing numbers of the rural migrants as a cultural and political threat to their very existence.

According to one account, in 1993, the number of *gecekondu* residents was 1.6 million, with the vast majority living in Turkey's seven largest cities. Nearly

750,000 had settled in Ankara, Istanbul, and Izmir alone. According to other estimates, the *gecekondu* residents constituted 17 percent of the national electorate (İlgu 2000: 40). By the year 2000, *gecekondu* residents in Istanbul constituted 75 percent of the city's total population (Yalçıntan and Erbaş 2003: 94). The sociocultural hierarchies between the periphery and the center came to the fore when the *gecekondu* dwellers came into closer contact with the old-timers in the cities. The increasingly negative representations of the *gecekondu* dwellers by the urbanites galvanized sociocultural grievances of the periphery. In this context, the *Imam Hatip* schools addressed both social and cultural concerns of the periphery.

The Origins of the *Imam Hatip* Schools

The reforms implemented in the area of education formed an important part of the Republican revolution. The Law on Unification of Education, passed on March 3, 1924, abolished Ottoman pluralism in education and established total state control over the new unified education system. Just after the passage of this law, all the *madrasas* (religious schools) were shut down. The implementation of the Law on Unification of Education meant that all the students of the new Republic would be educated according to the new secularist, modernist world-view. This showed how the Republican elites saw education as a political tool through which they could mold their children into the future citizens of modern Turkey.

Nevertheless, Article 4 of the Law on the Unification of Education stipulated that vocational schools for the training of religious functionaries needed to be opened under the Ministry of Education. Subsequently, in 1924, the state opened 29 new vocational schools under the title "*Imam Hatip* schools" (preacher and prayer leader schools) in order to train religious functionaries. The number of the *Imam Hatip* schools, which provided a four-year education similar to other middle schools, decreased in the 1920s due to a lack of demand, and the last two schools were closed down at the end of 1929–30 academic year.

In 1947, one year after the introduction of the multi-party system, the RPP made some reforms regarding religious education and reopened these schools in the form of "*Imam Hatip* programs." These new programs provided ten months of education and a certificate to middle-school graduates who wanted to become religious functionaries (Ayhan 2004: 186). With the new government of the Democratic Party (DP), which was more sympathetic to the cultural values of the conservative masses than the Republican RPP, the *Imam Hatip* programs were transformed into full-fledged vocational high schools, which provided students with seven years of education. Between 1951 and 1972, the student body of these state-based religious high schools increased. Despite this increase, the number of *Imam Hatip* students as a percentage of the entire student body was marginal and never exceeded 4 percent (see Figure 7.1).

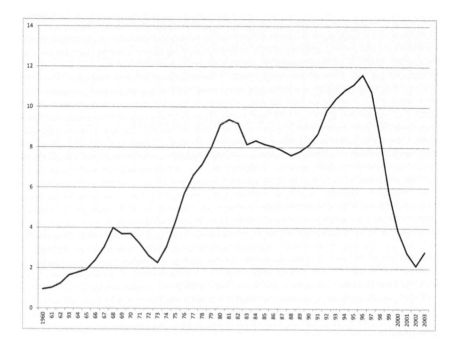

Figure 7.1   Number of students in *Imam Hatip* schools as a percentage of students in all middle and high schools in Turkey (1960–2003)

Source: Ministry of Education, *Statistical Indicators (1923–2005)* (Istanbul: Turkish Statistical Institute). Calculations are the author's.

Politicization of Religious Education and *Imam Hatip* Schools

The participation of the religiously oriented National Salvation Party (NSP) in the coalition government of 1974 was an important turning-point for state religious education in Turkey. The origins of the NSP go back to 1969, when Necmettin Erbakan, the then-president of the Chamber of Commerce, formed the National Outlook Movement (NOM).[2] The NSP represented a watershed in Turkish politics:

---

2   The National Outlook Movement (NOM) is an Islamist movement formed by Necmettin Erbakan in 1969. The National Order Party was formed as the political party of NOM the following year. When the National Order Party was shut down during military intervention in 1971, NOM was reorganized under the National Salvation Party in 1972. Afterwards, the political party that represented NOM was closed by the military or by the Constitutional Court three more times. Yet, each time, the cadres of NOM formed a new party. Therefore, in this article, I refer to NOM or to the National Outlook Parties to capture the political activities of the five parties, namely, the National Order Party, the National Salvation Party, the Welfare Party, the Virtue Party, and the Felicity Party, which shared the

for the first time, a religiously oriented political party was participating in Turkish politics. This party emerged as the champion of the economic interests of the small merchants in Anatolia against the big industrialists' interests in Ankara and Istanbul. The party also addressed the periphery's cultural grievances regarding the top-down secularization of Turkish culture and the erasure of Islam from the public space. Thus, the party's dual agenda on economic and cultural issues was reflected in its party program as material development *(maddi kalkınma)* and spiritual development *(manevi kalkınma).*

During the NSP's coalition partnerships in the latter half of the 1970s, first with Ecevit's RPP and then twice with Demirel's center-right Justice Party, both the number and the status of *Imam Hatip* schools changed significantly. During the ten months of the RPP-NSP government, 29 new schools were opened. Because of the NSP's key role in the Nationalist Front governments in the second half of the 1970s, the opening of new *Imam Hatip* schools speeded up, and in 1980, *Imam Hatip* school students constituted over 9 percent of all middle and high school students.

In addition to the quantitative changes in the students who attend *Imam Hatip* schools, the NSP succeeded in changing the public's perception of these state religious schools. The NSP never hid its interest in the *Imam Hatip* schools and saw them as a tool, through which it could realize its self-declared goal of spiritual development for Turkey. Many Islamist activists I interviewed claimed that religious education was a significant source of Turkey's moral transformation:

> First of all, we think that the moral and spiritual fabric [of this nation] needs to be strengthened. This can be achieved through education. To state it more clearly, it can be achieved through religious education, moral education. A shared destiny, spiritual fabric, morals, respect for one another's rights ... these are at the basis of the elements that keep a nation together. This is how a sound social fabric and family structure are formed; this is how people with strong moral and spiritual values, a strong society, a strong family, comes into being ... For that reason, we call all of these [elements] spiritual development. (C. Ayhan, personal communication, February 22, 2007)

It was clear that what Ayhan and other NOM activists meant by religious education was state-funded religious education provided in *Imam Hatip* schools. In its political propaganda, NSP activists portrayed the graduates from the *Imam Hatip* schools as "a new and moral generation" (Yavuz 2003: 126–7), which would transform Turkey. For instance, the coalition agreement of 1975 attributed to

---

same ideological core. When the Virtue Party was closed down by the Constitutional Court in 2001, a split occurred in NOM. The "old generation" created the Felicity Party, while the reformist "new generation" established the Justice and Development Party (JDP). Although the JDP was formed by the same cadres, the leadership explicitly stated its break from the ideology of political Islam represented by the NOM. Many, including the author of this article, label the JDP as a "post-Islamist" party.

Imam Hatip graduates new roles. According to this agreement, which was signed by the center-right Justice Party and Erbakan's NSP:

> ... the morality lessons in the elementary and high schools will be foremost taught according to their philosophy by the graduates of the divinity faculty, Institute of Islamic Higher Education or *Imam Hatip* schools; the place of religious functionaries in [the Turkish] society will be recognized by utilizing them in social and economic development.

Moreover, the NSP also attempted to give the graduates from the *Imam Hatip* schools the opportunity to become officers in the Turkish Army, but failed in its attempt (Ahmad 1992: 383–4). According to the political statements of the NSP, the best students, who would be able to rule the country without corruption, came out of the *Imam Hatip* schools (Gökaçtı 2005: 219).

Therefore, by depicting the *Imam Hatip* schools as the source of spiritual awakening, the NSP politicized the issue of religious education in Turkey in the late 1970s. Many pious families started to see the *Imam Hatip* schools as an alternative educational track to the secular schools. During the latter half of the 1970s, which was a period of extreme political volatility in Turkey, the campuses of these schools became places where the youth organizations of different political parties struggled for hegemony. The main competitors were *Ülkücüler*, the youth organization of the ultranationalist Nationalist Action Party (NAP) and the *Akıncılar*, the youth organization of the NSP. It was the latter which most frequently had control over the campuses of the *Imam Hatip* schools (Gökaçtı 2005: 224).

In the 1980s during the governments of the Motherland Party (MP), which contained a religious faction under its roof,[3] the debates around the *Imam Hatip* schools continued. Despite the fact that the number of religious schools did not considerably increase during the MP period (1983–91) because of the remaining military influence in politics, the quality and the capacity of these schools improved significantly. Rather than opening new schools, the education ministers opened new buildings as additional campuses of already existing high schools. When the MP assumed power in 1983, 207,006 students attended *Imam Hatip* high schools, while in the 1990–91 academic year, their number increased to 309,553 (Öcal 1994: 68–9). Moreover, the MP established "Anatolian *Imam-Hatip*" high schools, which provided a more elite education including the instruction of a foreign language.

In the 1990s, political discussion around these schools became more heated with the increasing political fortunes of the Islamist WP, the reincarnation of Erbakan's NSP. The secularist parties and social actors constantly accused the

---

3   Erbakan's NSP was closed down by the military coup of 1980, like all the other political parties of the pre-coup era. The MP, which was headed by Turgut Özal, emerged as the most powerful new party in the aftermath of the 1983 elections. The MP claimed to unite four different factions under its roof. One of the factions was the Islamist faction, which contained politicians and bureaucrats from the pre-coup NSP team.

Imam Hatip schools of being the Islamists' political "backyard" or even the Trojan Horse within the Turkish state. The religious-secular divide in Turkish politics culminated in the 1997 military intervention into politics during the coalition government led by Erbakan's WP. The National Security Council demanded that the government implement its decisions taken on February 28, 1997. When Erbakan refused to implement those decisions, the army pressured the parliamentarians of the True Path Party, the junior partner of the coalition, to resign from their party. As a result, the coalition collapsed and the WP was ousted from power. The next year, the party was banned by the Constitutional Court. The military continued to demand that the new government, now led by Mesut Yılmaz, implement the February 28 decisions, which included the closing of the middle-school sections of the *Imam Hatip* schools and a change in the status of vocational schools in the university entrance examination. This latter provision, which specifically targeted the *Imam Hatip* schools, practically prevented all the *Imam Hatip* graduates from entering any department other than the Divinity Faculty in higher education. After 1998, the middle-school sections of the *Imam Hatip* schools were closed down and the number of students who attended the remaining high-school sections plummeted due to the difficulties imposed on the graduates in the university entrance examinations.

Currently, both the graduates and students are disgruntled with the existing restrictions put on their *Imam Hatip* schools. The governing post-Islamist JDP, which has political roots in NOM, is sympathetic to the concerns of the *Imam Hatip* students. Considering that many JDP politicians are themselves *Imam Hatip* graduates, this should not come as a surprise. According to the party program of the JDP, "the graduates of all high schools and equivalent institutions would be accorded equality in the university entrance examinations" (as cited in Hale 2006: 78). This stipulation meant getting rid of the restrictions put on *Imam Hatip* schools with the 28 February Decisions and granting their graduates equal opportunities with the secular schools in university entrance examination.

The JDP acted on its commitment when a bill prepared by the Education Minister, Hüseyin Çelik, demanded improvements for all vocational schools, including the *Imam Hatip* schools, in university entrance examinations. Although the bill passed the Grand National Assembly on May 13, 2004, it was vetoed by Turkey's former president, Ahmet Necdet Sezer, who claimed that the provision violated the principle of secularism (Kuru 2006: 151). After the bill was vetoed, Prime Minister Erdoğan said that they were shelving the law (Hale 2006: 79).

Up until recently, the JDP has not taken an activist stance on the status of *Imam Hatip* schools, as it did not want to draw any anti-secularism charges from the judiciary upon itself. This hesitance is not unwarranted, considering that the Republican Prosecutor Abdurrahman Yalçınkaya filed a case in the Constitutional Court to close down the JDP in 2008. Remarks made by the prime minister, ministers, JDP parliamentarians, and mayors regarding the *Imam Hatip* schools constituted an important part of the indictment. According to the Public Prosecutor's argument, promotion of *Imam Hatip* schools as alternatives to secular schools violated Turkey's constitutional principle of secularism. The document refers to the words "*Imam Hatip*" 70 times. While the JDP was not closed down, the Constitutional Court found the JDP guilty of engaging in anti-secularist activities and cut half of its public funding.

However, due to its unmatched electoral power in the last few years and considerable weakening of the staunch secularist actors, particularly the higher judiciary and the army, the emboldened JDP passed a new law on educational reform on March 30, 2012. The new law, which is popularly known as 4+4+4 formula, increases compulsory education to 12 years, where pupils have to study four years in an elementary school, followed by another four years of middle school, and four years of high school education. According to this new educational reform, the middle sections of the *Imam Hatip* schools will be reopened, and the pupils will be able to receive religious education at an earlier age. These new educational provisions that will go into effect in the 2012–13 academic year have been drawing much criticism from educational experts and parents because of the Turkish public education's lack of infrastructural and pedagogical preparation to accommodate such a major restructuring. Although not explicitly stated, JDP's main aim in this complete education overhaul is opening the middle sections of the *Imam Hatip* schools and provision of religious education. While the generals changed the entire educational system to close the middle sections of the *Imam Hatip* schools in 1998, the JDP now tinkers with the entire system to reopen them. As this political bickering shows, religious education and the status of *Imam Hatip* schools is still a salient and contentious political issue.

Islamists, the JDP, and State-centrism

A closer look at the views of Islamist NOM as well as the post-Islamist JDP politicians reveal that they do not challenge the state's control over religious education. *Imam Hatip* schools are part of a religion-state constellation which grants the Turkish state extensive authority over religious affairs in all spheres of life. For instance, the Directorate of Religious Affairs is responsible for the building of mosques, the appointment of imams in the mosques, as well as providing religious services in Turkey and abroad. Moreover, the Directorate provides basic religious education in the Quranic courses operating under its purview. As of 2010, the Directorate had a budget of over \$1.75 billion. The 1982 constitution put "Culture of Religion and Knowledge of Morals" courses into the curriculum of each school and made them compulsory. When asked how NOM perceives state-religion arrangements, a longtime NOM politician explained:

> In Turkey there is a legal foundation of religiosity … The Turkish Penal Code stipulates legal sanctions against the defamation of religion, defamation of religious people, and defamation of religious values … Even more important than these, the Political Parties Law states that a political party which puts the

abolition of the Directorate of Religious Affairs in its party program should be closed down ... Hence, in Turkey both in the constitution and in the laws there is respect for religion and religious values. Yes, there are deficiencies, but the main problem is in practice. For instance, to remove the spiritual weakness [of the Turkish society], religion needs to be made much more active, much more functional, because—according to published statistics—in Turkey today 25 million people go to Friday prayers. Now, this is very important—such an organization does not exist in any other country. For the peace of the society, for the strengthening of the society, this [opportunity] needs to be used. In Turkey with a population of 70 million, there are nearly 25 Divinity Faculties. The curriculum of these Divinity Faculties needs to be reevaluated and the number of students accepted into them needs to be increased ... The Directorate of Religious Affairs needs to be reorganized. The imam should not just be a person who leads the Friday prayer and the five prayers, he also needs to be an opinion leader, he needs to be more active and functional. (Ş. Malkoç, personal communication, February 22, 2007)

As the quotation shows, the aim of NOM is not to get rid of the state's control over religion, but to use the institutional infrastructure of the Turkish state to disseminate its own ideology of religious revival. Hence, similar to the Kemalist elites, many NOM activists perceive the state as a "sacred" institution that is crucial for running the affairs of the society.[4] Similar to Malkoç, many of my interviewees claimed that the Directorate of Religious Affairs' authority over religion should be preserved. As one NOM activist claims: "Religion is a very sensitive subject, it can be exploited very easily. [The] Directorate of Religious Affairs is a significant authority; it is accepted [by the people]. Now you have to satisfy people's [religious] demands through these institutions. If not, you would leave it to the clowns to do it" (C. Ayhan, personal communication, February 22, 2007). Along similar lines, Islamist and JDP politicians argue that the state should continue to provide religious education rather than leaving religious education to civil society. For instance, Ali Turan, a JDP politician, who began his political career in NOM says: "Definitely, the state should provide [religious education] and it should be provided by specialists" (A. Turan, personal communication, March 1, 2007).

Ayhan and Turan's claims reflect a common understanding among the Islamist and post-Islamist politicians regarding religion's place in the Turkish religion-state arrangements. According to this understanding, the state should have the sole authority to provide religious education, and this authority should not be extended to the civil society, namely to different religious communities (*cemaatler*). If these religious communities would have a right to give religious education, the argument runs, then false religious beliefs would be disseminated by unqualified people, and Turkish citizens would be manipulated. This argument, which is also frequently

---

4   For an argument on the similarity of statisms of both the Kemalist and Islamist actors, see Navaro-Yashin 2002.

used by many Kemalists to thwart legitimate societal demands, assumes that there is one correct interpretation of Islam, and that the state should disseminate this correct interpretation through its institutions.

Yet, the Islamist movement in Turkey is not monolithic. A more liberal minority group within NOM articulates a more society-centered approach and is critical of the state-centered political approach of the party leaders. Mehmet Bekaroğlu, who was one of the fiercest critics of this state-centric approach, articulates this criticism eloquently:

> The modernism of the WP comes from this: they aim to capture the government and transform the society from top-down. They want [to create] the "Great Turkey." In this manner, they are similar to the Kemalists, hence they want a strong, developed, industrialized Turkey. There is only one difference: Muslim morality, spiritual development. They aim to come to government with their spiritually-developed cadres and to rehabilitate Turkey with these cadres. This is the ideological basis. Hence, this is the basis of the conflict. There is an authoritarian state..and there is an ideology named Kemalism within this state ... They [the WP activists] do not challenge the authoritarian state. They oppose the totalitarian ideology in this authoritarian state, namely Kemalism. Hence, they will take out Kemalism and put in an ideology that is inspired by Islam. (M. Bekaroğlu, personal communication, March 11, 2007)

According to Bekaroğlu, there is a need to dismantle the over-extensive state institutions that regulate religious affairs. Bahri Zengin, another Islamist who takes a pluralist position, claims that the state should grant autonomy to each religious community in providing its own version of religious education. The role of the state in this constellation should be limited to enforce peace among different communities (Zengin 2001).

My interviews show that many National Outlook activists, with the exception of a small liberal group led by Bekaroğlu and Zengin, do not question the "strong state" ethos of the Turkish Republic, but only want to utilize the institutions of the "strong state" to implement their own world-view. In this "strong state" ethos, religious education is seen as one of the important state institutions to be used to transform the society. While the JDP is much more moderate than its predecessor NOM on a number of issues, JDP politicians concur with NOM on retaining the state's control over religious education. These views are surely shaped by the institutional constraints set by the Turkish Constitution, which entrenches the state's control over religious institutions in different realms.

Imam Hatip Schools as Institutions Addressing the Sociocultural Needs of the Periphery

While the discussion above can show how and why religious entrepreneurs politicized state-religious education starting with the 1970s, it cannot explain why they succeeded in their attempt to do so. As seen in Figure 7.1, the number of students attending the *Imam Hatip* schools declined significantly after 1997 because of the new provisions regulating the university entrance examination of *Imam Hatip* graduates. Yet, it is imperative to explain why *Imam Hatip* schools became so popular among the periphery of the Turkish society between 1974 and 1997, and how they became a successful vehicle of political mobilization for the Islamists. I argue that the *Imam Hatip* schools became popular starting from the mid-1970s because they successfully addressed the cultural aspirations of the periphery as well as their economic needs.

First, *Imam Hatip* schools emerged as institutions that provided economic benefits to the poor families from the periphery. At the same time, and maybe more importantly, these state religious schools addressed the cultural needs of the periphery. A focus on the framing processes that occurred within and around the *Imam Hatip* schools can reveal how they empowered the conservative segments of Turkey culturally. These empowerment framing played a critical role in political recruitment and the provision of popular support for the Islamists.

Imam Hatip Schools as Social Providers

As discussed above, the relationship between the periphery and the center was transformed with increasing rural-urban migration. Hence, the sociocultural hierarchies between the two groups became more pronounced in the urban encounters of the rural immigrants with the "modernized" city-dwellers. The changing residential backgrounds of the *Imam Hatip* students also reflect the movement of the periphery from the villages to the cities. Akşit (1986) found that 55.8 percent of the *Imam Hatip* students in his study in 1977 were from rural origins, while Akşit and Coşkun (2004) found in their study in 1997 that only 14 percent of the students came from rural backgrounds. In this context, the *Imam Hatip* schools attracted poor students from the *gecekondu* and low-income neighborhoods in big cities by providing extensive scholarships and free boarding opportunities. Since the *Imam Hatip* schools are state educational institutions, they receive income from the state budget. More importantly, they receive material resources from societal sources. From the 1970s onwards, grassroots organizations around these schools proliferated (Yavuz 2003: 124). Civil society organizations provided material and logistical support to students and graduates alike. For instance, the Association for the Dissemination of Knowledge (*İlim Yayma Cemiyeti*), which has 85 branches in 45 cities across Turkey, has provided material help to the *Imam Hatip* students since 1963 and to successful graduates in their university education since 1973 ("İlim Yayma Cemiyeti," http://www.iyc.org.tr/, accessed on November 25, 2010). The organization also runs 60 boarding houses, which provide accommodation for the students in secondary and higher education. Similarly, the Alumni Association of *Imam Hatip* High Schools *(ÖNDER)* and Ensar Foundation provide scholarships primarily for *Imam Hatip* students based on need and academic merit.

Furthermore, social organizations collected charities from citizens in order to construct new buildings for the *Imam Hatip* schools and to donate them to the state. Accordingly, 65 percent of the school buildings of all the *Imam Hatip* schools were built by private donations, while only a little over 9 percent were built by the state with no help from citizens (Ünsür 2005: 202–3). For instance, Ünsür's (2005) study shows that Üsküdar Imam Hatip High School, a prestigious religious school in one of the city centers of Istanbul, received three times more money from the Istanbul Üsküdar Imam Hatip Beneficent Society (*Istanbul Üsküdar Imam Hatip Lisesi Koruma Derneği*) than from the state budget. These funds were used both to increase the quality of education by contributing to the infrastructural needs of the school and to help students from disadvantaged families (Ünsür 2005: 209–11).

According to data provided by the Education Ministry, in the academic year 1996–97, 28.1 percent of all boarding facilities in primary and secondary education belonged to the General Religious Education Administration (Çakır et al. 2004: 73). If we consider that the percentage of *Imam Hatip* students was about 12 percent of the entire student population in the same year, we can see that the boarding facilities available for *Imam Hatip* students far exceeded those facilities available for other students. This difference is primarily due to the fact that many of the boarding houses are donated to the state by civic associations or private foundations to be used specifically as boarding facilities for *Imam Hatip* schools.[5]

These material incentives made *Imam Hatip* schools very attractive for students from a lower socioeconomic background. A NOM activist explained this function of the *Imam Hatip* schools eloquently:

> [In the past] in Turkey, which is ruled by a political and economic elite, a big segment of the population could not send their children to the schools. They could not do that due to a lack of material opportunities ... *Imam Hatip* schools constituted the most important social project in the history of the Republic ... I met many people who told me: "We couldn't have studied if these schools had not existed. We wouldn't have a profession, if these schools had not existed." Hence, [these schools] became the only place where the poor and deprived masses could get an education. (N. Kurtulmuş, personal communication, March 4, 2007)

Thus, these schools provided a venue for the children of the deprived masses who were seeking upward mobility. While some parents chose to send their children to *Imam Hatip* schools due to economic accessibility and a good quality of education,

---

5   According to Turkish law, if a building is donated for a specific purpose to the Ministry of Education, it cannot be used for something else.

others preferred it due to the expectation that their children would have a guaranteed job in the Directorate of Religious Affairs once they graduated (Çakır et al. 2004).

Framing Processes and Cultural Empowerment through Religious Education

Material incentives were not the only reason for the increasing popularity of the *Imam Hatip* schools among conservative Muslims. Many families sent their children to the *Imam Hatip* schools because of cultural motives. In order to grasp how these schools addressed the cultural needs of the conservative sectors of Turkish society, it is necessary to unpack some of the frames constructed in and around the *Imam Hatip* schools.

First of all, *Imam Hatip* schools built a positive pious Muslim identity through the use of empowerment frames. The creation of a positive collective identity for pious Muslims was important because the Republican elites had tried to erase such a positive social identification around Islam for so many years. This positive collective identity partly stemmed from the socialization process within the schools and was expressed in different ways. Some of the *Imam Hatip* graduates whom I interviewed pointed to a special consciousness that existed within the schools. Zeynep, a graduate from Kütahya Anadolu Imam Hatip High School, said that there was a different type of atmosphere in her school compared to the secular schools.[6] This atmosphere, which she called "emotions" *(hissiyat)*, inculcated spiritual principles in the students, such as valuing others because they are Allah's creations. Another graduate, Metin, claimed that there was a spiritual atmosphere in his school because "we could talk with others about religious matters, we could pray in the mescid [mosque] within the school" (personal communication, March 31, 2007). This spiritual atmosphere created a consciousness of being an *Imam Hatip* member *(İmam Hatiplilik şuuru)*. According to Metin, this consciousness is "not something that is taught in the classes, rather it is a situation that emerges during your years of education in the school" (personal communication, March 31, 2007).

This atmosphere on the school campuses also affects the religiosity and ideological orientations of the students. Akşit (1986) reported that during the 1977–78 academic year, *Imam Hatip* students were a lot more religious compared to the secular school students. Akşit and Coşkun (2004) reported that their survey conducted in the 1997–98 academic year showed a significant cultural and ideological gap between the students in the *Imam Hatip* schools and the students in secular high schools. For instance, while more than 55 percent of the *Imam Hatip* students read Islamic/conservative newspapers, in secular high schools only 5 percent did. Similarly, Onay (2005) found in his survey, conducted among university students in the 1999–2000 academic year, a significant difference between the *Imam Hatip* school graduates and secular high-school graduates in their level of attitudinal and behavioral religiosity.

---

6   All the names used in the text for the *Imam Hatip* graduates are pseudonyms.

Secondly, prognostic frames are constructed in the *Imam Hatip* schools. These frames represent religious schools as institutions that remedy the ill-effects of modernization. These frames are not only constructed within the school, but also reproduced by religious newspapers and conservative politicians. According to this frame, *Imam Hatip* students and graduates avoid improper behavior, such as violence, criminal activities, or drug use, because of their religious education. In comparison, as the frame goes, students in the secular schools are more likely to engage in those illicit activities, due to a lack of religious teaching. Metin, an *Imam Hatip* graduate, sums up this claim eloquently:

> Currently, you can observe that students engage in strange movements, such as Satanism, or commit homicides. I think this happens due to a lack of religious knowledge. Let me give you an example. For instance, you tell people not to steal. Yet, if you cannot make the person internalize this, if this person cannot assimilate this spiritually and conscientiously, then [this instruction] is to no avail. Hence, I want to say that education is not solely mental. Today, you see that people who received a very good education go and rob banks, embezzle state resources, steal. Why? And [they do these] despite the fact that you gave them a good education ... The reason is because you approach education one-dimensionally. (Personal communication, March 31, 2007)

Similarly Osman Yumakoğlu, the head of the Istanbul organization of NOM says:

> One of the reasons why people prefer *Imam Hatip* schools is because of criminal activities, such as drug abuse, physical injuries, that were occurring in secular schools ... In *Imam Hatip* schools, students who are engaged in these types of activities don't pass 1 percent [of the school's student body]. (O. Yumakoğlu, personal communication, March 23, 2007)

This frame is sometimes supplemented by a more activist prognostic frame that emphasizes the proactive social role *Imam Hatip* students should take in their larger social setting. According to this frame, *Imam Hatip* students and graduates are expected to be role models for the larger Turkish society. As one graduate puts it: "Once you say that you are an *Imam Hatip* member *(imam hatipli)*, you need to be aware of your behaviour, because you subscribe to a mission. Hence, you develop an auto-control mechanism" (cf. Çakır et al. 2004: 126).

Others go one more step and claim that the *Imam Hatip* generation should be seen as the engine of societal Islamization in Turkey. Hayreddin Karaman, who is one of the first graduates of the *Imam Hatip* schools and an authoritative figure in *Imam Hatip* circles, summarizes this argument very cogently:

> How does Islamization occur? What is the means to achieve Islamization? ...
> According to my opinion, Islamization occurs through education and instruction.
> It occurs through generating faith and action among those we educate ... As

a result our people will become Muslims again ... Those who are deficient Muslims will become complete Muslims. The more you turn people into complete Muslims, the more the country becomes Muslim with her morality, with her image, with her actuality, with her institutions, and with her order ... But who will undertake this effort? ... We claim that under current conditions the most suitable community for this job is the *Imam Hatip* community, this generation. (Karaman, 2005: 11–12)

Another frame that is used by the *Imam Hatip* community is that these schools became the only venue for the education of pious girls, since they offer a dignified educational context for them. According to this claim, conservative families, which would not send their daughters to regular schools, were more likely to send them to *Imam Hatip* schools because of the more acceptable gender relations within the schools. The majority of the parents interviewed by Pak (2002) for his study in three *Imam Hatip* schools affirmed these claims and asserted that these schools were the only option for the education of their daughters due to the propriety standards they provided. The spatial segregation between the sexes in curricular and extra-curricular activities and the lack of mingling between boys and girls played an important role in the maintenance of these propriety standards (ibid.: 184–5). While girls were accepted to the *Imam Hatip* schools for the first time in the 1977–78 academic year, the number of girls in religious education rose exponentially in the following years. In the academic years after 1990, girls have always constituted at least 40 percent of all *Imam Hatip* students (Çakır et al. 2004: 13).

Secularist circles in Turkey often voice dismay on the acceptance of girls to the *Imam Hatip* schools, since it is impossible for the girls to become either *Imams* or *Hatips*. Most of the female graduates from *Imam Hatip* schools, like most of the boys, move to secular professions or attend universities to study secular subjects. In this way, the female graduates from the *Imam Hatip* schools played an important role in the upward mobility of the periphery. Moreover, this led to the increasing visibility of Islamic symbols, such as the headscarf, in professional jobs and institutions of higher learning.

Finally, the *Imam Hatip* schools were put at the center of injustice frames, which depict these religious schools as victims at the hands of the secular establishment. This frame became much more prevalent and persuasive after the draconian February 28 decisions of the NSC. However, victimization has always been a major narrative emphasized by conservative politicians and media. According to this frame, the reason for the proliferation of the *Imam Hatip* schools was the society's embrace of Islamic values. In spite of the demand from society for more *Imam Hatip* schools and religious education, secular intellectuals and state elites, who are alienated from their Turkish-Islamic roots and aspire to become westerners, try to malign these schools by depicting them as sources of religious extremism (Çiçek 1994). Furthermore, throughout the 1980s and 1990s, religious newspapers, like *Tercüman, Zaman,* and the *Milli Gazete* have periodically published reports about *Imam Hatip* school buildings, which were donated to the state by private initiatives and awaited the approval of the education minister to open. The subtext of these news reports emphasizes state-society tensions. According to this message, the *Imam Hatip* schools represented the demands of the society for more religious education. Nonetheless, these demands were not sufficiently met by the authoritarian Turkish state, which was controlled by a powerful secular minority elite. Hence, the *Imam Hatip* schools were at the center of this injustice frame that portrayed the victimization of a religious society at the hands of a secular state. This frame resonated with the cultural grievances of the periphery and led the families from peripheral segments of the Turkish society to embrace *Imam Hatip* schools.

Social Networks and the Dissemination of Frames

In order to understand how these frames are translated into social and political power, it is important to explain how they are disseminated to the larger society through social networks formed around the schools. The graduates of the *Imam Hatip* schools come together around several associations and foundations and form a tight-knit community. The Ensar Foundation, Alumni Association of Imam Hatip High Schools, Community for the Dissemination of Knowledge, and the Foundation for the Dissemination of Knowledge are the main organizations that bring the *Imam Hatip* community together. These organizations provide several opportunities for social and political mobilization. Through their meetings and publications, they actively disseminate empowerment frames that emphasize the positive collective identity formed around the *Imam Hatip* community, as well as prognostic frames that highlight the significant role *Imam Hatip* students play in transforming Turkish society. The Ensar Foundation has a prolific publishing house which has five different publishers. The Alumni Association of *Imam Hatip* High Schools has close to 2 million members that consist of both students and graduates (Y. Kara, personal communication, March 20, 2007). The organization publishes a quarterly magazine called *Tohum* (Seed), which discusses the concerns of *Imam Hatip* schools, as well as the success of its students. The cartoon below (Figure 7.2), which is published in *Tohum,* is just an example of how prognostic frames disseminate through publications to wider audiences.

This cartoon, which is drawn by the cartoonist of the Islamist daily *Vakit*, depicts a pious *Imam Hatip* student 'cleansing' the society of corruption, bribery, adultery, prostitution, drug use, burglary, terror, treachery, and dirt. The aim is clearly to portray *Imam Hatip* students as agents of social change who will cleanse Turkish society of social and political ills, and create a less corrupt social order.

Secondly, these social networks provide spaces, where the members of religious political parties and the *Imam Hatip* graduates can physically meet and interact. It is widely known that certain members of NOM, as well as the governing JDP, are *Imam Hatip* graduates. These politicians preserve their ties with other alumni, who later have become prominent members in other social or business circles. Mukadder Başeğmez, a member of the Turkish National Assembly from the

KEMAL GÜLER
Vakit Gazetesi Karükatüristi

Karikatür

Figure 7.2 "Karikatür"

Source: Güler, K. (2006). Karikatür. *Tohum*, 125: 91 (Istanbul: Imam Hatip Schools' Graduates and Members Association Publication).

Islamist Welfare Party (1991–99), explains how social networks of *Imam Hatip* graduates turned to political and economic networks:

> I am a graduate from the *Imam Hatip* [schools]. The most effective aspect of the *Imam Hatip* [schools] is this—we received a better education than other schools in all subjects such as physics, chemistry, foreign language, biology, law, health. But at the same time, we were also learning religious sciences. For this reason, we were raised as individuals who had a strong social side, but at the same time we knew the religion. Afterwards, these [*Imam Hatip* schools] have proliferated. Their proliferation was not forced. People were giving the money themselves, they were building [the schools] themselves. Hence, this was a popular demand. *But those who could not create such organizations felt uneasy. These cadres [from the schools] became at the same time political cadres, at the same time commercial cadres.* (M. Başeğmez, personal communication, February 26, 2007)

As Başeğmez mentions, the secular camp, which lacked such effective networks to mobilize its supporters, felt uneasy about the social, economic, and political potential of the *Imam Hatip* graduates, and therefore demonized these schools as the breeding ground of political Islam. Hence, the capacity of these networks to mobilize the *Imam Hatip* constituency through its social networks not only helped the Islamist actors to strengthen themselves politically, but also sharpen the religious-secular cleavage by drawing strong criticism from secular actors.

Finally, through their participation in these social networks, *Imam Hatip* graduates were able to talk about and act on political issues that were their common concerns. For instance, many of the graduates were engaged in political protests against the headscarf ban in universities, and these social networks emerged as the hotbeds of such protests. Naturally, these social networks were active on the policies on religious education. For example, on May 11, 1997, the Ensar Foundation, the Alumni Association of Imam Hatip High Schools, and the Community for the Dissemination of Knowledge organized a huge rally in the Sultanahmet Square against the draconian February 28 decisions of the NSC ("İmam Hatipe Yakışır Şekilde," 1997). Three hundred thousand people, including many prominent figures from the Islamist and center-right parties, gathered in order to protest the change in the education law, which closed the middle sections of the *Imam Hatip* schools.

Conclusion

The status of *Imam Hatip* schools became a hotly debated, emotional, and polarizing public policy issue in contemporary Turkey. The origins of this conflict go back to the politicization of religious education by the Islamist NOM during its participation in coalition governments in the 1970s. Erbakan's party changed the public's perception of *Imam Hatip* schools as vocational schools to be seen as alternatives to secular education, and the party increased state funding to these schools by using its leverage in government. The NOM and JDP politicians' views on state-religion arrangements in Turkey also affirm that their aim is not to challenge the state's control over religion, an arrangement set up by the Republican elites, but rather to translate the state's cultural and material resources to political capital.

A closer look at processes of ideological construction in these state institutions contributes to the debate between institutionalist and ideational theories of political change. The analysis of state-funded religious education shows us how political institutions and ideas interact in creating political change in line with the claims of discursive institutionalism. Islamist NOM's reinterpretation of the vocational state schools as alternatives to secular schools had important political consequences. *Imam Hatip* schools later became important institutional sites where the Turkish Republic's official ideology of secular nationalism was challenged and alternative frames were constructed. These institutions brought together religious intellectuals, students from culturally marginalized backgrounds, and political activists as producers, consumers, and subjects of cultural artifacts (Wuthnow 1989). The frames produced in and around these religious schools resonated with the cultural grievances of the periphery who felt empowered by the *Imam Hatip* schools' projection of a positive collective identity based on Muslim piety. Those frames not only emerged within the schools through students' interactions with each other or their teachers, but also in the social networks formed around the schools. As SMT suggests (Singerman 2004), these informal networks played an important role in translating those ideas to political power by transmitting the alternative frames to audiences that extended the students and their parents. They were also critical in forming close ties between the NOM, the JDP, and the *Imam Hatip* community.

References

Akşit, B. (1986). "Imam-Hatip and Other Secondary Schools in the Context of Political and Cultural Modernization of Turkey." *Journal of Human Sciences* 5(1): 25–41.

Akşit B. and Coşkun. M.A. (2004). "Türkiye'nin Modernleşmesi Bağlamında İmam Hatip Okulları." In Y. Aktay (ed.), *İslamcılık*. Istanbul: İletişim Yayınları.

Ahmad, F. (1992). *Demokrasi Sürecinde Türkiye (1945–1980)*. Istanbul: Hil Yayın.

Ayhan, H. (2004). *Türkiye'de Din Eğitimi*. Istanbul: Dem Yayınları.

Barlas, D. (1998). *Etatism and Diplomacy in Turkey: Economic and Foreign Policy Strategies in an Uncertain World, 1929–1939*. New York, NY: Brill.

Benford, R.D. and Snow, D.A. (2000). "Framing Processes and Social Movements: An Overview and Assessment." *Annual Review of Sociology* 26: 611-639.

Boratav, K. (2003). "İktisat Tarihi." In Akşin, S. (ed.) *Yakınçağ Türkiye Tarihi 1908–1980* (pp. 297–379). Istanbul: Milliyet Yayınları.

Çakır, R., Bozan, I., and Talu, B. (2004). *İmam Hatip Liseleri Efsaneler ve Gerçekler*. Istanbul: TESEV Yayınları.

Çiçek, Cemil (1994). "Milletin Gözüyle İmam Hatip Okulları ve Beklentileri." In *Kuruluşunun 43. Yılında İmam Hatip Liseleri* (pp.73–83). Istanbul:Ensar Neşriyat.

"Erdoğan İmam Hatipliler Kurultayında Konuştu" (2010, December 5). <http://www.hurriyet.com.tr/gundem/16454307.asp>.

Gamson, W.A., Fireman, B. and Rytina, S. (1982). *Encounters with Unjust Authority*. Homewood, IL: Dorsey Press.

Gökaçtı, M.A. (2005). *Türkiye'de Din Eğitimi ve İmam Hatipler*. Istanbul: İletişim Yayınları.

Güler, K. (2006). "Karikatür." *Tohum*, 125, 91. Istanbul Imam Hatip Schools' Graduates and Members Association Publication.

Gürsel, S. (1999). "Cumhuriyet Döneminde Türkiye Ekonomisi." In M. Tunçay (ed.), *75 yılda düşünceler tartışmalar*. Istanbul: Türk Tarih Vakfı Yayınları.

Hale, W. (2006). "Christian Democracy and the JDP: Parallels and Contrasts." In H. Yavuz (ed.), *The Emergence of a New Turkey: Democracy and the AK Parti* (pp. 66–87). Salt Lake City: University of Utah Press.

Hall, P.A. and Taylor, C.R. (1996). "Political Science and the Three New Institutionalisms." *Political Studies* 44: 936–57.

İlgu, Ş.Ö. (2000). "Politics of Gecekondu in Turkey: The Political Choices of Urban Squatters in National Elections." *Turkish Studies* 1(2): 39–58.

"İlim Yayma Cemiyeti," http://www.iyc.org.tr/, accessed on November 25, 2010

"İmam Hatipliye Kapı Kapandı" (2011, March 2). <http://www.sabah.com.tr/Egitim/2011/03/02/imam_hatipliye_kapi_kapandi>.

"İmam Hatipe Yakışır Şekilde" (1997, May 12). <http://www.zaman.com.tr/haber.do?haberno=463630&title=imam-hatipe-yakisir-sekilde&haberSayfa=0>.

Karaman, H. (2005). *Imam Hatiplilik Şuuru*. Istanbul: Ensar Neşriyat.

Keyder, Ç. (2000). *Türkiye'de Devlet ve Sınıflar*. Istanbul: İletişim.

Kuru, A. (2006). "Reinterpretation of Secularism in Turkey: The Case of the Justice and Development Party." In H. Yavuz (ed.), *The Emergence of a New Turkey: Democracy and the AK Parti* (pp. 136–59). Salt Lake City: University of Utah Press.

Laitin, D.W. and Wildavsky, A. (1988). "Political Culture and Political Preferences." *American Political Science Review* 82: 589–96.

Levi, M. (1997). "A Model, A Method, and A Map: Rational Choice in Comparative and Historical Analysis." In M.I. Lichbach and A.S. Zuckerman (eds), *Comparative Politics: Rationality, Culture, and Structure* (pp. 19–41). Cambridge: Cambridge University Press.

Mardin, Ş. (1973). "Türkiye Siyasasını Açıklayabilecek Bir Anahtar: Merkez-Çevre İlişkileri." In M. Türköne and T. Önder (eds), *Şerif Mardin Bütün Eserleri 6 Türkiye'de Toplum ve Siyaset* (pp. 35–79). Istanbul: İletişim Yayınları.

—— (1993). "Religion and Secularism in Turkey." In A. Hourani, P.S. Khoury, and M.C. Wilson (eds), *The Modern Middle East* (pp. 347–74). Berkeley: University of California Press.

Navaro-Yashin, Y. (2002). *Faces of the State: Secularism and Public Life in Turkey*. Princeton, NJ: Princeton University Press.

Onay, A. (2005). "Imam Hatip Liselerindeki Din Eğitimi ve Dindarlık Yansımaları." In Mahmut Zengin (ed.) *Imam Hatip Liselerinde Eğitim ve Öğretim* (pp. 97–112). Istanbul: Dem Yayınları.

Öcal, M. (1994). *Imam Hatip Liseleri ve İlk Öğretim Okulları*. Istanbul: Ensar Neşriyat.

Pak, S. (2002). *At the Crossroads of Secularism and Islamism*. (Unpublished doctoral dissertation). University of Wisconsin, Madison.

Schmidt, V.A. (2008). "Discursive Institutionalism: The Explanatory Power of Discourse." *Annual Review of Political Science* 11: 303–26.

—— (2008). "From Historical Institutionalism to Discursive Institutionalism: Explaining Change in Comparative Political Economy." Paper presented at the American Political Science Association Meeting, Boston, MA.

Singerman, D. (2004). "The Networked World of Islamist Social Movements." In Q. Wicktorowicz (ed.), *Islamic Activism: A Social Movement Theory* (pp. 143–63). Bloomington: Indiana University Press.

Snow, D.A., Rochford, E.B., Worden, S.K., and Benford, R.D. (1986). "Frame Alignment Processes, Micromobilization, and Movement Participation." *American Sociological Review* 51(4): 464–81.

Swidler, A. (1986). "Culture in Action: Symbols and Strategies." *American Sociological Review* 51(2): 273–86.

Ünsür, A. (2005). *Kuruluşundan Günümüze İmam Hatip Liseleri*. Istanbul: Ensar Neşriyat.

Wiktorowicz, Q. (2004). "Introduction: Islamic Activism and Social Movement Theory." In Q. Wicktorowicz (ed.), *Islamic Activism: A Social Movement Theory* (pp. 1–34). Bloomington: Indiana University Press.

Wuthnow, R. (1989). "Communities of Discourse: Ideology and Social Structure in the Reformation, the Enlightenment, and European Socialism." Cambridge, MA: Harvard University Press.

Yalçıntan, M.C. and Erbaş, A.E. (2003). "Impacts of 'Gecekondu' on the Electoral Geography of Istanbul." *International Labor & Working-Class History* 64: 91–111.

Yavuz, H.M. (2003). *Islamic Political Identity in Turkey*. New York: Oxford University Press.

Zald, M.N. (1996). "Culture, Ideology, and Strategic Framing." In D. McAdam, J.D. McCarthy and M.N. Zald (eds), *Comparative Perspectives on Social Movements: Political Opportunities, Mobilizing Structures, and Cultural Framings* (pp. 261–74). New York: Cambridge University Press.

Zengin, B. (2001). Sivil Anayasa Yeni Bir Toplum Sözleşmesi Önerisi. Ankara: Mart Matbaacılık.

Bibliography for Further Reading

Demiralp, S. (2009). "The Rise of Islamic Capital and the Decline of Islamic Radicalism in Turkey." *Comparative Politics* 41(3): 315–35.

Göle, N. (1997). *The Forbidden Modern: Civilization and Veiling*. Ann Arbor: University of Michigan Press.

Kaplan, S. (2006). *The Pedagogical State: Education and the Politics of National Culture in Post-1980 Turkey*. Stanford: Stanford University Press.

Kuru, A.T. (2009). *Secularism and State Policies toward Religion: The United States, France, and Turkey*. New York: Cambridge University Press.

Lee, R.E. (2010). *Religion and Politics in the Middle East: Identity, Ideology, Institutions, and Attitudes*. Boulder, CO: Westview Press

Tuğal, C. (2009). *Passive Revolution: Absorbing the Islamic Challenge to Capitalism*. Stanford, CA: Stanford University Press.

Turam, B. (2006). *Between Islam and the State: The Politics of Engagement*. Stanford, CA: Stanford University Press.

White, J.B. (2002). *Islamist Mobilization in Turkey: A Study in Vernacular Politics*. Seattle: University of Washington Press.

Yavuz, H.M. *Secularism and Muslim Democracy in Turkey*. New York: Oxford University Press.

Chapter 8

Uncertainty in Governance Processes: The Political Economy of Biosafety Policies in Turkey

Ebru Tekin

Throughout the 1990s, the governance concept as a new way of market making emerged in the discussions about *complex sovereignty* and *technical democracy*. Governance processes have generated new areas of politics where the private has become public while becoming responsible rather than accountable. Turkey has 75 percent of the total number of plant species found in Europe (Baran and Yılmaz 2008), yet biotechnology in Turkey is one of the new areas of governance that entails numerous legal adjustments. This study investigates the governance processes and thus the laws and regulations that have been enacted since 2009 on biosafety policies in Turkey on the entry of Genetically Modified Organisms (GMOs). These processes include uncertainties, and thus within the framework of politics of the uncertainty and political economy of law, this chapter questions how uncertainty is made a normal component of policy making, according to which even the unknown is socially constructed. Analyzing risk as uncertainty, the only risk becomes the objective risk that is created naturally while uncertainty is the social creation of objective risk.

Since the 1990s, the constitutive concepts of modernity in Turkey have been shaped by the shift from the dominance of a national bureaucratic state to the inclusion of diverse groups and private actors. The shift has included policies and regulations initiated by international institutions, namely the IMF, the World Bank and the WTO as well as the EU, through *complex sovereignty* (Paul and Grande 2005). Therefore, the modernity concept indicates the inseparable interaction between state and society through market and law-making mechanisms.

Beck's (1992) *risk society* is derived from the complexity of modernity through technology and industrial development, where modern institutions fail to control risk. In a risk society, risk is associated with the development of rational control. As such, the regulatory aspects of modernity envisage rational control. However, for Callon et al. (2009), political institutions can organize and control overflows of science and technologies (that is, GMOs); yet, they cannot prevent, contain, or eliminate them. Moreover, the rational control mechanisms disregard locality and power configurations at the local level as well as the dichotomy between the accountability and responsibility of institutions. Shaped through the governance process at the local level, the local constitution of modernity is a point of discussion throughout this chapter. By means of a case study approach, the economy of biosafety policies will be analyzed in this chapter, with particular attention given to the mechanisms of the governance processes.

The role of governance mechanisms in terms of responsibility, transparency, the rule of law and accountability become significant in the institutional transformation that aims to minimize transaction costs. What is of importance for the institutional approach is that transaction costs have been identified as obstacles to market development and thus it is believed that the removal of these costs will lead to economic growth (North 1990). The identification and elimination of, as well as intervention into, transaction costs produce contested areas of politics on the way to the implementation of neoliberal policies and creation of global markets. Therefore, uncertainty in policy creation, policy sharing and policy implementation generate transactions costs during governance processes.

However, such a rational approach is not adequate to understand the governance as a communicative process and to understand the constitutive mechanisms of uncertainty. This is an approach shared by constructivist institutionalists, who argue the inefficient, ineffective and contingent nature of institutional struggles (Hay 2006, Blyth 2002). The uncertain nature of the new governance arrangements due to the convergent and resisting mechanism is taken for granted in the literature (Fung 2002).

The general discussion has been derived from uncertainty regarding the lack of biosafety policies in Turkey and the intervention of an international organization into this uncertainty. In 2005, the governance process was initiated by a multi-tiered global project, United Nations Environment Program–Global Environment Facility (UNEP–GEF), with the conduction of a series of workshops, seminars, presentations, training, and discussion sessions at both the national and local levels in Turkey. From 2005 to 2011, it analyzed the dynamics of decision making as well as agenda-setting processes, the shifting of governance processes from one sphere to another, and how the process shapes the patterns of regulatory changes. These shifting spheres include the enactment of the biosafety regulation before the biosafety law, the uncertainties that arose due to the institutional, administrative, legal, and technical gaps, as well as the converging and resistance mechanisms.

This chapter does not include a discussion on risk or its consequences; instead, it focuses on uncertainty and its creation. Furthermore, uncertainty is not about unknowns, but about how actors and institutions intervene into unknowns. Although the methodology of the governance approach is useful in the context, the content needs to be analyzed using a profound approach. Therefore, the focus of this chapter is on the constitutive and constructive dynamics of uncertainty in governance processes.

Providing a critical and analytical perspective on the bases of secondary resources, this chapter is based on legal documents, and council and committee reports, as well as the archives of the Turkish *Official Gazette*. In addition, face-to-face interviews and individual opinions were retrieved through newspapers, the official websites of public and private institutions and organizations—that is, the United States Grain Council (USGC), the Ministry of Agriculture and Rural Affairs (MARA), and the United Nations Environment Program–Global Environment Facility (UNEP–GEF).

This chapter is structured as follows. The first part includes a conceptual framework as a reference to the concepts of the constructivist and discursive aspects of the institutionalist account in relation to the creations of uncertainty and risk during the governance processes. The second part presents the introduction of the governance process in Turkey with a case study approach on the economy of biosafety regulations and laws in relation to the concepts of transparency, top-down governance, countervailing power and participatory governance. The following part includes an overview on the shifting governance processes and how uncertainty and countervailing power shape these shifts. This chapter concludes with a brief summary of the main arguments.

Conceptual Framework

This chapter examines two constituting concepts of policy making: governance and uncertainty. In the literature, the concept of uncertainty is identified with rational aspects such as risk, complexity, lack of information, unknowns, probabilities, and calculations. Indeed, there is little about the social construction of uncertainty through discursive actions in policy making and how governance processes are constituted by uncertainty production. Therefore, analyzing the constitution of uncertainty provides insight into governance processes that are generated from objective uncertainties (that is, the entry of GMOs) and that also shape subjective uncertainties as discursive and rhetorical actions.

Institutions as the Constituting Power of Governance

The early theoretical foundations of the institutional approach were laid in the work of Karl Polanyi (1944), who argued the significance of regulatory institutions to maintain market mechanisms, which can only be sustained by institutions as areas of power struggle. Through his analysis of market economies and institutions, he criticized the arguments of neoclassical economists based on the assumption that markets come into being on their own if the state does not intervene. In that sense, there is no perfectly self-regulating market due to the contested relationship between market and institutions. Similarly, Bates (2005) criticizes the neoclassical position from two perspectives. First, the neoclassical economics approach does not probe institutions; hence, this is their failure to adequately deal with institutions. Secondly, they disregard institutions as areas of decision making to analyze politics within the institutions as well as by the institutions (ibid.).

As a common ground, the neo-institutionalist approach analyzes institutions as tools to increase efficiency and growth in both political and economic activities

(Walker 2004, Nash and Kovic 1997, Apeldoorn 2001), as well as a "negotiated economy," including various institutions to overcome global competition to create a new economic common sense (Campbell and Pedersen 2001). The institution, as a concept, is defined as "any collectively accepted system of rules (procedures, practices) that enable us to create institutional facts" (Searle 2005: 21), with a general reference to the governance concepts of communication and transparency. The institutionalist stance also analyzes individual behavior as conditioned by preexisting institutions within models raised as human constructs (Caldwell and Boehm 1992).

The governance approach that transcends the rational choice approach (Campbell and Pedersen 2001) due to its very nature includes societal partners and also social ties such as alliances, trusting partnerships, long-term relationships, friendships, informal patterns of reciprocal obligations (Lorenz 1992), and untraded interdependencies between local traders (Storper 1995). It is the constructive and deliberate features of the discursive processes throughout the "coordinative" policy sphere and the "communicative" political sphere (Schmidt 2000). The rational approach, by taking resistance mechanisms for granted as natural components of policy making, disregards the limitations of rational design of institutions (Pierson 2000, Leibfried and Pierson 1995).

Callon et al. (2009) introduces hybrid forums, where the uncertainty and complexity of the actor's views prevail, including diversity in participants, among them experts, non-experts, ordinary citizens, and politicians. The dynamics of the actors within these hybrid forums as yet remain unexplored in terms of power dynamics within hybrid forums, interactions between participants, mechanisms, and tools of hybrid forums, and the results of decisions. The interpretation of uncertainty requires the analyses in terms of not only spheres of politics and science, but also their constitutive processes of governance. For this, it is necessary to examine how uncertainty produces politics. Marris (1996) identifies "politics of uncertainty" in terms of its management by individual endeavor. More importantly, he writes, "… because the power to control uncertainty is very unequally distributed, the greatest burden of uncertainties tends to fall on the weakest." This is a "kind of power, which emphasizes control over contingencies rather than the control over resources" (ibid: 1).

Based on the approaches on the politics of uncertainty and its socially constructed processes, it is the argument and contribution of this study that these processes have been constituted through the governance processes and the discursive actions on the way of the neoliberal transformation that entails profound and unexpected changes in principle and ambiguities in practice. The states of uncertainty are based on socially constructed risk discourses as well as time frames, rather than on rational risk estimations and control.

How Uncertainty in Governance Generates Risks

Dosi and Egidi (1991) introduce the concept of procedural uncertainty, which indicates the relationship between complexity and the ability of actors to transmit the necessary information (Dequech 2003). Considering the policy-making process, such a complexity is attached to governance coalitions and corporate network relations as well as multivocality (Stark 2001). The multiplicity (Frey 2009), plurality, or networking in policy influencing (that is, "complexity of biopolitics") includes actors from the market, universities, research institutions, and government representatives (Yu and Liu 2009). However, by analyzing the relational and causative enclosure of power dynamics, it is also necessary to focus on how uncertainties (that is, the lack of legal adjustment for biosafety) are constructed during the policy making process and how the shift from policy creation to policy implementation includes power politics.

The institutional transformation distinguishes the concepts of ambiguity and fundamental uncertainty that are related to creativity and structural changes (Dequech 2000). The discussions on uncertainty have been studied in the literature in terms of institutional change (Beckert 2009), and in relation to risk and ambiguity as uncertainty about probability and the lack of information (DiMaggio 2003). Similarly, the creation of institutions is generated through uncertainty and incomplete information (Bartley and Schneiberg 2002), as well as through uncertain and scientific risks (Asselt et al. 2009). The risks they have discussed, indeed, are about the social construction of uncertainties, rather than real and unknown natural risks.

In light of the network governance approach, Koppenjan and Klijn (2004) define network uncertainty as "substantive uncertainty" in relation to the lack of knowledge, as "strategic uncertainty" in terms of the multiplicity and diverse choices that arise from multiplicity, and as "institutional uncertainty" that is created due to institutional relativities. What they propose to overcome these uncertainties is "cooperation" between the actors through a learning process.

Stewart and Jones (2003) define the governance concept as "policies, structures and processes" in relation to the mechanisms of control and coordination in the decision-making process of the social partners and suggest a depoliticized institutional setting to overcome uncertainties. However, the studies on risk and uncertainty revealed "how concerns about risks to human health and the environment can turn into intensely contested political affairs" (Boholm 2003: 160, Boholm and Löfstedt 1999, Ferreira et al. 2001). According to Boholm (2003: 168), "there are known risks for which are people prepared and for which they have adopted strategies to mitigate"; whereas, there are also things where "knowledge is inadequate and where no established procedures for management exist" (Cancian 1972, Cashdan 1990). Contrary to the discussions that analyze uncertainty as risk, uncertainty also is seen as "making us free" and creative (Bernstein 1998). In fact, the unknown of economics is socially constructed (Kessler 2007: 122, Knorr-

Cetina 1999) through complexities of knowledge creation (Murphy 1992) during the policy-making processes (Beckert 2009).

Providing deeper profound insight, this study analyzes risk as uncertainty in a way that the only risk is objective risk and uncertainty is the social creation of the objective risk. The constructed nature of uncertainty challenges economic assumptions by focusing on how social relations frame the processes of decision, laws, regulations, and provisions. However, the approaches toward uncertainty, in terms of both systemic and individual stances, disregard its constituting mechanisms. Although the assertion includes references on causal mechanisms and human construct economic models, inner dynamics and comprising devices and power relations have remained largely unexplored.

Therefore, a multilevel thinking is asserted through the change in the governance dynamics to scrutinize the constitution, maintenance, and perception of uncertainty and also to depict how governance processes are produced through politics and institutions and how they are taken on the ground by individuals. Within these processes, one might need to scrutinize power dynamics and interaction between actors. Rather than questioning the process of win-and-take relations (who wins/ who loses), the focus is on the nature of the governance process itself in terms of how governance processes create uncertainties and vice versa.

Biosafety Governance in Turkey

Since the 1990s in Turkey, globalization has taken place through international institutions, which have shaped structural changes (Apeldoorn 2002, Önis 2006, Köse et al. 2007). In particular, the transformation in agricultural has been shaped by agricultural policies that have been implemented within the framework of the neoliberal reform measures of the IMF, the World Bank, the WTO and the EU governance. Following the EU Accession Program, in 2006, Agriculture Law No. 5488 was launched with a plan to introduce the principles and priorities of agricultural policies that guarantee harmonization through international commitments. The law proposed the adoption of governance concepts such as sustainability, human health, environmental responsibility, decentralization, participation, transparency, and accountability.[1]

With the Agriculture Law, a holistic approach was included in governance processes such as local and international institutions, state institutions, councils, expert boards, farmers, private sector initiatives, civil society organizations, agricultural cooperatives, unions, foundations, and voluntary organizations. However, although the law referred to the inclusion of non-state

---

1   The law also included changes in the support instruments and the role of producers' organizations to ensure the prevention of any market distortions. Also, the law insisted on the increasing significance of the private sector and the active involvement of producers in market activities.

organizations and farmers, the incorporation of these actors into the system was restrained to the areas of education, consulting, research, and publication of educational materials. The responsibility of civil society organizations (such as product councils and producer organizations) is therefore delimited in the technical duty, coordination, and partnership with decision-making bodies. Therefore, the system might be called just technical governance due to the fact that only state actors are involved in the decision-making process, while limiting the functions of non-state actors to technical responsibilities.

Two concepts—risk and uncertainty—are operationalized during the governance process in relation to the economy of biosafety policies in Turkey. On the one hand, the risk concept signifies the entry of GMOs to the country without any control or monitoring. On the other hand, the uncertainty concept indicates the gap in the implementation of the proposed legal arrangements regarding control and risk assessment. As such, while risk becomes delimited knowledge and ignorance, uncertainty becomes the power relations during the governance process of biosafety law. The delimited knowledge is related to the (socially constructed) unknown risks of GMOs while the ignorance is the lack of measurement and control mechanisms.

Deregulation of Risk Without Transparency

A motion questioned on October 14, 2004 by a deputy member of the Grand National Assembly of Turkey on the importation of genetically modified (GM) corn and soybeans can be used as evidence to show that the entry of GMOs and their products to Turkey have not been controlled or monitored. According to the response document, published on November 2, 2004, a state minister mentioned that since there was no legal regulation on GMOs, there was no specific control on either domestic procedures or importation. More importantly, the minister stated that it was not known whether the imported corn and soybeans were genetically modified or not. According to Law No. 53 on the State Statistical Institute and Its Duty, Responsibility and Foundation, specific information cannot be revealed to any individual or institution. Therefore, the amount of imported GM corn and soybeans had not been revealed. This led to the lack of transparency (GNAT 2004). Therefore, the detailed data about the imported GM products, the exporters and the usage must be questioned.

Nevertheless, the entry of products with GMOs has continued without any legal control. In 2003, the country imported 1.8 million tons of corn and 900,000 tons of soybeans, according to the Union of Chambers of Engineers and Architects in Turkey. In 2005, the amount of soybean imports increased to 1.2 million tons. In 2008, the country imported 435,378 metric tons of corn gluten feed and 465,212 tons of dried grain with solubles from the United States. In 2009, Turkey imported 285,631 metric tons of corn gluten feed and 377,707 metric tons of distiller's dried grain with solubles (USGC 2010a). In Turkey, there was an intense and hasty process of policy making on the control of the importation of GMOs that was not detected until 2011. The lack of information in the usage of GMOs in the domestic market has signified the lack of transparency and the ignorance of the public. The lack of transparency has led to uncertainty and risks.

The Governance of the Draft Biosafety Law: Regularized "Assistance"

From September 22, 2002 to March 18, 2005, the project on the Development of the National Biosafety Framework of Turkey between Turkey and the UNEP–GEF was carried out under the supervision of MARA and the assistance of the UNEP–GEF. The UNEP–GEF is an international organization that regulates the trade, production, processing, distribution, and consumption of GMOs. Since 2000, the Council of the Global Environment Facility (GEF) has targeted to *assist* countries that are in the preparation process of the biosafety regulations that are stipulated in the National Biosafety Frameworks (NBFs). The idea is to alleviate the "potential risks posed by Living Modified Organisms (LMOs) resulting from modern biotechnology" (UNEP–GEF 2005; Jank and Gaugitsch 2001).

The components of the NBF initiated by the UNEP–GEF Project were determined by a commission with the completion of four workshops with the participation of 82 experts and representatives from 51 institutions, including governmental and non-governmental institutions, universities, and the private sector. Under the NBF project framework, the agenda of the National Biosafety Framework included the creation of the institutional basis and legal and regulatory infrastructure. Between March and October 2004, the commission conducted 35 meetings and created the Draft Biosafety Law, which also was discussed at the local level (UNEP–GEF 2005).[2]

The NBF project is a mechanism to produce policies and strategies to regularize the GMOs and their products. The executive agency of the NBF project has assisted the nation-level committees that have requested assistance to overcome the difficulties that have arisen from the diverse institutional setting of the governance process (ibid.). Under the NBF project, the Cartagena Protocol on Biosafety[3] was introduced and signed by the Ministry of Foreign Trade on May 24, 2000. Since the adoption of the protocol on June 17, 2003 (Law No. 4898), the Ministry of Foreign Trade has started addressing the protocol regulations. Under this protocol, the procedure of the importation of GMOs has been simplified

---

2   The Draft Law was included in the NPF Project Document. Throughout this chapter, the expression "Draft Law" also will be used in relation to the Project Document (UNEP–GEF 2005).

3   The Protocol, under the Convention on Biological Diversity 1998, which is operated by the General Directorate of Agricultural Research under the Ministry of Agricultural and Rural Affairs, applies to three categories of Living Modified Organisms (LMOs): LMOs for intentional introduction into the environment (for example, seeds), LMOs intended for direct use as food or feed or for processing (for example, agricultural commodities), and LMOs for contained use (for example, scientific experiment).

and GM products became open for direct use as food, feed, or for processing. Accordingly, two arrangements were introduced for the entry procedures. First, firms could apply the domestic regulations that were consistent with the protocol objectives or, in the case where there was no domestic regulatory framework, the protocol regulations were applied under the information exchange mechanism of the Biosafety Clearing-House[4] within 270 days (Duthie 2010).

On May 27, 2004, Law No. 5179 on the Production, Consumption and Control of Food was enacted. On June 23, 2005, the Regulation was published in relation to the Foundation and Duties of Control Laboratories to create public and private laboratories for food safety, hygiene, and the quality analyses of foods and materials that came into contact with foods, as well as public laboratories for feed, feed materials, animal diseases, and seed. Nevertheless, the entrance of GM products was not controlled due to the lack of any legislative arrangements until the time the law on biosafety was enacted in 2010 and the regulation was created in 2009.

Since 1998, the pending importation and domestic production applications have been assessed by MARA as trials, according to the NBF project document, yet the finalization of these applications has not occurred due to the legislative, administrative, institutional, and technical gaps on biosafety. Although the regulations on food safety have been worked on during the EU accession process, the legislative chanlges have generated uncertainties, gaps, and insufficiencies during the implementation of control and auditing procedures. Throughout the time gaps and legislative uncertainties, the entrance of GMOs to the country has not been monitored and GM products have been entering without any control or auditing (UNEP–GEF 2005).

The Draft Biosafety Law included in the NBF project document was prepared with coordination between MARA and the Ministry of Environment and Forestry (CBD 2010). The National Coordination Committee was created with 27 representative members from MARA, the Ministry of Health President of Environmental Health, the Ministry of Foreign Trade, the Turkish Patent Institute, the Ministry of Industry and Trade, the Ministry of Environment and Forestry, the Ministry of Justice, the Scientific and Technical Research Council of Turkey, the General Directorate of Custom Enforcement, the State Planning Organization, the Turkish Seed Industry Association, the Union of Turkish Chambers of Agriculture, the Turkish Association for the Conservation of Nature, the Turkish Feed Manufacturers Association, the Consumer's Rights Association, the Ankara University Agricultural Faculty Department of Plant Protection, and universities (veterinary faculties and science biology departments) under the Draft Biosafety Law, as was stipulated in the EU National Program accepted on July 24, 2003.

---

4   The Biosafety Clearing-House (BCH) is "a mechanism set up by the Cartagena Protocol on Biosafety to facilitate the exchange of information on Living Modified Organisms (LMOs) and assist the Parties to better comply with their obligations under the Protocol. Global access to a variety of scientific, technical, environmental, legal and capacity building information is provided in all 6 of the UN languages" (BCH 2010).

The Draft Biosafety Law included several research phases involving institutional, legal, infrastructural, and technical research circles.

The Draft Biosafety Law aimed to control the possible impacts of GMOs in terms of the invasion or spread to the environment, safety and health, the freedom of choice of consumers, the ecosystem and the sustainability of biodiversity. The Draft Biosafety Law also included the creation of the institutional legal, administrative and technical bases for measurement and control such as laboratories. According to the Draft Biosafety Law, the importation of GMOs was allowed and the production and processing of GMOs were restricted in some aspects.

The Draft Biosafety Law created a Biosafety Council and scientific committees to implement the control and risk assessment procedures. Since the central authorized institution was MARA, the ministry was responsible to assess the applications in terms of their content with the assistance of a scientific committee. In terms of evaluating the applications on the basis of the relevant law, the creation of a National Biosafety Committee constituted by the representatives of stakeholders was proposed. Also, the Biosafety Council was to be created as a decision-making organ to which the units of MARA were to provide information and data. The Biosafety Council was to consist of the members of the National Coordination Committee, the NGOs, and the private sector, as well as public organizations. The Biosafety Council would have nine members, four of them appointed by MARA, two by the Ministry of Environment and Forestry and one by each of the ministries of Health, Industry and Trade, and Foreign Trade. The head of the Biosafety Council was to be appointed by MARA.

In the Draft Biosafety Law, the aim is not to prevent or prohibit the entry of GMOs, but to regularize through regulatory arrangements under a legal framework. These prohibitions have been initiated to regulate the entry of GMOs to the country and to identify conditions, procedures, actors, and roles. The prohibitions have included only any unpermited use and/or making use of GMOs and GM products, the use of GMOs and GM products in baby foods, the importation and distribution of baby foods containing GMOs and GM products, and the production of GMOs within a given distance and in places protected for biological diversity and allocated for organic agriculture. Only GMOs specifically developed or judged as safe for babies have been allowed. Nevertheless, the application of simplified procedures provides flexibility in the control and risk-assessment process. The NBF project document included the following:

> Consent is required for first import; placing on the market for environmental release and/or as food and feed or for processing; contained use; export; and, transit of each GMO and products thereof. Simplified procedure might be applicable in the cases of import and marketing of GMOs if there is evidence of safety for biodiversity, environment and human health. (UNEP–GEF 2005)

Although the decisions that were taken or discussed during the governance process were obligatory or binding, the Draft Biosafety Law and the NBF project provide insight into the nature of an unbinding character of the governance approach. The governance process of the creation of the Draft Biosafety Law only included policy communication restricted among institutions. The Draft Biosafety Law assigned the MARA as the responsible and authorized institution to create the agenda for a biosafety law and to determine its components as well as the infrastructure. However, the UNEP–GEF is not accountable to the public. In fact, the governance needed to include both public communication and policy communication, as a reference to the *technical democracy* that ensures the democratization of the experts and the corporation of professionals and laypeople (Callon et al. 2009).

Regulation Without Law: 'Top-down' Governance

The concept of the "top-down" governance has been adopted from Fung (2002: 6) as a concept that is defined as follows: "Once the rules have been set by bargaining among interests, agencies implement these rules upon stakeholders and the general public. But interest groups themselves have no direct responsibility for devising solutions or implementing the rules." On October 26, 2009, the Regulation on Importation, Processing, Exportation, Control and Audit of Genetically Modified Organisms and Products for Food and Feed[5] was published in the *Official Gazette*. The Regulation 2009 was introduced "suddenly" (USGC 2010c) as a top-down approach of MARA without informing any of the governance actors.

The Regulation 2009 included the requirements of control documents on the entry of GMOs to the country as well as the prohibitions of GMOs in violation of the condition set by the regulatory provisions. The Regulation 2009 was enacted at the time of its publication, before the Biosafety Law was created. Following the publication of the Regulation 2009, widespread uncertainty was experienced in the market. After the Regulation 2009 came into effect, there were discussions among different groups on the condition provisions for the importation of GMOs, with the aim to understand the condition provisions.

NGOs and private organizations created social platforms against the regulation of GMOs. The argument of these social platforms was the de facto legitimation of the entry of GMOs through *fait accompli* regulations. The Regulation 2009 also upset the importers, who had not expected a law that would include provisions for the entry of GMOs to the country. More importantly, they had already shipped GM products to the country and the cargo ships had been waiting for a long time for inspection and were being charged rent at the ports.

According to Joe O'Brien, the Regional Director of the United States Grains Council in the Middle East and Subcontinent, the legal representatives made diverse comments. According to him,

---

5   Throughout this chapter,the regulation will be referred to as "the Regulation 2009."

> It is chaotic at the ports as vessels arrive and no one knows what to do ... there are vessels near the region that are not able to come into port to deliver essential feed ingredients only available through exports and are circling the area or consigning the cargo into costly bonded facilities, driving up costs. (USGC 2010b)

Following the initiation of the Regulation 2009 and as a result of the uncertainty in timing and policy implementation, prices increased and trade relations remained uncertain. During the process of uncertainty, the power relations at the local level were roused. The importers started to contact local trade representatives as well as government officials against such an "irrational regulation" (USGC 2010b, 2010c). After the Regulation 2009, importers do not need to produce the necessary documents for their GM products to be able to enter the country.

Re-regulation and the "Countervailing Power"

Uncertainty in the market created a new governance process. On November 2, 2009, MARA announced the foundation of laboratories for the analysis of GMOs and specified the names of 27 products. One week later, on November 9, the number of products to be treated under the GMOs analysis was decreased to nine, due to insufficient laboratory infrastructure. Following the publication of the Regulation 2009, the Health and Food Security Movement Foundation opened a case against MARA with the aim to cancel and suspend the implementation of the Regulation 2009 against the entry of GMOs to the country. On November 20, 2009, the Regulation 2009 was amended and a temporary article was added to release the importation of products for those that had received the control documents before October 26, as well as for those that were suitable under EU criteria.

On the next day, the Council of State decided to suspend the implementation of the Regulation 2009 due to its lack of necessary legislative framework. In fact, since the decision was dependent on MARA's decision, after the opposition of MARA, the Council of State accepted the opposition on December 24, 2009. On January 20, 2010, the provisions of the Regulation 2009 in terms of importation were eased and changed by postponing the prohibition on the importation (of products with GMOs in violations of the provision conditions set by the Regulation 2009) until March 1. Therefore, GM products with over 0.9 percent continued to enter the country without any inspection or risk assessment.

The regulatory function of MARA during the governance process was shaped through power relations. Therefore, one might say that the countervailing power led to the changes in the Regulation 2009. The importers and local trade representatives who trade GM products insisted on the postponement of the MARA decision on the condition provisions on GMOs. The process of uncertainty and obscurity included a waiting and preparation process, policy production and the political economy of power. The uncertain and unsteady governance process that emerged was created because the Regulation 2009 was enacted before its law was published. The regulation was enacted without the law. Although the

Draft Biosafety Law created the detailed framework for legal, regulatory, and institutional changes, the Regulation 2009 changed this framework.

Finally, on March 18, 2010, the Biosafety Law was accepted in the Parliament, published in the *Official Gazette* on March 26, 2010 and enacted on September 26, 2010. A new regulation was published on August 13, 2010 and the Regulation 2009 was abolished. In the new regulation, the prohibitions were in parallel with the Draft Biosafety Law. The law prohibited the GMOs' entry without approval; the use of GMOs and GM products contrary to the Biosafety Council decisions; the production of genetically modified plants and animals; the use of GMOs and GM products in places prohibited by the Council, and the use of GMOs and GM products in baby food and baby formula. Furthermore, the Law proposed the creation of the Biosafety Council as the authorized institution,[6] as well as the labeling conditions and the socio-economic risk assessments on GMOs.

The "Participatory" Governance Without the Public

The governance process on the way to create the biosafety law in Turkey has included both public and private actors. As such, a participatory type of governance has been applied in terms of policy generation. The concept has been defined as "the effort to achieve change through actions that are more effective and equitable than normally possible through representative government and bureaucratic administration by inviting citizens to a deep and sustained participation in decision making" (Kearney et al. 2007: 80). However, what this chapter reveals is that participatory governance only includes the active participation of institutions and their representatives rather than individuals on the ground.

The NPF project referred to public awareness and public communication in a way that "it was not possible to determine the exact opinion of the public about GMOs and products thereof at the current stage in Turkey due to the lack of information on or misunderstanding of the issues on GMOs and biosafety in general" (UNEP–GEF 2005: 16). The creation of public awareness and participation were delimited to organizations at the regional level, consultation meetings at the national and local level, and the distribution of publications to the "general public, farmers, operators, managers, decision-makers and the Parliament" (ibid: 17) Such an approach excluded and alienated the public and the people from the governance processes that had shaped the policy making.

Nevertheless, despite the lack of public participation, responsibility was transferred to individuals outside of the spheres of expertise and the state apparatus. While public institutions were only responsible for information gathering and providing as well as training, it was ensured that individuals would be aware of and responsible for the possible risks of GMOs through public awareness. Table 8.1 lists the selected targets of the NBF project for public awareness in biosafety

---

6   Although the Biosafety Council was created as an authorized institution, its members are selected by the Ministers. The head of the Council is selected by MARA.

policies with a shared responsibility of the possible risks of GMOs. In that sense, no institution is assigned as accountable.

Table 8.1   Project targets for public awareness and "public participation"

Rising awareness on biosafety and the dissemination of information
Ensuring the rights of farmers to participate in decisions
Ensuring the rights of consumers
Getting the support of the public in the implementation of biosafety measures and NBF
Ensuring the implementation and common understanding of NBF
Ensuring the awareness and education of young people on the subject of biosafety
Ensuring future human resources for biosafety
Ensuring that the public is informed quickly and correctly
Keeping the attention of the public on biosafety issues and ensuring public participation in decisions
Inclusion of biosafety issues in academic programs and primary education programs
Informing and giving roles to NGOs
Regular programs in the media
Participation of famous people at events

Source: UNEP–GEF 2005

As a part of shared responsibility, on June 21, 2011, the Biosafety Council decided on the presentation of the Council's Decisions to the public opinion via the Biosafety Information Exchange Mechanism of Turkey (TBBDM).[7] The decisions were presented to the public, with 21 days allocated for natural persons and legal entities to fill the public opinion form via the form of Public Opinion Form (TBBDM 2011b).[8] Although this was a mechanism to create public awareness and signified partial integration to the decision-making mechanism, the process lacked a systematic voting and a legal infrastructure. The aim to create public awareness was to let the public become aware of the entry of GMOs and the sharing of

---

7   The website of TBBDM (<http://www.tbbdm.gov.tr>) includes information on the Biosafety Council, its members, the law and regulations on GMOs, and so on.

8   The results of the public opinion have not been presented yet.

responsibility. The voluntary nature of public participation had been foreseen, yet no legal framework was proposed for this kind of arrangement. Instead, the target was to engage and regularize the concepts of the discussion of the public/persons through "systematic awareness" and "common terminology" (UNEP–GEF 2005).

The Politics of Uncertainty

The governance process includes inconsistencies in regulating risk and discrepancies in information on risk, which creates uncertainty in terms of the accuracy of the content. The Biosafety Council decisions must be analyzed to understand these inconsistencies. The Draft Biosafety Law has proposed that each GMO application will be evaluated by separate committees of eleven members and these subcommittees will be dependent on the Council. However, the Regulation 2009 proposed the creation of the Committee assigned by the MARA. Until the enactment of the Biosafety Law, the scientific committee, which is created within the framework of Regulation 2009, has worked as Biosafety Council. Finally, with the Biosafety Law, the Biosafety Council has been created with its subcommittees to be selected by the Council. These members of committees will be appointed by experts from TUBITAK (the Scientific and Technological Research Council of Turkey), universities, and research institutes.

On September 27, 2010, the first Biosafety Council gathered with the agenda of creating a list of experts, to set the next meeting time and cite "wishes and requests." With this meeting, the Committee decided to make announcements to universities and TUBITAK, to create the list of experts to be selected among the scientific committees. The duty of these committees is to conduct risk analysis and the socioeconomic assessment.

On October 26, 2010, the Council met with the agenda of approving the release of GMOs and GM products into the market for food, animal feed, and processing; the release of these products for scientific experiments, and the use of GMOs in enclosed places. The agenda of the meeting also included importation provisions for soybeans and soy residue. The Council decided on the specification of the threshold value as 0.9 percent and the allowance of products with 0.9 percent of GMOs without labeling. They also decided to submit the application files reserved by the TBBDM committee members to be analyzed in terms of risk, socioeconomic, and ethical considerations. Although firms are required to label products with GMO content higher than 0.9 percent, firms, except in the feed industry, do not apply the labeling procedures.

On November 1, 2010, the Council decided to evaluate the application of the Feed Manufacturers' Association of Turkey.[9] Since the application had included the usage of GMOs only in feeds, the Council decided to apply simplified procedures.

---

9   On January 27, 2011, the name of the applicant institution was changed to the Feed Manufacturers' Association Enterprises of Turkey, which organizes the financial activities of the Foundation.

On January 26, 2011, the Council decided on the usage of two genes in the production of animal feeds after an application was made by the Turkey Feed Manufacturers' Association. In light of the report of the Scientific Risk Assessment Committee and the Socioeconomic and Assessment Committee, the Council approved the application with a number of restrictions such as risk management and market control, labeling, and follow up. Following the decision, Risk Management Plans were to be submitted by the firms. In this way, private actors were made responsible for exploring risks and for informing the state authority. However, no control or audit mechanism in terms of the accountability of these firms was implemented. In light of this process, the control governance indicates how policy enactment was initiated by private and market actors and how science shaped the market as well as prevailed over politics (Moore et al. 2011).

On October 28, 2010, Federation of Food and Drink Industry Associations of Turkey submitted an application on the release of 29 GMOs under simplified procedures. According the Regulation 2009, the scientific committee has allowed these GMOs entrance under the simplified procedures. However, on January 10, 2011, the Biosafety Council decided to abolish the decision of the previous scientific committee created by the Regulation 2009 and to initiate a new process of risk and socioeconomic assessments.

The politics of uncertainty becomes visible through the Socio-Economic Report prepared by the scientific committee (TBBDM 2011a). The report started the discussion on GMOs with a common understanding in relation to scarce resources and the need of GMO production. With a reference to scientific literature on GMOs, the report depicted the potential costs and benefits of GMOs. These costs included the changes in food quality, resistance to antibiotics, toxicity, and the potential for GMOs to cause cancer. Focusing on the case of GM corn, the report provided the statistics of corn production in Turkey, which depicted the increasing volume of corn production with an 80 percent rate of coverage of the national consumption. Accordingly, the report discussed the potential impacts of GM corn importation on small-scale corn producers in relation to the lack of support systems and decreasing agricultural employment.

Despite these discussions within the report, the committee decided to release the importation of the products with GMOs with a set of measurements. It was advised to take a "cautious approach" towards GMOs in law making (that is, to decrease the validity period of each GMO application from ten to five years) (TBBDM 2011a). However, any system of audit and inspection is still inadequate in Turkey.

In light of the discussion on the damages on the importation and usage of GMOs, the report referred to the presentations of stakeholders, particularly conducted by the Turkey Grain Board (TMO).[10] On these presentations, it has

---

10   The Turkish Grain Board, founded in 1938, is "a limited liability and autonomous state economic enterprise running on state capital in accordance with the provisions under Decree Law No. 233 of 08/06/1984 on State Economic Enterprises" (TMO Official Website 2011).

been mentioned that the country needs to import GM feeds. Also, as the report mentioned, the scientific committees have been asked to make decisions within the framework of international law. The report started therefore a discussion on legal and regulatory framework that has been "imposed" by the international regulations. The report clearly specified that a legal evaluation cannot be possible without scientific studies. Providing a legal assessment, throughout the report, it refers to the struggle of the actors in policy making on GMOs (TBBDM 2011a).

Therefore, the advisory role of the scientific committees does not guarantee the changes in the laws and regulations on how to control the risks that were clearly defined in the report. Also, the scientific uncertainty was discussed at the end of the report, in relation to the "lack of knowledge," "variations," "indeterminable" process, as well as "real unknowns" (TBBDM 2011a). Although the scientific committee specifies the potential costs and damages, the committees decide in parallel to international regulations. Callon et al. (2009) offers the exploration of scientific results not only with *secluded* research, but also research that include laypeople (that is, field trials of GMOs). Therefore, the decision of scientific committees which approve the usage of GMOs in feed proposes a number of control items against undefined risks. The undefined risks are not unknowns, but stem from ignorance. More importantly, the decisions of the scientific committee do not prevent risks, yet this presents how risk is regulated rather than contained. Uncertainty in this process is not about unknowns, but about the inability to intervene into unknowns. Therefore, their decisions become part of the politics of uncertainty and delimited within the international regulations.

Shifting Governance Process

Fung (2002: 3) focuses on the shifts between the governance processes in relation to the concept of countervailing power as "the presences of powerful actors in most decision-making venues, and to the possibilities that those actors may be challenged and even defeated from time to time by the weak and less organized." Table 8.2 is adopted from Fung's conceptualization on governance processes in relation to countervailing power. In light of this analysis, the case study on the Turkish biosafety policies depicts how uncertain the shift is between governance processes under the impact of countervailing power and also how uncertainty strengthens the impact of the countervailing power.

In the case of biosafety governance in Turkey, it depicts how the governance process moves from a participatory type of governance in policy creation toward a top-down type of governance in policy implementation. The governance process on biosafety policies has been initiated, regulated, and assisted by an international organization, namely UNEP–GEF. The interaction between UNEP–GEF and social partners, as well as its relations with these participatory agents, constitute the basis of complex sovereignty where private actors are made responsible rather than accountable.

During the NBF project and thus the creation of Draft Biosafety Law, as depicted in the first governance process (I), a participatory type of governance was executed with the participation of public and private institutions, as well as NGOs and universities. The shift from the Draft Biosafety Law (process I) to the initiation of the Regulation 2009 (process II) indicates the top-down governance executed by the state apparatus. The Regulation 2009 was not expected by the market actors and thus the unexpected conditions provisions generated uncertainties in the market where the countervailing power was in a situation of unexpectedness. Furthermore, the Regulation 2009, which was enacted before the Biosafety Law, included arrangements that were inconsistent with the proposal of the Draft Biosafety Law. Similarly, the majority of the proposals initiated, especially in relation to public awareness and participation, in the Draft Law have not been enacted in the final version of the law, as depicted in the third governance process (III).

Table 8.2   Governance processes under the impact of countervailing power

		Countervailing power	
		Low	High
Governance processes	Top-down governance	(II) The Regulation (2009)	(III) The Biosafety Law (2010)
	Participatory governance	(I) Draft Biosafety Law (2005)	(IV) Public awareness and resistance

Adopted from Fung (2002)

During the process of biosafety governance in Turkey, the countervailing power, as depicted in the third governance process (III) with the initiation of the final version of the Biosafety Law, has been executed through local and global representatives as well as private-sector initiatives against the condition provisions on the importation of the GMOs and its products. In this governance process, the governance approach has been applied under the influence of the countervailing power, which is generated through private-sector representatives.

The following table also provides insight into the governance process from inception to policy making and implementation. The selected points below that are included in the NPF project were treated as high priority during the workshops, meetings, and discussions. In fact, several of the arrangements were treated as high priority in the Draft Biosafety Law prepared by the governance parties, but the Biosafety Law did not include the effective regulatory, executive and assessment mechanisms to implement the points as high priority (UNEP–GEF 2005).

Most of these proposals have only been enacted through the supportive regulatory changes. Furthermore, there are gaps in the control and inspection mechanisms. Although the Biosafety Law was enacted, the application of the

Table 8.3   Level of enactments of the points proposed to be treated as high priority

The points proposed as high priority
Administrative, institutional, technical, and legislative gaps in risk assessments
The lack of studies on the creation of public awareness
The lack of sufficient laboratory capacities in controls and inspections
The lack of efficient border control systems
The lack of emergency measures in the danger of transit
Inadequate human resources
Lack of coordination between research institutions and laboratories
Lack of regulation to prevent intentional and unintentional environmental release
Lack of a single competent institution for biosafety
Lack of an Information Management Center for biosafety
Lack of the protection of the country's genetic resources
Danger of the possibility of studying GMOs

Source: UNEP–GEF 2005

provisions cannot be implemented with a systematic mechanism. The law and its inserted regulations have been enacted without any well-defined, well-implemented, or systematic institutional basis. More importantly, the provisions of the law have not been implemented properly, due to the lack of monitoring and auditing.

For future research, one might hypothesize that the fourth governance process (IV) might be analyzed in terms of resistance mechanisms through participatory means, where the countervailing power comes from general public. For instance, the process of public opinion assessment of the Biosafety Information Exchange Mechanism of Turkey may be analyzed in relation to the effectiveness of public participation, results, evaluation, and integration into the decision-making process. This type of governance process hypothesizes that if the participatory governance includes not only institutional representatives but also public means through individual initiatives on the ground, a high countervailing power generates a wide range of public awareness and collaborative resistance mechanisms (for instance, the activities of Greenpeace against the GM products) against both the content (the lack of systematic control and monitoring mechanisms for the risk assessment and ignorance of the risk revealed from the entry of GMOs and its products to the country), and the methodology (the dominance of private institutions in policy and decision making and the lack of the participation of local initiatives on the ground) of biosafety governance.

Conclusion

The changing nature of the governance process includes non-state actors as well as international initiatives. The interaction between international and local actors generates a "complex sovereignty" through which the legitimacy of the state is questioned. In the case of the economy of biosafety policies in Turkey, the lack of legislative arrangements has been met by an international organization that is accountable neither to the state nor to the public.

The policy making is set on policy communication between social partners that include national and international actors as well as local representatives and experts. However, this communication has drawbacks. First, non-state actors are excluded in decision-making processes. Their duties and responsibilities are delimited to participation in workshops and seminars, but not in decision making. Secondly, laypersons and individuals are isolated not only due to the nature of the decision making, but also to the *secluded* scientific research. Scientific committees make decision in terms of current literature, rather than an original scientific research, within the framework of politics and international law. Third, the process of policy implementation becomes inconsistent with policy communication and thus the governance process.

As such, delimited knowledge (that is, politics in scientific decisions) and ignorance (that is, the lack of public awareness) create uncertainties that lead to shifts in governance processes. The shift is based on countervailing power, which is the ability to intervene into unknowns. The natural risk becomes a socially constructed risk through uncertainty due to the lack of transparency. As a result, this study concludes how uncertainty generates different governance processes and how uncertain the shift from one governance process to another in relation to the changing countervailing power. Uncertainty is not about complexity, but unexpectedness and shifting patterns of the interaction of countervailing power.

References

Apeldoorn, B. (2001). "The struggle over European order: Transnational class agency in the making of embedded neo-liberalism." In A. Beiler and A.D. Morton (eds), *Social Forces in the Making of New Europe* (pp. 70–89). Basingstoke: Palgrave.

Apeldoorn, B. (2002). *Transnational Capitalism and the Struggle over European Integration*. London: Routledge.

Asselt, M.B.A., Vos., E., and Rooijackers, B. (2009). "Science, knowledge and uncertainty in EU risk regulation." In M. Everson and E. Vos (eds), *Uncertain risks regulated* (pp. 359–415). Oxford: Routledge.

Baran, M. and Yılmaz, R. 2008). "The biosafety policy on genetically modified organisms in Turkey." *Environmental Biosafety Research* 7: 57–9.

Bartley, T. and Schneiberg, M. (2002). "Rationality and institutional contingency: the varying politics of economic regulation in the fire insurance industry." *Sociological Perspectives* 45(1): 47–79.

Bates, R.H. (2005). *Beyond the miracle of the market*. Cambridge: Cambridge University Press.

BCH. (2010). *Welcome to the BCH Central Portal*. http://bch.cbd.int/

Beck, U. (1992). *Risk society: towards a new modernity*. London: Sage.

Beckert, J. (2009). "The social order of markets." *Theory and Society* 38: 245–69..

Bernstein, P.L. (1998). *Against the gods: The remarkable story of risk*. New York: Wiley.

Blyth, M. (2002). *Great transformations: Economic ideas and political change in the twentieth century*. Cambridge: Cambridge University Press.

Boholm, A. (2003). "The cultural nature of risk: Can there be an anthropology of uncertainty?" *Ethnos: Journal of Anthropology* 68(2): 159–79.

Boholm, A. and Löfstedt, R. (1999). "Issues of risk, trust and knowledge: The Hallandsås Tunnel Case." *Ambio* 28(6): 556–61.

Caldwell, B.J. and Boehm, S. (eds) (1992). *Austrian economics: Tensions and new directions*. Boston, MA: Kluwer.

Callon, M., Lascoumes, P. and Barthe, Y. (eds) (2009). *Acting in an uncertain world: An essay on technical democracy*. Translated by G. Burchell (2009). Boston: Massachusetts Institute of Technology.

Campbell, J.L. and Pedersen, O. (2001). "Introduction." In J.L. Campbell and O. Pedersen (eds), *The rise of neoliberalism and institutional analysis* (pp. 1–24). Princeton, NJ: Princeton University Press.

Cancian, F. (1972). *Change and uncertainty in a peasant economy: The Maya corn farmers of Zinacantan*. Stanford, CA: Stanford University Press.

Cashdan, E. (ed.). (1990). *Risk and uncertainty in tribal and peasant economies*. Boulder, CO: Westview Press.

CBD (2010). *Projeler (Projects)*. Ministry of Environment and Forestry <http://www.cbd.gov.tr/projects/doga_koruma_projeler.doc>.

Dequech, D. (2000). "Fundamental uncertainty and ambiguity." *Eastern Economic Journal* 26(1): 41–60.

Dequech, D. (2003). "Uncertainty and Economic Sociology: A Preliminary Discussion." *American Journal of Economics and Sociology* 62(3): 509–32.

DiMaggio, P. (ed.). (2003). *The twenty-first century firm: Changing economic organization in international perspective*. Princeton, NJ: Princeton University Press.

Dosi, G. and Egidi, M. (1991). "Substantive and procedural uncertainty." *Journal of Evolutionary Economics* 1(2): 145–68.

Duthie, D. (2010). *Biosafety and biosecurity in the context of the Cartagena Protocol on Biosafety* http://www.opbw.org/new_process/mx2008/BWC_ MSP_2008_MX_Bio_UNEP_En.pdf.

Ferreira, C., Boholm, A., and Löfstedt, R. (2001). "From vision to catastrophe: A risk event in search of images." In J. Flynn, P. Slovic, H. Kunreuther (eds), *Risk, media and stigma: understanding public challenges to modern science and technology* (pp. 283–300). London: Earthscan.

Frey, B.S. (2009). *A multiplicity of approaches to institutional analysis. Applications to the government and the arts IEW.* Working papers <http://www.iew.uzh.ch/wp/iewwp420.pdf>.

Fung, A. (2002). *Collaboration and countervailing power: Making participatory governance work* <http://www.archonfung.net/papers/ CollaborativePower2.2.pdf>.

Grand National Assembly of Turkey. (GNAT) (2004). *Motion to the Ministry of Foreign Trade replied to by State Minister Kürsat Tüzmen.* B.02.1.DTM.0.03.07.01.24.

Hay, C. (2006). "Constructivist institutionalism." In R.A.W. Rhodes, S. Binder, and B. Rockman (eds) (2006). *The Oxford handbook of political institutions* (pp. 56–74). Oxford: Oxford University Press.

Jank, B. and Gaugitsch, H. (2001). "Decision making under the Cartagena Protocol on Biosafety." *Trends in Biotechnology* 19(5): 194-97.

Kearney, J., Berkes, F., Charles, A., Pinkerton, E. and Wiber, M. (2007). "The role of participatory governance and community-based management in integrated coastal and ocean management in Canada." *Coastal Management* 35: 79–104.

Kessler, O. (2007). "Performativity of risk and the boundaries of economic sociology." *Current Sociology* 55(1): 110–25.

Knorr-Cetina, K. (1999). *Epistemic cultures: how the science make knowledge.* Cambridge, MA: Harvard University Press.

Koppenjan, J. and Erik-Hans, K. (2004). *Managing Uncertainties in Networks: A Network Approach to Problem Solving and Decision Making.* New York: Routledge.

Köse, A., Senses, F., and Yeldan, E. (eds). (2007). *Neoliberal globalization as new imperialism: Case studies on reconstruction of the periphery.* New York: NOVA Science.

Leibfried, S. and Pierson, P. (1995). *European social policy: Between integration and fragmentation.* Washington, DC: Brookings Institution.

Lorenz, E. (1992). "Trust, community, and cooperation: toward a theory of industrial districts." In M. Storper and A. Scott (eds), *Pathways to industrialization and regional development* (pp. 194–210). London: Routledge.

Marris, P. (1996). *The politics of uncertainty: Attachment in private and public life.* London: Routledge.

Moore, K., Kleinmann, L.D., Hess, D., and Frickel, S. (2011). "Science and neoliberal globalization: a political sociological approach." *Theory and Society* 40(5): 505–32.

Murphy, J.W. (1992). "Reason, bounded rationality, and the lebenswelt." *American Journal of Economics and Sociology* 51: 293–304.

Nash, J. and Kovic, C. (1997). "The reconstitution of hegemony: The free-trade act and transformation of rural Mexico." In J. Mittelman (ed.). *Globalization: Critical reflections* (pp. 165–85). Boulder, CO and London: Lynne Rienner.

North, D.C. (1990). *Institutions, institutional change and performance.* Cambridge: Cambridge University Press.

Önis, Z. (2006). "Globalization and party transformation: Turkey's Justice and Development Party in perspective." In P. Burnell (ed.), *Globalizing democracy: party politics in emerging democracies* (pp. 122–40). London: Routledge.

Pauly, L. and Grande, E. (2005). "Reconstituting political authority: Sovereignty, effectiveness and legitimacy in a transnational order." In E. Grande and L. Pauly (eds), (2005). *Complex sovereignty: Reconstituting political authority in the twenty-first century* (pp. 3–21). Toronto: University of Toronto Press.

Pierson, P. (2000). "The Limits of Design: Explaining Institutional Origins and Change," *Governance* 13(4): 475–99.

Polanyi, K. (1944). *The Great Transformation: The Political and Economic Origins of Our Time.* Boston: Beacon Press.

Searle, J.R. (2005). "What is an institution?" *Journal of Institutional Economics* 1(1): 1–22.

Schmidt, V.A. (2000). "Values and discourse in the politics of adjustment." In F.W. Scharpf and V.A. Schmidt (eds), *Welfare and work in the open economy. Volume I: From vulnerability to competitiveness* (pp. 229–309). Oxford: Oxford University Press.

Stark, D. (2001). "Ambiguous assets for uncertain environments: Heterarchy in postsocialist firms." In P. DiMaggio (ed.), (2003). *The twenty-first century firm: Changing economic organization in international perspective* (pp. 69–104). Princeton, NJ: Princeton University Press.

Stewart, J. and Jones, G. (2003). *Renegotiating the environment: The Power of Politics.* Sydney: The Federation Press.

Storper, M. (1995). "The resurgence of regional economies, ten years later: the region as a nexus of untraded interdependencies." *Journal of European Urban and Regional Studies* 2(3): 191–221.

TBBDM (2011a). *Biyogüvenlik Kurulu'na sunulmak üzere Sosyo-Ekonomik Değerlendirme Komitesi tarafından hazırlanan rapor (report prepared by Socio-Economic Assessment Committee to be submitted to Biosafety Council)* <http://www.tbbdm.gov.tr/Libraries/Regulations/sosyo_MON88017XMON810.sflb.ashx>.

TBBDM. (2011b). *Genetik yapısı değiştirilmiş organizmalarla ilgili bilimsel komite raporlarinin kamuoyu görüşüne sunulmasina ilişkin usul ve esaslar (Guidelines and Procedures on the Presentation of Scientific Committee Reports on GMOs to Public Opinion)* TBBDM Website http://www.tbbdm.gov.tr/Libraries/Regulations/8top_ek_kamuoyu_usul_esas.sflb.ashx.

TMO Official Website. (2011). *History of Turkish grain board (TMO)* <http://www.tmo.gov.tr/Main.aspx?ID=232>.

UNEP–GEF. (2005). *Draft national biosafety framework for the Republic of Turkey prepared in the scope of the UNEP-GEF project on the development of the national biosafety framework by the Ministry of Agriculture and Rural Affairs General Directorate of Agricultural Research* <http://www.unep.org/biosafety/files/TRNBFrep.pdf>.

USGC (2010a). *USGC discusses Turkey's new biosafety law with officials in Ankara, Istanbul* <http://www.grains.org/index.php/2012-04-30-15-22-26/2318-usgc-discusses-turkeys-new-biosafety-law-with-officials-in-ankara-istanbul>.

USGC (2010b). *Biotech import ban creates feed ingredient shortage in Turkey* <http://www.grains.org/index.php/2012-04-30-15-22-26/2041-biotech-import-ban-creates-feed-ingredient-shortage-in-turkey>.

USGC. (2010c). *Turkey puts kibosh on biotech imports* <http://www.grains.org/index.php/2012-04-30-15-22-26/2005-turkey-puts-kibosh-on-biotech-imports>.

Walker, R.A. (2004). *The conquest of bread: 150 years of agribusiness in California.* New York: New Press.

Yu, J. and Liu, J. (2009). "The new biopolitics." *Journal of Academic Ethics* 7(4): 287–96.

Epilog

As the studies in this volume suggest, the complexity of the region underscored, in turn, by the presence of diverse local traditions, colonial experiences, and competing assumptions of religious values and practices, poses a challenge to conventional scholarly interpretations of the process of modernization in the Middle East. The individual case studies provide an insight into the varied approaches that characterize the attempt to come to terms with a changing international system, while simultaneously attempting to preserve and draw upon the repositories of tradition. It is clear that the impact of Western traditions and ideas have had an impact on the process of transformation, although the strategies have varied depending on the strength of local traditions.

There is also a clear sense that linear interpretations of modernization obscure the necessity for a nuanced approach and an appreciation of the role played by culture, identity, and history. This has resulted from the changing interpretations of Middle Eastern societies and cultures by Westerners and by Middle Easterners themselves. As modernization studies have moved away from being an exclusively Western interpretation of social and political change, the concepts concerning what constitutes an authentic analysis of a culture or society has changed dramatically. One constituent which provides analytic continuity is the relevance of political and personal identities as an organizing framework for associations and networks that parallel or limit the authority of the state.

The contributions to this volume demonstrate the limitations of the kind of modernization theory that attempts to explain social change solely as a manifestation of the embrace of a more rationalistic cultural position. Interpretations of modernity as a progression from unthinking obedience to tradition to a set of attitudes more suited to existence in a changing technocratic world exemplifies the either/or approach that is less than helpful in understanding the developments of the Middle East. This methodology understates the critical acumen, diversity, and dynamism that is present in traditional cultures. By making attitude modification a central explanatory factor for a broad range of social transformations, this type of analysis ignores the political and cultural underpinnings of regional transformation.

Understanding the dynamics of twenty-first-century governance in the Middle East requires an acknowledgement of the distinctive experiences of countries in this rapidly changing region.

Many questions arise from these analyses that warrant a continuing effort to disentangle the strings that connect societies in this broad aggregation of states.

One cluster of questions is suggested by the examination of traditional Islam as well as contemporary interpretations to assess its broader influence as a global movement as well as its more particular manifestations at the local level. It is essential to understand how the wider currents of Islam engage the local traditions and practices. It is also important to identify the reaction of religious thinking to the rapidly moving economic and political contexts of a globalizing world in which it must remain relevant. One conventional approach that characterized some of the previous studies of the region suggested that religious standards and criteria were increasingly irrelevant in the issues, conflicts, and policy processes of modern Arab politics. This sense of the diminishing influence of Islamic authorities on political development has been challenged by recent events .The states of the region, whatever their political leanings, are facing a situation where significantly varying interpretations of Islam are held by the citizenry and in many cases it is evident that Islam has direct practical application to political and economic affairs.

A second set of issues involves cultural identity. In a region as complex as the Middle East, with its overlapping linguistic and ethnic traditions, its national distinctions, and its class divisions, the manner in which personal and collective identities are affirmed and how they are manifest in differing historical and political contexts is of great significance.

A third set of questions concerns the political aspects and consequences of governance. Many governments in the region are straggling participants in the politics of a newly awakened public. They are still deeply caught up in the assumptions, conflicts, and constraints of the old order. As the communications revolution continues to enable ideas to be widely shared on social networking websites and other media outlets, traditional rulers are increasingly confronted with the challenge of responding to non-governmental organizations and external influences.

Many of these issues are raised in this volume, while further studies of societies not covered in this collection of essays would contribute to our understanding of change in the region, both as distinctive occurrences and as representative of broader generalizations.

Index